YOU ARE G8,
WE ARE 6 BILLION

Also by Jonathan Neale

Memoirs of a Callous Picket
The Cutlass and the Lash
The Laughter of Heroes, a novel
Mutineers, a novel
The American War: Vietnam, 1960–1975
Tigers of the Snow
Lost at Sea, a novel for children

YOU ARE G8, WE ARE 6 BILLION

The Truth Behind the Genoa Protests

Jonathan Neale

First published in Great Britain by Vision Paperbacks,
a division of Satin Publications Ltd.

Vision Paperbacks
101 Southwark Street
London SE1 0JF
UK
e-mail: info@visionpaperbacks.co.uk
website: www.visionpaperbacks.co.uk

Publisher: Sheena Dewan
Cover design © 2002
Printed and bound in the UK by Biddles Ltd.

ISBN: 1-904132-13-8

For John Molyneux, Richard Moth and Richard Peacock

Contents

Acknowledgements

Great thanks, most of all, to Tom Behan, Chris Nineham, Nancy, Martin, Kalpana Lal, Nicola, Richard Moth, Richard Peacock, Richard G, Ruard, Barbara Neale and Terry Neale for reading the manuscript and commenting on it. I didn't always take their advice, but the book is far better for it.

Richard Moth and Nicola told me their stories in detail; the book would be far less without them. And I am grateful to Kalpana Lal for her letting me quote at length from her diary.

Thanks to my agent in London, David Smith of the Annette Green Agency, above all for his tenacious determination to make sure the book was published, and to Laura Langlie in New York. Stella Wood at Vision has been an encouraging and insightful editor. Martin Moss of Proof Positive was a careful and helpful copy editor.

And thanks to Maria, and yet again to Nancy.

Lastly, the book is dedicated with thanks for everything to John Molyneux, Richard Moth and Richard Peacock, loved comrades over many years, and men I much admire.

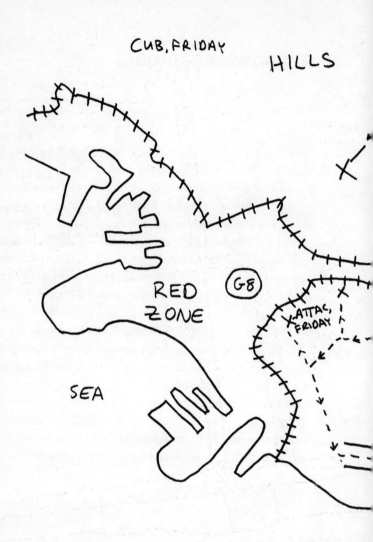

Map of the Genoa protests

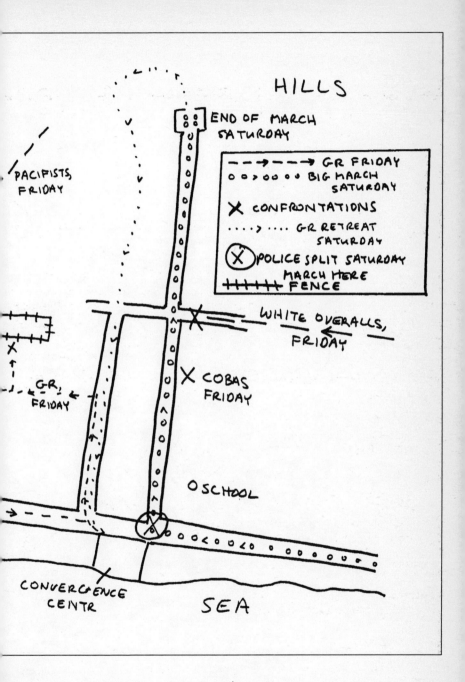

1 | **Beggars**

In July 2001 there were three days of demonstrations against the G8 summit of world leaders in Genoa. This book is a personal account of those days. I was one of the organisers of the protests, and I was on the street every day. Friday I was part of the direct action, trying to break down the fence around the summit, facing tear gas and water cannon. Saturday, on the mass demonstration, I was happier than I have ever been in my life. Sunday I was terrified for people I loved.

Hundreds of thousands of people went to Genoa, for many reasons. The best way I can explain why I went is to tell a few stories about beggars.

I'm 53 now, and I live in London. I was born in New York and grew up in Connecticut, Texas and India. In 1965, at the age of 16, I was a student at Colvin Taluqdar's, a high school in Lucknow, India. With two school friends I went to Darjeeling in the foothills of the Himalayas. On the way we changed trains at Patna, in Bihar.

There was a man lying on the Patna station platform. He was naked, and next to him was a begging bowl. The man had elephantiasis, a disease carried by mosquitoes that leads to swelling in the lower extremities. As is often the case with the disease, his testicles were swollen to the size of watermelons. I was a teenage boy. Just looking at him frightened me. I'd seen a lot of beggars, and given to them. I couldn't go near him. My two friends were fascinated, in a smutty teenage boy way, poking me and pointing at him. I thought: why don't the station staff move him on? Why do they leave him here? This is a prudish country. How can they allow this?

I thought about that on the train to Darjeeling, as it wound slowly back and forth, up the steep green hills of the tea plantations. I imagined that I was one of the station staff. That man must have no other source of income. Otherwise he would not be humiliating himself in this way. If I were the station manager, or a platform guard, I would not want to make that man move. It was pity, I realised, and kindness, that let the station staff leave him there.

Thirty-five years later, in 2000, I was sitting on the floor, like everyone else, in the entrance hall of the New Jalpaiguri railway station at the foot of the Darjeeling hills. It was early evening. My train wasn't due till the middle of the night, and I had a long wait. But I had a good book. It was May, a hot night. A woman about 10 years younger than me went from family to family, begging. She whined as she begged, in the high-pitched wheedling voice such women use. Her thin red sari was cheap, old and torn. She wore it hitched up, and her legs were thin and muscular. Her stomach and the upper part of her chest were so thin as to be almost wasted. The man who ran the station tea stall decided she was driving away his business, and called a policeman to get rid of her.

Indian policemen patrol alone, not in pairs. They are unarmed. They just have thick bamboo sticks to hit people with. This cop told the woman to leave the station. She sat on the stone floor of the station, head lowered, not speaking. He clubbed her, whack, whack, whack, hard about the head and chest. She screamed with each blow. When he was finished she wailed in a high keening voice, like a mourner, huddled on the ground, hugging herself. But she would not move.

The young man running the tea stall, a poor man in a vest with a small moustache, laughed as the policeman hit her. No one else, including me, moved.

The policeman began beating her again. I looked round the crowded entrance hall. Many people were in family groups, sharing a cloth spread across the floor to keep their clothes clean. They were all looking at the ground. On my left, six feet away, a man in his late twenties squatted tensely, watching the policeman hit the woman. The squatting man was good-looking, with a thick black moustache. On his face was the hatred I felt for that cop. We were about 20 paces from the beating. Like me, the man made no sound, just watched. The woman left the station, muttering defiance over her shoulder.

When I was a child, any Indian crowd would have commented on the beating to each other, criticised the woman, defended the cop, criticised the cop, raised their voices at each other in argument. Now, whatever we were thinking, we were silent. Neo-liberalism, the right-wing politics that dominates the world, had come to India. That man with the swollen testicles would never be allowed on Patna railway station today.

My brother, sister and I always called our mother Mom, and our father by his name, Terry. At some point in the late 1970s or early 80s Terry was visiting me in London from his home in Tennessee. He went shopping on the Holloway Road at the bottom of our street. Terry came back with whatever he'd gone to buy. He'd forgotten his key, so he rang the bell and I went downstairs to let him in. Terry was shaken, his face open like a child. When he saw me he began to cry. He said there were beggars on the Holloway Road. He had grown up in America in the depression, and there were beggars everywhere then. As a grown man he'd seen them enough in India, but he never expected to see beggars in the West again. He thought all that was done. But now it was back.

My daughter Siobhan was born in 1978. She never knew the forty years when there were no beggars on the Holloway Road. They look normal to her. I usually give 50 pence or a pound to the first beggar I see in a day, and then nothing to the rest.

Siobhan was really angry at me one day when she was 13. I had just given to a beggar's outstretched hand on the Holloway Road. 'Never do that again,' Siobhan said. 'You didn't look at that man.'

'I gave him the money,' I said.

'Doesn't matter,' she said. 'You can give him the money or not. Either way, look him in the face. He's a person.'

I still can't do that.

On the bright side, when I go to India now the beggars don't worry me much. I'm used to them.

The economic and political forces that were making and punishing beggars were changing the lives of billions of other people. Over most of the world work had become harder, the welfare state had been cut, public services had been privatised and mass unemployment was normal. Some people were desperate, and everywhere greed seemed to rule. The complex processes involved went under the name 'globalisation'. By 2001 many people had had enough. In July of that year I went to Genoa for a mass anti-capitalist protest.

I write books for a living: novels, history and politics. This book is a bit like all three of those. I have written my own experiences and feelings like a novel, but with nothing invented. If you were in Genoa yourself, you will often think while reading this 'That wasn't how I was feeling then.' And of course it wasn't. Each of us brought different things to Genoa, and had a different experience. But by concentrating on my own time, and what happened to my small group of friends from home, I hope to take you inside the feeling of a great demonstration. One of the most important things about the anti-capitalist movement is how it feels. But I have also tried to write a history of the demonstrations in general, to tell the story of what happened to other people.

There is politics here too, because there is a danger in just writing about marches, tactics and tear gas. On most of the issues we protest about (global warming, the lack of cheap drugs for Aids, poverty, sweatshops, Star Wars, and the rest) we have the support of the majority of people in every country in the world. The leaders of the world know this. Whenever we protest, they try to shift the argument away from the issues, and the media talk only of street fighting. So each chapter about Genoa is followed by a shorter chapter, like this one, about the reasons we went there.

A final introductory point. This book uses the phrase 'third world'. This has become a rather old-fashioned phrase to some, and many now say 'global south'. Whatever term we use, what we all mean is the poor countries of the world.

2 | The weeks before

At Genoa the mountains come down to the sea. From the air, as you fly in, the city is a long thin ribbon of white along the shore of the dark blue Mediterranean. From the coast sharp hills rise, green with trees, the last outliers of the Alps to the north. In the centre of the city is the arc of the port.

Genoa is a city of narrow lanes, steep hills, stone staircases and old palaces. It was one of the two great ports of the Italian renaissance. Ships went from there to the Arab coasts, Istanbul, the Indies and the Americas. Christopher Columbus was born in Genoa, and Marco Polo spent time in prison there. Much of the old city survives in the centre that rises steeply from the port.

It's still a working city. In Europe, Florence or Canterbury can feel like museums. Genoa is a port. In the protests of July 2001, the police lined the streets with empty ship cargo containers. The great ferries to Corsica, Sardinia and Tunisia filled the quays. Seven hundred thousand people live here. Most of them are in apartments up the steep hills, or in the suburbs along the coast: the city is 15 miles long and half a mile or a mile wide along that length.

The streets are hot in summer. But the lanes and homes of the old centre are cool. There's a breeze off the sea. The narrow alleys are always in the shade of the brick and plaster of the old buildings that tower over them. In the rooms the walls are high, the wooden shutters swing open, and the floors are marble or old stone.

It's a tough city, like any port. The Genoese dockers are a

byword for union militancy all over Italy. At night, in June, I stopped for an ice cream on the street down by the shore. Every few yards, a prostitute stood under the covered stone arches. They were young, African, each beautiful and a long way from home. I wondered what the less beautiful ones did. These women called to each other, swung their arms, tried to seem insouciant. They wore jeans, and colourful tops, looking like friendly young women, careful not to be slutty. Men stared at them, and called out remarks.

Two months before the G8 met in Genoa, the local police had already called in every 'undesirable' who worked or lived in the old city. That meant the prostitutes, but also all the other Africans, the other immigrants, and everybody with a criminal record. The police told them they would have to leave home, or stop work, for the three days the world leaders would be in town. In May I asked a waiter in a pizzeria how he felt about it. He resented losing the work for those days. 'I'm from Kosovo,' he said. 'I came here to escape a war. All I want to do is work. Now war follows me here.' And he spread his arms high, his fingers extended, as if in prayer, meaning: 'But what can you do?'

It's lovely to walk around a city full of history and beauty that's still a workers' town. Ordinary people, bus drivers and teachers, live in the apartments in the centre. The only ugly thing is a raised motorway that runs along the coast, cutting off the port from the old city. They say the construction was a political boondoggle, and everybody knew that nobody needed it. The road is called Via Antonio Gramsci, after the great communist intellectual who ended his life in Mussolini's prisons.

When the G8 summit was first planned, George W. Bush was supposed to stay at a four star hotel on the Via Antonio Gramsci. (The protesters were later allocated Piazzale Kennedy and Piazzale Martin Luther King for their meetings.) Historic Genoa seemed like a good choice for the G8 summit then.

★

The G8 started as the Group of Seven (G7) in the 1980s: the USA, Canada, Japan, Germany, France, Britain and Italy. These were the seven biggest economies of the rich West. The idea was that their leaders would hold a summit in each country in turn to discuss the world economy. It would be a junket, but with a serious purpose. The three great regional power blocs of capital (North America, Western Europe and East Asia) could meet every year to discuss what to do about the world economy. They could talk more or less in private, because the smaller countries and the poor ones were not invited. The hope was that the G7 could coordinate to make sure the world economy didn't crash again the way it had in 1929. After the fall of the Soviet Union in 1989, the leader of Russia joined what now became the G8.

Most people didn't much question the G8. In 1997 the churches in Britain brought 50,000 people to protest about third world debt outside the G8 meeting in Birmingham. That was important, but it didn't make much of an impact outside Britain.

Then came the protests outside the World Trade Organisation meetings in Seattle, in November 1999. Many of the protesters were environmentalists and campaigners for the third world, but the majority were workers brought by their trade unions. The spirit and numbers of the protests were unexpected, and they succeeded in closing down the first day of the summit. Suddenly there was a movement.

In the USA the movement was more commonly called 'anti-globalisation', and in Europe usually 'anti-capitalist'. In either case, people all over the world were looking for international meetings and thinking: 'Where can we have our Seattle?'

There were many answers to that, many elite and exclusive gatherings (the Davos meetings of bankers and politicians, the World Bank, the International Monetary Fund, the European Union, the Free Trade summit of the Americas). The new movement tried them all. But two were clearly the biggest and best meetings to protest.

One was the next meeting of the World Trade Organisation

after Seattle. But they were holding that in Qatar, a brutal dictatorship in the Persian Gulf, precisely so protesters couldn't get to them.

The other obvious target was the G8: eight rich men trying to rule the world. Japan hosted the 2000 meeting. They held it on the island of Okinawa, a long way even for most Japanese, and avoided protests. But the 2001 G8 was scheduled for Genoa, in Italy. Two hours away from the industrial heartland of Turin and Milan, the old centres of the Italian left. Right near the French border. 'Italy!' we said to each other on the European left, gloating. The G8 country with the most radical mass movements in the last 60 years, we said. They might have been quiet for a while, but Italians? Yes!

It didn't feel that easy in Italy, of course.

The Genoa Social Forum was the body trying to organise protests against the summit. As time went on, it included activists from all over Italy. But it began as a local organisation, and all the way through the volunteers and many of the rank and file organisers were local people.

They held their first international meeting the first weekend in May. I went along as a representative from a group in Britain. The G8 summit was 10 weeks away.

Genoa is roughly the same size as Leeds, in Yorkshire, or Austin, Texas. It felt a bit as if Leeds Trades Council or the left in Austin had been told there would be a confrontation bigger than Seattle in their town. They had been chosen to organise one side of this, the one without any power. After all the demonstrators had gone home, they would have to live with the consequences. It's Armageddon, the activists in Leeds or Austin would tell each other, but don't panic. The Housing Aid office down the road in Pudsey say they'll help, or the Legal Aid Centre in San Marcos is sending two people to the meeting. And the local branch of the World Wildlife Fund is on board. All the other side has is the United States Army.

I'm exaggerating, but not a lot. That first international

planning meeting was only 150 people. It was disorganised. The local organisers seemed to feel a bit like rabbits trapped in the headlights, waiting for the car to come down the road.

They were afraid of a violent confrontation, and being held responsible afterwards. But they had clearly decided to do the best they could. Oddly enough, history had asked the activists of Genoa to do this, so they would. It was their duty.

These people in Genoa were like me, I thought. I would have felt the same in their place: overwhelmed and determined.

I'd grown up in the United States, been part of the anti-war movement there in 1969 and 1970. After that I moved to Britain and eventually joined the Socialist Workers Party in 1974. I'd been in squatter politics, the Anti-Nazi League, collected money for the striking miners, refused to pay my poll tax and organised my street to do the same. I'd been a health worker for years, a shop steward for most of that, and I'd lost track of the one day strikes I'd been on.

Those were bad times, the era of Thatcher, Reagan and defeated strikes. The union work held me together. I love watching the way ordinary people grow when they become trade union reps. Even in bad times, people could be persuaded to defend each other and try to save the hospitals we worked in.

But I remember one day in 1994. I spent the afternoon in a long meeting of the shop stewards committee for the Barnet hospitals in North London. That evening my local branch of the Socialist Workers Party met in Islington. Both meetings felt the same: depressed. Both were small groups of ageing militants, trying to hold something together, waiting for class struggle that never seemed to come, trying not to blame each other, complaining about the full time officials, deeply tempted to blame the workers.

I held on, hoping for a return of the movement of my youth, the feel and hope of 1968. When Seattle happened and the anti-capitalist movement came along, I threw myself into the new movement.

In September 2000, I went to the protests against the IMF and the World Bank in Prague. We were 20,000 people at most. In a classic piece of military stupidity, the organisers split our forces into three marches. Now we were even weaker. I was with the socialists, and we marched with the people from the Non-Governmental Organisations (NGOs) and the Italian left.

We walked through the empty streets, unaccompanied by any police. Then we came up to a bridge over a deep valley. On that bridge, and behind it, were row after row of what people said were armoured cars, but they looked like tanks to me. On top of them sat men with machine guns. In front were riot police in black visors, clubs ready. In front of them a line of tear gas canisters fizzed on the ground. We could stay where we were, with no police, in the sun. Or we could walk onto that bridge and maybe be pushed off to our deaths.

We sort of pushed the police a bit. *Ya Basta* (Enough), the hard men and women of the Italian street left, were there with us. They had no more intention of getting onto that bridge than anybody else. So we went back into the centre of town and surrounded the opera house, preventing a special performance of *La Traviata* for the IMF delegates.

The meetings were supposed to last three days. We had demonstrated on the first day, and then most people went home. On the second day Czech TV showed pictures of IMF conference rooms designed to hold 400, with 20 people scattered amid empty rows. The bankers were refusing to leave their hotels. Late that afternoon the World Bank and the IMF cancelled the third day of the conference. I flew out of Prague the next morning on a plane full of demonstrators, press photographers, and African bankers who had opted for an unexpected stopover in London.

We'd won. At first I couldn't understand it. We had been comprehensively shut down on the streets. The 'pink' anarchist march had got closer to the conference than us, and even briefly managed to get to some bankers, because they had the sense not to try to cross a bridge. But there hadn't been enough of us to break through in force. After the marches a few people had broken the windows of a few McDonald's in the city centre. But no bankers had been attacked, none barricaded in their hotels. So why were they scared to come out?

The only way I could explain it was that they were demoralised. In the countries they came from, we were winning the argument about the IMF. They felt isolated back home. The third world delegates, in particular, had often been responsible for cutting wages and social programmes and raising the prices of necessities at the behest of the IMF. They may have been believers, as dedicated to greed as any first world yuppie. But they had to know they were reviled. That's why the bankers couldn't face us.

Looking back, I think there was another reason I didn't understand at the time. The protests had been small because there were few Czechs on the marches. Those who came almost all did so as individuals, not organised groups. The majority of the demonstrators came from across western Europe, and the banners were almost all from foreign groups. Yet on the evening after the main march, and the next day, the Czech police arrested over 800 people on the streets of Prague. Most of them were Czechs. Many of them were tear gassed in jail, and some were badly beaten in their cells. Others were sexually abused, and some had bones broken. This was a clear attempt to restore order, to say 'Those foreigners may have got away with what they did, but don't think you can.'

The fact that the majority arrested were Czech, though, meant that Czechs were changing. I suspect that one reason for cancelling the meetings was that Vaclav Havel, the president of the Czech Republic, wanted the meetings out of his country before they caused more unrest.

We had demonstrated against the market, chanting 'Our World is Not For Sale.' Three months later the workers at the Czech state television occupied their newsroom in protest against a new boss sent in to privatise the station. One night 100,000 people demonstrated in Wenceslas Square in their support, and they won. I think our demonstrations had something to do with that.

I came back to Britain from Prague in September 2001 feeling 10 feet tall. It was a new experience, winning, and hard to make people back home believe it. The newspapers had not reported the cancellation of the conference. But the report back meetings were well attended. Then in January the Socialist Workers Party approached members of the Green Party and a lot of the NGOs to see if we could organise a series of one-day anti-capitalist conferences around the country. They were up for it. We got Kevin Danaher from the US, who had been at Seattle, to speak, and Boris Kagarlitsky from Russia, who had been at Prague. Eight hundred people came in London, 500 in Glasgow, and in the other towns we did far better than anybody expected. More important, at the London conference we announced an organising meeting the next week for Genoa, still six months away and 220 people came. We knew we had a movement, and decided to call it Globalise Resistance (GR).

Our first problem was to unite the disparate groups and individuals who wanted to do something. We had the Socialist Workers Party, including me, on board. With several thousand active members, the SWP was by far the largest political party on the British left, and we certainly did know how to organise. But we needed a lot more than that. Luckily, a lot of full timers from the NGOs very much wanted us to succeed. Their organisations could not affiliate: GR was political, and they were charities. But the full timers spoke tirelessly from our platforms, night after night, travelling all round the country. We also got activists from the Green Party involved, and from Workers Power, another left-wing group.

The whole of the British left was having to learn to leave our narrow prejudices behind us. It wasn't easy. The word we used for our deep-seated sneering at each other was 'sectarianism'. This was not a personal failure. It came from years of defeat and isolation on the left. When you're losing, you look for somebody to blame. If there is no struggle that teaches you to unite, you can sneer at the other groups and tendencies around you. In the SWP, we had spent years in meetings, keeping our political arguments sharp. That meant we survived the years of defeat. It also meant a habit of ranting at people without letting them interrupt.

Sectarianism was a classic problem on the left. The left of the Labour party seemed to have it as bad as we did. The anarchists had it even worse. Around much of the country, they refused even to sit in organising meetings for Prague and Genoa with the rest of the left.

All this made no sense to the new people coming into GR and the movement. Some of them said they were anarchists, some socialists, some greens, and many weren't sure what label they wanted, if any. For those of us used to behaving badly, it was hard to change. We might argue passionately for unity, but then as the 'other side' spoke our noses would crinkle into the habitual sneer. But the important thing was that we were trying. And just to be polite, to buy each other's newspapers and sit on the same platforms, was exhilarating. Travelling back on the train from Swansea, late at night, with the man from the World Development Movement, chatting about his children and mine, was wonderful. The bad times were over.

It was not just the anti-capitalist movement that was leaving sectarianism behind. In the Socialist Alliance election campaigns, in the movement against the war that began in 2001, and in a thousand local and union struggles, we were all learning to unite.

As you read these pages, however, you may well ask yourself, 'If Jonathan is so non-sectarian, why does he spend so much time arguing about tactics and disagreeing with other groups in the movement?' My answer is that arguing inside the movement is not automatically sectarian. Anti-capitalism is a new movement. It throws up new problems and new dilemmas. I went through the movements of the 1960s and 70s in the USA, Britain and Afghanistan. We got it wrong, and were defeated. I learned that it makes an enormous difference what decisions the movement makes, how you fight and what you say. You do the right thing, and you win. You do it wrong, and you lose. The way you learn what is right and wrong in any situation is by arguing it out among yourselves. It matters enormously whether the anti-capitalist movement wins or is defeated over the next 10 years. Arguments are necessary to that. That is why in every great political movement in history, the air has been alive with arguments on every street corner. Arguing isn't sectarian. Sectarianism is refusing to act together because you haven't won the argument.

Two things about the new movement were particularly important to me. First, all the young people. There were perhaps 400 people camping in the stadium in Prague when I got there. Only two of them were anywhere near my age. Everybody else was in their teens and twenties. I'd been part of an ageing movement a long time. My white hair had fitted right in. And then at a Globalise Resistance London meeting of 50 people, everybody but me under 40 and most under 30, somebody from the Green Party said we should get older people involved. Others liked that idea. Could we possibly find issues that might appeal to them? Hospitals? Pensions? I sat in my chair like a cat in the sun, saying nothing, basking in the feeling.

The other thing that touched me deeply was that this was a movement about both the West and the third world. I had lived three years of my childhood in India, and five years of my adult life in India, Afghanistan, Nepal, Venezuela and Turkey. I knew those places, felt the issues, wanted the same changes there I wanted at home.

I quickly started speaking from GR platforms, got elected to the national steering committee, and did interviews for the press. This was where my heart was. I understood the issues. I was up for this. So there I was in Genoa, one of the two delegates from Globalise Resistance to the international meeting.

The meeting was held in the hall of the local branch of the dockers' union. The first speaker was Bruno Rossi, a docker in his early sixties. He said how important this was to him, how much an honour, to speak to this new movement.

Three portrait photographs hung at the front of the union hall. On one side was Togliatti, the leader of the Italian Communist Party (CP) from the late 1920s to 1964. On the other side was Lenin. Somebody had put large vases of fresh red flowers in front of both, so you couldn't see them. I didn't think this was an accident. In the middle, slightly larger, was a photo of a docker from Genoa who had been shot by the Red Brigades, the left terrorists, in the 1970s. He was not hidden.

The communists had led the dockers' union, as they had led most organisations of the Italian working class from 1944 to 1989. The communists had been the partisan heroes, the leaders and much of the rank and file of the resistance to Mussolini. In the years after that they got a pretty steady third of the vote. That meant perhaps half the working class vote, and in northern cities like Genoa well over half. Most workers who didn't like their bosses, or the system they lived under, became communists. That was the decent heart of the party.

At the same time, the Italian party was one part of a world communist movement led by the Soviet government. What the Soviets wanted the Italian Communist Party to do, when push came to shove, was not to build communism. They wanted the CP not to take power. This may seem odd. But the Soviet and US governments had divided Europe into spheres of influence. For 45 years the agreement was that neither would really mess with the other. So the Italian CP was always trying not to go too far.

In the end the Russian link sank the communist party. In 1989 the communist dictatorships of Europe fell, to the obvious relief of the crowds of workers celebrating on the streets of Berlin, Prague, and Bucharest. Those regimes were revealed for what they were: dictatorships run by violence and greed. Western communist parties started to fall apart.

At almost the same time, the middle of the road Socialist Party and the right-wing Christian Democrats went into crisis as well. When the dust cleared, there were two major parties in Italy. One was the Left Democrats, made up of the shards of the communists, the socialists and some old Christian Democrats. The other was the coalition of the right led by Silvio Berlusconi.

What was paralysing the Genoa Social Forum (GSF) at that meeting in the dockers' hall was the prospect of Berlusconi coming to power. The elections were a week away, and the right was in front in the opinion polls. The militants in the GSF feared the right would simply ban our protests if they won. They might close off the city, shut the train stations, and put roadblocks on the motorways.

If that happened the GSF people were quite clear they would go ahead with the protests. But they were scared.

Silvio Berlusconi was a corporate tycoon, his fingers in a lot of pies, but his holdings centred on football, newspapers, magazines and all the private television stations in Italy. If he won the election, he would control the state TV too. He led a party of his own creation, '*Forza Italia*', named after the football slogan meaning 'Go Italy'. The ideology was unclear, except that business was good. But basically Berlusconi was heir to the old Christian Democrat right, with support from about 35 per cent of the voters.

He was also accused of being a white collar crook on a grand scale, under investigation by prosecutors in both Spain and Italy. One of the main reasons he was running for office was to be able to rewrite the Italian law on fraud and accounting, so that three of the offences for which he faced prosecution would no longer be illegal.

The second party in his coalition was the National Alliance, with about 12 per cent of the vote. They called themselves 'post-fascists', and had succeeded the old 'neo-fascist' party, which in turn had looked back to Mussolini's plain old fascist party. The leader of the National Alliance, Fini, now wore a suit and talked softly. But these were rebranding exercises. The third party in the coalition was the Northern League, another far right group, with about 5 per cent of the vote.

So the GSF activists were worried about what Berlusconi would do. At the same time, they were demoralised that Italians as a whole would vote for such a bunch of crooks and racists. It undermined their feeling of legitimate protest. People they knew said to them 'You are the far left, and Italians won't even vote for the moderate left. Who do you pretend to speak for? And why do you think Berlusconi will let you?'

The next weekend Berlusconi's coalition won the election. Three weeks after that I went back to Genoa for another round of meetings.

Berlusconi had indeed decided to shut down Genoa for the G8. The borders would be closed to trains and buses bringing foreign demonstrators. They might even be closed to all traffic. The train stations in and around Genoa would be shut, and the roads into the city blocked. The authorities were refusing to meet the GSF to negotiate routes for the marches. Everything the GSF did, it seemed, we would have to do illegally. The people coming from outside the city might have to fight their way in. The people already there would have to demonstrate in small numbers, surrounded by police.

I kept reminding myself and everybody else in Britain what the American government had done during the Vietnam war protests 30 years ago. They had banned all the big marches in Washington until a day or two before they happened. Then they had approved legal routes at the last minute and offered full facil-ities. Everything we had done in Prague had been illegal too, up to and including the last minute, but the police had not tried to stop us marching. During the anti-capitalist protests in Nice, in December, the local police had refused us permission until the last minute, and then the right-wing municipality had given all the protesters accommodation.

So, we said to each other, Berlusconi is bluffing in order to scare people out of coming. Chris Nineham from Globalise Resistance said 'I bet they've already ordered the mobile toilets. We just have to keep our nerve.' I did that in public, but in private my nerve kept slipping away from me.

Which I think was more or less where the other organisers in the GSF were when I got there in early June. But they had grown in the last month in a way I had not. The experience of standing out against the might of the government was changing them. More people were getting involved around Italy. The election result, when it finally came, had stiffened people too. At least that's out of the way, they thought. Now everybody who wants to show what they think of Berlusconi can come to Genoa.

There were to be two days of meetings this time. The first meeting was on Sunday, in the local offices of the World Wildlife Fund. This was just for one or two people from each broad political grouping, maybe 40 people in all, so we could have a whopping argument in private.

That week Ya Basta, the most important radical left group, had issued a leaflet defying Berlusconi and making a 'declaration of war' against the G8 summit. Many of the other groups in the GSF were furious. Berlusconi had been saying the protestors would be violent. The newspapers had been carrying stories about people planning to bring guns and throw acid at the police. The activists who lived in Genoa said Berlusconi's propaganda was working. The people they knew in their daily lives thought the protestors would break their windows, burn their cars, and might attack them. Late July was holiday season in Genoa, and many people were booking themselves out of the city for that weekend. The 'declaration of war' had made it much harder for the GSF to win local support.

Of course Ya Basta didn't actually mean they wanted a real war. This was left-wing rhetoric. But behind the words there was serious disagreement about tactics.

Ya Basta was one of several autonomist, or 'White Overalls', groups. The autonomists come out of the defeat of the Italian revolutionary movement of the 1970s. The older men among their leading thinkers came mainly from one of the parties of those years, *Potere Operaia* (Workers Power). As the movement fell apart in the late 70s, the people who founded the autonomists decided they had made two central mistakes. One was concentrating on leadership and being undemocratic. The other was concentrating on workers. So now they decided to be looser, more anarchist in feel. They built networks around 'social centres' in each city, large squatted buildings where the left and any dissident movements could go for a meeting, a drink, a film, a cheap theatre performance, or just to hang out. At the same time they turned away from organising in unions, or among workers. Their theoreticians said the working class had splintered into many different fragments and interest groups. Therefore, they said, the margins of society were a better place to build opposition. People at the margins were less likely to be brainwashed and more open to new ideas. In practice the social centres concentrated on three marginal groups: immigrants, students, and young people living a counter-culture lifestyle.

Their central activity, though, was demonstrations. I stayed in the same stadium in Prague with 90 people from Ya Basta. They had a bugler to wake them up in the morning, and fantastic costumes. The day before the march they practised putting them on. First they put on big shoulder pads like American football players, and knee and shin pads. They had helmets, and big shields like riot policemen. On top of all this they wore baggy white overalls made from the same thin material that asbestos removal teams wear. And around their necks, gas masks. They looked like space cadets, and well ready to be beaten by riot police without much damage. I was really interested to see what happened on the march the next day. And quite a lot of people from Britain who watched them were impressed by the gear, the discipline and the playful feel about them.

Ya Basta was at the head of our part of the march. They went to the front, up against the riot police and the tanks at the bridge. Then they began dismantling the various barriers the police and soldiers had put up. At the back of their contingent, they made a line with linked arms to prevent anybody else getting to the front.

The group I came with were marching with the British SWP and the allied International Socialist groups from all over Europe. (We didn't have Globalise Resistance yet.) Some of us tried to push to the front. Ya Basta pushed back, and hit us. Eventually they did let some of us get to the front; not me, though, thank God.

From their politics, this made sense. The White Overalls (in Italian 'Tute Bianche') felt they were the shock troops of the movement: padded, protected, experienced, and disciplined. They also knew each other. They had gone up against the riot police in Italy many times. Their strategy was to confront the police, try to push into their lines, and then to hold their own position. They were not into smashing up the police; this was a strategy of heavily padded non-violence. From their point of view, if we got to the front undefended we might be massacred. Or, for all they knew, we might lay into the police and involve everybody in a bloodbath.

From my point of view, they were being elitist. They were making themselves into the vanguard of the crowd, the people who do the demonstrating for you. I have the same problem with both violent urban guerillas like the IRA and non-violent groups like Greenpeace. In all these cases, a small group of experts do it for us, and we support them. It's undemocratic, and it also weakens our side. For our one strength is that we are many and the people at the top are few. If you have experts, you have to limit the number of people in your contingent. If you're not worried about experts, then you can say to everybody you meet: 'Join us.'

The White Overalls had two main spokespersons in the meeting in Genoa. Luca Casarini was 35, with hair down past his shoulders, a bit of a belly, intense but a joker. He was the politician. Luca reminded me of me. Francesco Caruso was about 30, black haired, with glasses, talking in blocks of speech, with a far more abstract turn of phrase. He was the theoretician.

We all sat round a big polished wooden table, like a boardroom. Because it was the World Wildlife Fund there were posters of friendly animals on the walls, and signs telling us not to smoke. The White Overalls were in one corner by a window. The non-violent pacifists, the liberation theology Catholics, and the other moderates faced them from another corner. Around and between them were the radical trade unionists, various Italian socialists, people from local organisations in Genoa, and me.

The Genoa organisers began by explaining the state of play. The government was refusing to meet them. Everything was illegal, and it looked like Genoa might be cut off. The police had told the newspapers that they would be building a metal fence around the historic centre of the city. Inside that fence would be the Red Zone, where nobody would be allowed in without a pass. We planned three demonstrations. On Thursday evening there would be a march for the rights of immigrants. Many of the marchers would be refugees, some without legal papers, and we didn't want any of them arrested and then deported. So we would be very careful that there was no civil disobedience of any kind on Thursday. On this we were all agreed.

On Friday we would stage some kind of civil disobedience in or near the Red Zone. On Saturday there would be a much bigger march that would not go near the Red Zone. This would have no civil disobedience, so there would be no challenge to the police.

We all knew, however, that if there was bad trouble on the

Friday there might well be trouble on the Saturday. So the debate centred on Friday. People spoke angrily, at length, very clearly, again and again. But they told jokes too. The butt of the joke would laugh with the rest. It was a way of keeping the temperature down. They were mostly smokers; this was Italy, and the left smokes heavily everywhere. (We're nervous, it's hard to be in opposition all the time.) People glanced from time to time at the no smoking signs, looking guilty. They congregated by the high windows, trying to blow their smoke out. There, as others talked, Luca from the White Overalls would beg a cigarette from Rafaela of ARCI, the socialist cultural organisation, and she would light it for him. The two would exchange a few whispered words, to show each other and the room, 'We want to be friends'. Because, of course, if we couldn't unite we were well and truly fucked.

There were basically two positions around the table. What united both positions was that we were all very scared by what the police might do to us. One answer to this was self-defence. This was the argument from the White Overalls. But the man from COBAS, a radical trade union, put it best. 'We went on a demonstration in Naples three months ago against NATO,' he said, 'and there seem to be animals among the police now. We ended up with a lot of people in hospital, a lot of broken bones. Next time we're taking helmets and sticks to defend ourselves.'

Morally, this made sense. Every legal system in the world allows self-defence. There were two problems, however. The first was that if you go up to a Red Zone and try to get through a fence, the police will beat and gas you. Part of the reason is that on big demonstrations the police can't arrest many people, because they are outnumbered and can't spare the arresting officers. The more people they arrest, the more outnumbered they are. So they have to use violence if they want to disperse you. Going into non-violent disobedience intending to defend yourself is a bit like picking a fight with a mean drunk in a bar. Maybe he swings first, but you both know you're going to have a fight.

And self-defence doesn't work in the sort of situation we

would face. The other side has soldiers, gas, tanks, guns, and a habit of collective discipline. Sticks and helmets do not protect you when the police get serious.

There were flaws in the pacifist argument too. The pacifists wanted the demonstrators to stay non-violent and thus not provoke the police to violence. The difficulty here, though, is that the violence of the demonstrators is not the main determinant of police response. Their response is determined by the orders they get from above on the day. If a non-violent demonstration poses too great a challenge to people at the top, they will order violence to break it up.

The tradition of non-violence comes from Gandhi's independence movement in India and Martin Luther King's civil rights movement in the US. Both provoked a great deal of official violence. In 1919, in Amritsar, India, the British-led army herded a large crowd of non-violent protesters into a square, cut off all avenues of retreat, and opened fire, killing over 400 people. In Peshawar in 1931 the police again faced a crowd of non-violent Gandhian demonstrators. The police fired into the crowd repeatedly. The demonstrators stood their ground for four hours, non-violently refusing to disperse, and 131 of them died.

Again, the civil rights movement in the American South provoked police violence on the streets. Many organisers were killed in night time lynchings. Martin Luther King, like Gandhi, was eventually assassinated by political opponents. Moreover, both Gandhi and King understood that non-violence provoked violence. As an American trainer in non-violence said to me in Genoa, 'once the other side start hitting, we start winning.' In Birmingham, Alabama, for instance, King faced a police chief he could not budge. There was day after day of demonstrations, and the civil rights movement was getting nowhere in a key southern city. So King decided to send the high school and junior high school kids up against the water hoses and police dogs. The TV pictures of the dogs tearing at children raised such a storm that King and the kids won.

In the end, after hours of arguing and sharing cigarettes, the people round the table came to an agreement. We would not declare war. We would not carry any weapons, which meant no sticks or rocks. We would issue a statement assuring the people of Genoa that we would not attack them, and we would not break the windows of their shops. We would not attack any people at all. That included not attacking the police.

But, we said, force against things is not the same as violence against people. Some of us would try to take down the fence around the Red Zone. All of us would offer them moral support.

We would divide up into different groups on the Friday, on the basis of different strategies. Some nuns from the Jubilee movement to drop third world debt would pray at a church five miles away from the Red Zone. Some pacifists would try to get into the Red Zone to close down the summit, and some would not. Globalise Resistance would try to get into the Red Zone, but not fight the police. The White Overalls and COBAS would try to get into the Red Zone, and defend themselves if attacked. But we all agreed that people would only defend themselves with their hands.

Many of the pacifists were worried that when they sat down and prayed near the Red Zone, somebody would throw a rock from behind them, and the police would wade into them. (This was not a silly fear. Exactly this came to pass, and it had happened in Italy before.) So we agreed that we would all demonstrate separately. But each of us would respect the tactics of the others, and not criticise each other in public.

And on that, to my amazement, we left the meeting unified. Everybody else was amazed too, and suddenly proud of each other and what a new movement had made us do.

Then, far away, the Swedish police shot three people.

During the second weekend in June the leaders of the European Union met for a summit in Gothenburg, Sweden. They have been meeting every six months for many years. But in December the main French union federation, the CGT, had called an anti-capitalist demonstration outside the EU summit in Nice, France. A hundred thousand people, mostly workers, came.

Every anti-capitalist protest is consciously international, but at each one the majority come from the host country. In Seattle it was mostly Americans, in Quebec mostly Canadians, in Nice mostly French. Each demonstration leaves behind a new anti-capitalist movement. Gothenburg is on the south-west coast of Sweden, as close to Copenhagen and Oslo as it is to Stockholm. So this was the coming together of the all the Scandinavians. As a bonus, the first day of the summit featured George W. Bush on his first trip to Europe.

The government of Sweden had announced that they wanted a dialogue with the protesters. They provided schools for the protesters to sleep in, and facilities for the organisers. After all, this was Sweden, the home of tolerance and the welfare state. The government were Social Democrats.

There was a small White Overalls movement in Scandinavia and northern Europe, modelled on the Italians. They all got one school to stay in. Early on the morning of the first day of the protests, the police surrounded their school, confiscated all their padding, and arrested all of them.

From then on the policing was heavy, and deeply confusing for the Scandinavians gathered there. Gothenburg is a port, and everywhere ship containers blocked off the route. The police didn't use tear gas: there's a law against it in Sweden. But they used clubs and guns.

People who were there say guns were drawn many times that day, but only three protesters were hit. One of them was a 19-year-old Swedish transport worker, Hannes Westberg. John from New Cross was a few yards away when it happened. He says there was nobody near the police. He knows, because he was the closest to them, and he was running away.

A TV camera captured what happened. Hannes Westberg, a

stick or placard in his hand, shouted something at the police. Then he turned around to walk away, and the police shot him in the back. There is a moment on the tape when his body jerks and his face shows agony and surprise. Some people said the lad had shouted at the police, 'OK, shoot me.' Assuming, of course, that he was in Sweden, and they would not.

Of the three shot that day, he was the most badly wounded. He was in critical condition for two days, and we thought he was going to die. As he lay in hospital, his fate uncertain, the political leaders of Europe had to react.

The Swedish prime minister stood by his police, cutely quoting Lenin in his defence. So did the rest of his government. The Swedish left, stunned, hardly knew how to react. The British prime minister, Tony Blair, supported the police too. Nobody else from the governments of Europe did. But they didn't criticise the shooting either. And the newspapers and television apparently didn't ask them to.

I learned of the shooting watching it on the TV news in Britain. I breathed in. Maybe that'll be me in Genoa, I thought.

It seems obvious, but it needs saying over and over again: the reason that the police shoot somebody on a demonstration is that it scares other people. That's also the reason politicians support a shooting. And it's why they sent every policeman and woman in Gothenburg onto the streets with a revolver loaded with live ammunition.

There had been 25,000 people, more or less, on the demonstration the day Hannes Westberg was shot. The next day there were 40,000, mostly Swedes, and mostly trade unionists. That carried a message for Berlusconi. I think he asked himself what would happen if a demonstrator was shot dead in Genoa, and he didn't know the answer. In any case, when Berlusconi flew back from Gothenburg, he had a meeting with his generals, senior police officers, and the minister of the interior *at the airport*. They came out of that meeting announcing that Genoa would be open for the protests. They wanted a dialogue with us. The minister of the interior sat down and negotiated with the GSF. Suddenly all our demonstrations were legal. The central government told the local municipalities to put stadiums, schools, parks, and sports centres at our disposal. Of course the borders would be open.

We told the police that we planned to protest peacefully, and that some of us would defend ourselves. But we would use no weapons in self-defence. Fine, the police said. Negotiations stalled on gas masks. The police said they were a weapon. We denied this. But the police did agree that we could throw empty plastic mineral water bottles. These were not weapons, provided there was nothing in them.

The GSF negotiating team asked the chief of the police operation for Genoa to promise that his men and women would not carry guns or live ammunition. He said he could not do that. But he would take responsibility, personally, as a human being, that they would not use those guns.

We were happy with that. It did leave the problem of what those guns were for, of course, but we didn't want to think too hard about that.

I went back to Genoa for another meeting at the end of June. We'd won, we told each other happily. We'd kept our nerve, we'd stuck together, and Berlusconi had buckled. Globalise Resistance had 500 people coming from Britain on a chartered train, 150 on buses, probably 500 more by air or fitting Genoa into their holiday. Drop the Debt probably had 1,500 in all coming from Britain. Where could the GSF put these people, we wanted to know. Could we have a covered place? A school? Please? We were getting greedy.

In a classic spin doctor move, Berlusconi announced that he was inviting nine third world representatives to the G8 so the voice of the oppressed would be heard and they could mediate between the protesters and the G8. Nelson Mandela was one. So was Thabo Mbeki, the South African prime minister, President Obasanjo of Nigeria, Amartya Sen, the Indian economist who won a Nobel Prize for his work on the social causes of famines, and Rigoberta Menchu, a leader of indigenous Mayas in Guatemala.

At the GSF meeting I suggested that we ask all these people to speak on our platforms during the days of protest. Christophe Aguiton of ATTAC in France, far more experienced in these things, told me politely not to be silly. Wise heads around the table nodded. Mandela and the like will never speak for us, or even enter into a public dialogue with us, Christophe said. They are coming only as window dressing for the G8.

Which proved to be the case. And they weren't allowed into the G8 meetings either. But the fact that Berlusconi made a show of inviting them proved he was on the defensive.

Berlusconi's retreat unleashed a wind of feeling on our side in Italy. People had been nervous about coming to Genoa, not sure. Now it was safe. And after Gothenburg, in reaction to Gothenburg, people all over Italy wanted to come. A group of the country's leading porn stars announced their solidarity with the protests. From now until the G8, they would begin every scene they filmed wearing white overalls.

A priest from Genoa stood on the stage at a massive pop concert and called on the big union federations to stop mumbling and start supporting the protests. The heart of the old communist union federation were the metal workers, FIOM, whose oldest and strongest base was in the car factories. FIOM was holding a series of one-day strikes over the national contract. At each strike meeting and each demonstration the union had a representative of the GSF to speak.

My flatmate Silva went home to Turin for the weekend, and reported that all her friends, not just the political ones, were going to Genoa. My friend Hussein reported the same from Florence. It was going to be big. On Sunday 15 July I flew to Genoa.

3 | **Poverty and aid**

This chapter is about some of the issues that took us to Genoa: third world poverty, foreign aid and the IMF. Later chapters will cover AIDS, Star Wars, global warming, the roots of war in the Middle East, globalisation, and the alternative to capitalism.

There is a lot of assertion in what follows. When I write about Genoa, I am writing in detail and from my own experience, and can more or less support the arguments I make. When I write about the complex issues of globalisation in a small space, I cannot actually prove my case. But I can show you how I think the system works. If you want to pursue the arguments in greater detail and make up your own mind, there is a list of further reading material at the back of the book.

In 1971 I was in the town of Lashkargah, in south-eastern Afghanistan, about 100 miles from Kandahar. I was 23, a graduate student in anthropology trying to learn the language and do fieldwork. My wife and I were walking down the main street (there was only one street with shops in Lashkargah) to the only hotel in town, for supper. A boy, perhaps 16, stood there in the dark. He said something I didn't understand. When we got to the hotel restaurant I worked out what he'd said: 'Wuzhe yum (I'm hungry)'. It was the first thing anyone had said to me on the street in Pushtu that I'd understood. I was pleased with myself. I was also too embarrassed to go back out and down the street and give him money.

You didn't usually meet beggars in small town or rural

Afghanistan. The boy had probably come from the famine in the central mountains and north of the country, where there had been two years of drought. The nomads had watched their animals die, and then the harvest had failed. But no famine is simply a natural disaster. Famine is man-made, a socially constructed event. Some people eat in every famine, and some don't. Someone always makes a profit.

There was one road in northern Afghanistan. Foreign aid wheat, mainly American, came in on that road. The local officials of the royal government piled the grain high in the middle of small towns and put armed soldiers around the grain. The local merchants sold the grain for 10 times the usual rate. The poorer farmers sold their land to the merchants to buy the grain. The landless starved. The merchants paid a kickback to the local officials. The soldiers ate.

My friend Mike Barry, half French and half American, a romantic of the old school, bought a horse and rode through northern Afghanistan that year. Mike asked a group of starving peasants why they didn't simply storm the piles of grain in the centre of town. They said they could, but the king had planes, and he would send the planes to bomb them.

The planes were Russian MIGs. The pilots were trained in Texas. King Zahir Shah's government was careful to remain neutral in the Cold War.

Mike came back to Kabul and told the head of the US foreign aid mission (USAID) what he had seen. Mike asked him to do something. The head of mission said he couldn't. The head of mission's wife and daughter told me about this as I sat in their house in Kabul. It was full of American furniture, comfortable sofas. The Afghan, Persian and Bokhara rugs were dark red on the floor, seeming warm in the dim light. Like all USAID personnel, the family had an allowance to fly all their furniture to Afghanistan for a two-year tour of duty, and then back home again. USAID personnel got another allowance to send their children to private schools in America.

The head of USAID's daughter was a college student. She and her mother were both angry as they told me about what Mike had seen. They were liberal people, outraged by the father's failure to do anything. He came home from work, tired and distracted, and made me a Scotch. The cut glass glittered, the whisky a warm golden light. I said 'Thank you' politely.

That winter the UN mission decided to do something about the famine in the north. They ordered a rig from abroad to dig deep wells. The thinking was that in many parts of Afghanistan there was good water very deep down, too far down for traditional Afghan well diggers to reach. Western rigs, a bit like oil drills, could get to that water table. There wouldn't be enough water for irrigation, but nomads could water sheep and keep them alive.

When the digging equipment arrived, the first well they dug was in the United Nations compound in Kabul. The UN staff had long envied the people over at the US embassy. Kabul's water supply was not very clean, nor was an ordinary well. The Americans, always phobic about dirt and dysentery, had long had a deep well in their compound. Now, finally, so did the UN people.

By and large the UN is the most corrupt and useless of the aid agencies. When I was 16 and we were living in India, my mother was a graduate student learning Hindi and my father, Terry was an economist studying rural development. Terry and his friend Swarup, a senior Indian civil servant in charge of a rural development institute, drove round Lucknow in a UNICEF jeep that the United Nations programme for children had given to Swarup's institute. Until that year my parents had sent a cheque to UNICEF every Christmas. After they learned what happened to the jeeps, they never gave UNICEF anything again.

The UN usually pays the best of the aid agencies, but the others pay well too. Many of these salaries don't seem that high in Western terms. An aid worker starting a career now makes $30,000 (£21,000), and can expect to rise to $50,000 (£35,000). The majority of working people in the US or Britain make less, but it is not that much for a professional. Their standard of living, however, is far better than they would have back home. The allowance for shipping furniture and personal possessions helps. So do the allowances for private school fees. But the main difference is that every one around them is so much poorer than at home, and the prices of many things so much cheaper. Sound systems and new cars cost the same. But you can eat out every night.

Servants are ridiculously cheap. Aid people talk about the servant question quite a lot. The general consensus is that being waited on by poor people makes you feel a bit guilty, but the local rich people have servants too. And it's a lot better to spread the money around by having people work for you than just to hoard it. You treat them better than local people do, anyway. Of course you have to watch to make sure the servants don't steal. It seems so stupid of them to do that, and endanger a good job.

Back home, most of the aid workers would have jobs like social worker or college teacher. They might just be able to afford an au pair to help with the kids, or a part-time cleaner later in their careers. In Afghanistan or Nepal or Bangladesh, they can have a maid and a cook and a night watchman and a nice car with a driver. The driver makes sense. The local roads are packed and frightening. Aid people like their drivers, feel more at ease with them than with the other servants. They can imagine themselves working as a driver back home.

They have a nice house too, with a garden and a big wall. Back home they would be nobody. In Dacca or Kathmandu, they can be part of the local ruling class. They are invited to important dinner parties, have local friends who send their sons to the best private school in the country. They feel privy to the gossip of power, and there is no question about booking a table at the third best restaurant in a city of four million people. They feel they're doing something worthwhile.

When someone says that the USAID or Swedish aid or the

UN has spent a million dollars on some project in Sudan or Indonesia, that means they have spent $100,000 (£70,000) each on salaries, expenses, medical bills, drivers, cars and allowances per year for five experts for two years. Those experts know less than the Sudanese or Indonesians with a PhD in the subject who would work for a twentieth of the salary, or less.

In Nepal now a foreign expert on $30,000 to $50,000 a year works alongside local staff paid 10,000 rupees a month, which is $1,800 a year. That's not the driver. That's the wage for a Nepali with a wife and two children, a degree in ecology from a university in New Zealand and 12 years experience. Of course, that's two and a half times what he would make as a university lecturer in Kathmandu.

This inequality is built into all aid programmes, and leads to a deep and obsessive racism among aid personnel. In 1997 I was in an expensive ($3 a meal) tourist restaurant in Kathmandu. At the table next to me a young American man and a British woman were having lunch together for the first time. I listened. They worked for the same aid project, but didn't know each other well. It was the kind of lunch that is almost a date. They were trying to impress each other, so they spent half the lunch talking e-mail. He impressed her by explaining how he could pick up his American e-mail on his computer in Nepal every day. (This was 1997.) The other half of the lunch was spent telling stories about the local staff at the project, their stupidity and laziness.

I had heard such conversations so many times before. They go along with a general denigration of the local people. The reason they're poor, basically, is they're incompetent and dumb. This is rarely explained genetically; aid people are liberals. Instead, the framework is always cultural. The details of what's wrong with the local culture are always different. But what the stereotype explains, always, are the particular reasons why most local staff are useless. To be fair, the aid worker usually has one particular local friend, often their own assistant, who is trying to learn how to be Western and professional ... or 'modern', the code word for white.

The cultural stereotype about Nepalis, for instance, says that they are corrupt and their Hindu culture is hierarchical. It's mind-boggling listening to an American who pays his assistant five per cent of what he makes and his cook three per cent explain to you that the trouble with Nepalis is they take bribes and don't believe in equality.

The point of these prejudices, as of all racism, is to justify inequality. Because the inequality is so obvious and so large, the prejudice needs to be equally big. But aid workers are not totally stupid, and they often started out trying to do good in the world. So they worry, consciously or unconsciously, about the inequality that is feeding them very nicely. The more they worry inside, the more they obsess to each other about the natives.

What makes it worse is that some of the assistants know far more than the advisers. The advisers have trouble listening to them, of course. But someone who has lived in the country, done the job, knows the history and speaks the language is more likely to know what to do. This is why very few senior jobs in the American federal government in Washington are held by people in their twenties with four years work experience who can't speak English and are paid 10 times the salary of a Supreme Court Justice.

Then, too, foreign aid projects don't work. I don't mean they're inefficient or culturally inappropriate. I mean they fail relentlessly, in their own terms. In every country there are one or two aid projects people can point to and say 'That works.' (In Nepal, for instance, there is one German forestry project and Edmund Hillary's aid project in Solu Khumbu). In some lucky countries, there are 5 or 10 good projects out of 500 or 1,000. The others all fail.

I am not making this up. Sit down with foreign aid workers anywhere in the world, somewhere they can talk privately. On a warm night have a few of the old good colonial lagers, Tusker or Kingfisher or Cobra. The aid people will tell you of their guilt, their fury, their frustrations, story after story of corruption and failure and impotence.

This is astonishing. If the library system in Trenton, New Jersey, did not loan books or the social work offices in Kilmarnock, Scotland, did not get some help to the elderly, there would be questions. We expect those services to sort of work, more or less. But foreign aid projects don't work, and this upsets the foreign experts. They feel guilty and overpaid. They need an explanation. 'Culture' provides it.

The actual reasons lie deeper, and have little to do with cultural differences. Foreign aid projects try to help women, or children, or schools or health care. They try to change attitudes and 'empower' local people, though empowering never involves allowing people to vote on how to use the money. They do social work, or try to change the culture. The implication is that these countries are poor because of their customs, or how people think.

In fact, everybody in the world knows that the rich countries are rich because they have modern developed industries. The poor countries don't have big factories. The way you move from being a poor country to a rich one is the way the British, American, Germans, Russians and Japanese did it. You invest money and build those factories. For 50 years the very word 'development' meant changing a poor rural country into a rich urban one. Now it means aid that will do nothing of the kind. After all, the last thing the Western governments want is big competitive industries in Bangladesh or Nepal, unless, of course, the Western corporations own them.

Furthermore, development happens in cities. Foreign aid is directed mainly at villages. No country ever got rich by having productive small farms. Moreover, project money almost always goes to the richer peasants. After all, they own the land. I have lived in India, Afghanistan and Nepal. In all those countries half or more of the village people are sharecroppers or agricultural labourers. Foreign aid does not help them. If it did, if it made them more secure and more confident, the landowners would be furious. In any case, in Nepal the foreign aid money targeted at the villages is actually mostly spent in Kathmandu. It is there that the bureaucrats, the NGOs, the ministries and the four-wheel drive vehicles actually live.

It's the four-wheel drive vehicles I hate most. All over the third world, if you want to get a feel for the country, get on a bus. All human life is there, crowded, uncomfortable, pushed together, talking to each other. In countries where almost everyone takes the bus, the aid people always have four-wheel drive vehicles. These are not the cheap small cars the local rich drive. They are vehicles many of the aid people could not afford back home. In the United States, these 'Suburban Assault Vehicles' are the symbols of yuppie arrogance, of the soccer mom's reckless gas-guzzling contempt for the environment.

Driving the sort of car an ordinary working person in the USA can afford, a Nissan or a Ford, you live in fear. In any accident, the tall reinforced body of the four-wheel drive will pulverise you. Those four-wheel drive aid vehicles in Nepal say 'We are the rich.'

I trekked in Nepal in 1996 with two American college teachers from North Carolina. They had both worked on an aid project in Nepal several years before. One was an anthropologist. He was hired to find out what the villagers thought about a development project. He quit after three months. He said the last thing anyone in the project actually wanted to hear was what the villagers thought. His friend taught geology, and stayed a year, because Nepal is a geologist's heaven. He told me he did nothing for anybody that year. At the end of the year, he decided that there certainly were skills and goods that the Nepalis needed and did not have. Yet every one of those skills and all those goods were available from India, just over the border, far more cheaply than from the United States.

But the governments of the US, Japan and Europe and the United Nations do far more than supply foreign aid. They supply more military aid than economic. That military aid reinforces the power of dictatorships and ruling classes all over the third world. On top of that, there's the debt.

Some of this debt comes from foreign aid loans. These loans are provided to pay for Western experts, four-wheel drive vehicles and servants. Then the taxpayers of the poor country have to pay it back. Much foreign aid, military and civilian, is simply stolen by local politicians, who bank their takings in London, Panama and Geneva. That money then becomes a national debt.

More crushing is the private debt. In Britain, for instance, a government department guarantees most export deals to private companies in the third world. When those companies cannot pay, the British government compensates the British company. Then they add that private debt to the public debt of the third world country.

These debts accumulate interest beyond the ability of most poor countries to repay. Indeed, they are now usually not expected to repay the principal at all. What they have to do is keep paying the interest. Even this means that far more money leaves Africa in interest to banks than comes in aid: three times as much in 2000, according to a conference of Catholic bishops. For most countries in Africa, the debt interest they pay each year is much more than their combined spending on health and education. In 2000, Pakistan spent just half of one per cent of its budget on health, 2.2 per cent on education, and 60 per cent of repaying the debt.

The debt does something else too. The governments and international banks that hold the debt have regular meetings with the governments of the poor countries. Unless you run your economy as we tell you to, they say, we will insist on payment of all the debt. Their instructions on the economy are the same as those of the World Bank and the International Monetary Fund (IMF).

Both the IMF and the World Bank are effectively controlled by the US government. The IMF is larger than the World Bank, and far more important. It works like this. When a country runs into currency troubles, the IMF steps in. Take Turkey in 2000 as an example. Turkey's main export was textiles. The Turkish textile industry collapsed in the wake of the problems of the south-east Asian countries in 1997. They too made textiles, and now they were undercutting the Turkish industry. So Turkey was importing more than it exported. That meant Turkish companies needed dollars to import, and no one needed the Turkish currency, the lira. So the lira fell against the dollar, and then Turkish companies and the Turkish government could not pay their debts. They had to ask the IMF in Washington for loans. The IMF agreed, as they always do, to give on condition that Turkey agreed to certain economic policies. These policies, as always, were designed to lower the consumption of ordinary Turks and increase the profits of business. So pensions were to be cut, social services cut, hospitals closed, wages held down, unions faced down and subsidies to bread and the other necessities of life eliminated.

Always the consequences of an IMF policy are that unemployment rises, and workers' consumption goes down. That in turn does not even help local business. As people have fewer jobs, and those in jobs have less to spend, local companies have a smaller and smaller market. At the same time, the IMF always insists on the privatisation of public services and publicly owned industries. And they always insist that international capital, and particularly US capital, be allowed to buy up local companies.

These IMF polices are not abstract statements. The IMF makes lists in a 'letter of intent'. Those lists specify that the telephone company must be sold off, the pension age must be raised to 65, pensions must be reduced by 20 per cent, bread subsidies must be cut 50 per cent, and so on. The net result is always that international capital becomes stronger, and the workers suffer.

So far I have been talking about government agencies, US aid, the UN and the IMF. But since the early 90s there has been an explosion of Non-Governmental Organisations (NGOs) in aid.

These are charities, like Oxfam and Care and Save the Children, and hundreds of thousands more worldwide. Instead of the government of Nepal or Afghanistan getting aid for education and using some of it to pay teachers, more and more the NGOs get the money direct. This shift is driven by US government policy. The idea, any NGO person will tell you, is that there is something nebulous called 'civil society'. Civil society is better than governments. Better to give the money to Oxfam to administer than to give it to a government, even an elected government.

In practice, the NGOs are part of the privatisation of the world. The business of governments is privatised, and now the NGOs are responsible to no one except the funders. People assume that NGOs are charities who get their money from private contributions. In fact NGOs working in developing countries get most of their money from Western governments, Japan, the UN and the European Union. Of the large NGOs, only Greenpeace and Amnesty International refuse government money on principle.

So more and more of the work of aid is done by through contracts with NGOs. But it is still the same money, from the same governments, for the same purposes. The various projects the NGOs run in each country depend on that money. The NGOs have to do what the Western governments tell them, or lose that money.

The NGOs appear more democratic. In fact they are even less. In the old days you could blame the US government or the UN. Now no one is accountable. And the pay at the NGOs has gone up to meet the old salaries of the national aid agencies.

Living in the third world, I always hated the aid agencies and the NGOs that followed them. But then, in the anti-capitalist movement, I was suddenly working alongside all sorts of NGO people, all of us trying to fight the capitalist system together. Why?

Because the people who work for the aid agencies and the NGOs, by and large, do the work they do because they want to help the poor. There are some people in every agency who are simply corrupt and careerist. Much more commonly, people work in aid for two years or five or 10 or until they cannot bear it any longer. Frustration, rage and guilt build inside them.

They're not stupid. They do listen to what local people are telling them, even when they don't want to hear. They can see the structural features of the world economy that make what they want to do impossible. So throughout the 90s the people who actually worked in NGOs became more and more convinced that something had to be done.

You can see this clearly in the British magazine *New Internationalist*. The editors of the *NI*, and the people who write for it, are ex-aid workers. Month in, month out, the magazine reveals the failings of aid and the ravages of the world economy. The people who read it, avidly, all over the world, are the people who work in the aid agencies. It says what they really want to say, and can't.

Former aid workers in Britain have also set up political organisations like Drop the Debt or People and Planet. Oxfam, War on Want, and Doctors Without Borders have become more political, publishing reports on AIDS drugs in Africa, on debt, on the banks and IMF restructuring.

When our movement came along, the NGOs faced a crisis. They had always attended the meetings of the World Trade Organisation, the IMF and the World Bank. They had done two linked jobs there. First, they lobbied for policies that helped the poor of the world. Secondly, they lobbied for more grants for their own organisations. They saw no contradiction between these two aims, as their organisations were trying to help the poor.

Then suddenly there was a movement in the streets of Seattle outside the World Trade Organisation. That movement was campaigning for the same things the NGOs were lobbying for. Much of what we knew about the third world we had learned from the reports of the NGOs. The campaign in the streets had a

contradictory effect on the NGOs. On the one hand, the movement was a lever. Give us the money, they could say, and do what
we are advocating. Otherwise you will even more trouble with
these young people. The actual campaigners and workers in the
NGOs also felt in their hearts the same as the kids in the streets.
They felt they had no moral alternative but to be part of the
movement.

But there was the money. Since the movement started, the
governments, particularly the US, UN and EU, have been
threatening to cut off the money if the NGOs go too far. This is
why the NGOs are consistently on the right of the anti-
capitalist movement. It's why they always say 'anti-globalisation',
not 'anti-capitalist'. It's why they're often paralysed with fear of
non-violent civil disobedience on our side. It's why they don't
criticise governments directly, why they will attack the policies
of the IMF but never George W. Bush by name.

At one point in Genoa I was writing a leaflet for the GSF
with an activist from a Canadian aid NGO. We were listing the
reasons we were marching. I suggested saying that we were campaigning for cheap unpatented drugs for AIDS in the third
world. 'We can't say that,' the Canadian said.

'Why?' I said.

'My organisation doesn't have a policy on that,' she said.

You bet they don't. If they did, their funders would punish
them. But that woman was there in Genoa, writing that leaflet
with me, trying to build the protests. The money holds the
NGOs back. The decency of the actual aid workers pushes them
forward. Without the campaigns and propaganda by NGOs like
War on Want, the Jubilee Debt Campaign, Friends of the Earth,
Greenpeace and the rest, the movement would never have
started. They told us what needed fixing.

The policies of the IMF don't just hurt poor people in the third
world. They are not directed particularly against the poorest
people in those countries. The core policies (reducing subsidies

on essential goods, driving down wages, privatising public services, cutting any welfare state) hurt working people across the board. The same policies hurt workers in the west.

I was working in a hospital in London when Britain had a currency crisis in 1976. The IMF flew in and told the Labour prime minister, James Callaghan, what to put in his letter of intent. Callaghan did as he was told. The details of the letter of intent were never revealed to the newspapers in Britain. But what we got was cuts in the public services and wage controls.

Until that time Labour had always been the party of the welfare state, the people who gave Britain the National Health Service in 1948. Now Labour became the party that cut. They had never closed a hospital; in the next three years they shut 200. For the first and only time since the 1930s, the real wages of workers fell. In 1979 the Conservatives under Margaret Thatcher won the election. Fewer people voted for Thatcher than had voted for the Conservatives when they lost the election to Labour five years before. What had happened was that Labour voters stayed home.

After that, Labour local governments and the Conservative central government both pushed through cuts in public services year after year. Such a thing had not happened since the 1930s. The IMF letter of intent had made it respectable, inevitable, a fact of life. Every year the National Health Service lost beds and the hospital waiting lists lengthened. Fewer nurses, more stretched, provided a worse service. I worked in two geriatric hospitals where nurses on understaffed wards ran from one patient to another, always having to ignore somebody who was calling for a urine bottle. The patient, old, ashamed, helpless, would call but not scream. The nurse would be attending someone else, waiting for her tea break, hoping she would get that break, hating the patients in that moment, hating the job. And then the patient would piss herself and go silent in shame. Every day.

In 1993 I was teaching a course in the National Health Service to train nurses and doctors to do counseling for HIV tests. One of the students on my course was the director of nursing for obstetrics at the local hospital. On a coffee break from the course, standing outside in the sun in the car park, she told me about the waiting list for intensive care. Premature babies would go to the paediatric intensive care ward, where they would be put in incubators and tended carefully, and many of them would live. But there weren't enough incubators, because there weren't enough nurses for the ward. So some premature babies would go on the waiting list for the incubators.

'What happens to a premature baby on the waiting list?' I asked.

'They die,' she said.

'Is this just our hospital?' I said.

'No,' she said, 'I think there are waiting lists for paediatric intensive care in most maternity units in the country.'

Then she asked my advice. She said part of her job was to meet the parents of the baby after it died and counsel them. She always wanted to tell them the cuts had killed their child. But she felt, as a counsellor, that might leave them with a rage so deep they could never come to terms with the loss. So sometimes she told them about the cuts, but mostly she didn't. What did I think she should do?

'I don't know,' I said.

4 | **Thursday**

I arrived in Genoa on Sunday, part of the small advance party for Globalise Resistance. The first demonstration would be on Thursday. My job for the next few days was to sit in GSF committee meetings, talk to the press, and try to decide, with other people, exactly what we were going to do on Friday, and with whom. I was ever so proud of myself, being a leader like this, and quite unsure I would be able to do it.

Globalise Resistance was bringing 500 people on a chartered train. We had buses to take everyone from the assembly point in London to the ferry for Calais on Wednesday night. The chartered French train would take everyone from Calais to the Italian border. There buses would pick people up and take them to arrive in Genoa early Friday morning.

Two weeks before we left, *The Times* ran a scare story about a train full of 'English anarchists' going to Genoa. We were flattered. Then *The Times* made a formal approach to the French minister of the interior, asking him to ban the train. The minister asked the French railway company to cancel our booking. They refused. The man handling our booking at SNCF said they were a nationalised company threatened with privatisation. They supported our cause, and he was coming on the train with us.

Monday, two days before the train was due to leave, the French government banned it. The British and Italian borders were open, and any French people who wanted could cross France. But not us English anarchists. We didn't know what to do. I told everybody that we had better give refunds and everyone who could book a flight should fly to Turin or Milan.

That same Monday morning somebody sent a letter bomb to a police station in Genoa. It exploded in the face of the rank and file policeman who opened it. It was a small bomb, but he lost an eye.

Everybody in the GSF thought two things when we heard the news. First, some part of the security service had done it. Second, here we go again.

The Italians in the GSF had not forgotten the 'strategy of tension'. In the 1970s the CIA had been worried by the growing strength of the revolutionary left in Italy. They had been even more worried by the strike movement in the factories, particularly the 'Hot Autumn' of 1969. After that it looked more and more likely that the communist party would be invited into a government coalition. That was what disturbed the CIA most. So, in cooperation with parts of the Italian security services, they embarked on the 'strategy of tension': bombing. These bombings were carried out by police units, or by right-wing organisations with police support.

This sounds like a left-wing fantasy. It is now, 25 or 30 years later, after many official investigations and revelations, the general understanding in Italy, across the political spectrum, of what happened. But people also know it was not that simple. For the left fell right into the trap set by the right.

The bombings were in ordinary public places, and usually not against political targets. One in Bologna railway station killed 85 people in 1980. The idea was to blame them on the left, or anarchists. But this was done in such a way that people weren't really sure who did the bombings. The fact that they were in public places, that there was no predicting who would be hit, raised the level of public anxiety. The bombings were organised in the hope that people would turn to the politics of law and order. This might not simply be a turn to the right. It could be a turn to the centre, to the responsible people who would protect you from the bombings of the left and right.

In the late 60s and early 70s a new generation of striking workers and occupying students had flooded into the Italian left, many of them suddenly hoping for revolution. It didn't happen. By the mid-70s, as the militant workers' movement weakened, some of them began looking for another road to revolution.

For some, that meant guns and bombs. 'Urban guerrilla struggle' was popular with the left across the world in those years. Millions of people had a picture of Che Guevara on the wall, usually the one where he looks like an impossibly beautiful Christ. Che died leading a small band of revolutionaries in Bolivia. The theory behind this armed struggle was that a small group could pick up the gun and inspire a mass movement that would welcome them to power. Fidel Castro and Che had done exactly this in Cuba, and it could be done again.

Only it couldn't. When Fidel and Che and their small group were in the hills of the Sierra Madre in Cuba, the dictatorship of Batista had been falling of its own weight. The US Government, hedging their bets, had shifted their support to Castro. They were not about to do that again. There were armed struggles by small bands in many places in the 60s and 70s, in India and many parts of Latin America. All of them lost. In some cities there was 'urban guerrilla warfare', the rural model adapted to the city. All of them lost too. The Red Brigades in Italy were part of that.

The politics behind them was that a small number of people would lead the way. We fight in the mountains; you cheer when we come down into the city. This was just as elitist as the old communist parties, or the normal parliamentary socialists. There is no democracy in an urban guerrilla movement. There cannot be. Anywhere the struggle is fundamentally military, the relations within the movement have to be ones of command. So it was only natural that after Fidel and Che came to power in Cuba, there were no votes for anything.

But the real problem Che faced in Bolivia, and the Red Brigades faced in Italy, was that they had launched a war without the support of the majority. The Vietnamese communists did fight, and win, long and desperate wars. But they did it by building up support, village by village, so that when they finally launched a guerrilla struggle they had the people with them. Indeed, village by village, the Vietnamese communists were the fellow villagers who the poor peasants respected most. That is an enormous base to start from.

In Bolivia the miners had led a revolution that toppled a military dictatorship in 1954. Che decided not to try to win their support. Instead he took his band to a remote area occupied by indigenous ('Indian') people. Neither Che nor anybody else in his band spoke the indigenous language. He was shot by the Bolivian army, helped by the CIA.

The Red Brigades in Italy were smashed in the same way. Under a dictatorship, such as Mussolini's, people will support what they regard as legitimate resistance. When people are allowed to vote, as they were in Italy, it's different. If the revolutionaries take to violence without winning their point democratically, the police usually have some legitimacy when they start kicking down doors.

This repression was easier for the Italian state because they had infiltrated the Red Brigades from top to bottom. The Brigades had become part of the 'strategy of tension.' All this is known now in Italy, to everybody.

The security services didn't want to stop the Red Brigades. Indeed, in 1978 the Red Brigades kidnapped Aldo Moro, the prime minister. Moro had been negotiating to bring the Communist Party into a government coalition. The Red Brigades held him prisoner for weeks, and then killed him. Nothing could have pleased the security services more. Indeed, the secret service were part of the Red Brigades kidnapping group, and helped to stop any negotiations for Moro's release. There would be no communists in government now.

The defeat of the Red Brigades was traumatic for the Italian left, because of that picture of Che on the wall. Across much of the left in those years, there was a feeling that at the heart of revolution was violence. 'Power grows out of the barrel of a gun,' the dictator Mao had said, and many quoted him. The communist parties in Italy, France, Bolivia, India and many other places had mass support, but would not challenge the capitalist system. Many people felt sold out and thought the military road was the radical road. Almost all the models of revolution on offer, from Ho Chi Minh, Mao, Castro and Che to the more orthodox communists, were now deeply undemocratic.

This had not always been true. In 1887 Lenin was 17 years old. That year his older brother Alexander, an urban guerrilla, was hanged for his part in the assassination of the Russian ruler, Tsar Alexander II. Lenin spent several years deciding whether to follow his brother. In the end he decided not to. He wrote pamphlet after pamphlet arguing that his brother's movement, the Populists, were mistaken.

The only way to change Russia, Lenin said, was a mass movement of the new working class in the cities. The weapons of that movement would be the meeting, the newspaper, the vote, the strike, the demonstration, and the public insurrection. In that insurrection the people would not fight the army: they would talk to the soldiers, and bring them over to the side of the people. Lenin was not opposed to killing dictators like the Tsar on principle. For him the crucial point was that terrorism meant a small group of people trying to change the world, not a mass movement.

But that Lenin, the democrat, has been written out of history. Many Italian leftists who decided not to take the military road had a sneaking feeling that those who did were somehow more romantic, more principled or more revolutionary. So when the Red Brigades were broken, and gave evidence against each other in court, the radical left felt demoralised. Then it became clear how deep the police penetration had run. Crucially, it became clear that the police had not infiltrated the Brigades in order to stop them, but to encourage them for years and then arrest them only when it suited them. The left learned. And they had passed the lesson on to a new generation on the Italian left: beware of terrorism.

So when that letter bomb went off, everybody in the GSF assumed some part of the security services was recycling the 'strategy of tension'. The message the bomb would carry in the newspapers was clear. Those who believed left-wing terrorists sent the bomb would be put off both the left and Genoa. Fewer people would come to the protests. But those who thought it was the work of the security forces would be even more scared. They too might reconsider coming to Genoa.

We didn't think that Berlusconi had sent the bomb. What was happening, I was pretty sure, was that there were factions inside the security forces, arguing about what to do. One of those factions, in one part of the secret state, had sent the bomb.

The GSF held a press conference. Walden Bello, a fierce and decent economist in a suit, dark skin and neatly trimmed beard, spoke for us. Bello is probably the leading economic thinker in the anti-capitalist movement. He also used to be in the Filipino Communist Party. Bello knows that sometimes you have to lay the truth on the line. He told the press the secret state had sent the bomb.

The next day another bomb was discovered outside the Carlini stadium in the east of the city, where the White Overalls movement were all staying and practising their tactics. The bomb was small, and very obvious. Rumour said it was actually ticking. Again, we said, the 'strategy of tension'.

In Italy, most people seemed to believe this.

Wednesday afternoon we got a call from London. Our train was back on. The letter from the French government telling us this said they had changed their minds under pressure from the French railway unions. Joy.

What happened was this. Chris Nineham and I, representing GR in Genoa, didn't know what to do. But Tom Behan was with us to help with translation. Tom is a lecturer in Italian at a British university, and an academic expert on organised crime in Naples and the plays of Dario Fo. Since the train was cancelled, he'd been on the phone, the fax and e-mail, hour after hour, contacting the whole world, asking them to protest. And the French trade unions had delivered.

I'd given up while Tom kept trying. I told myself it was another piece of evidence that my brain was still stuck in the years of defeat. But I think it was also because Tom spoke Italian. He'd been talking to ordinary people outside the meetings ever since we got here. He could feel, in a way I couldn't yet, just how big and new this was going to be.

Back in London Guy and the others at the GR office were ringing people madly to tell them train was back on.

Wednesday is meetings, or chatting, encouraging people, ranting, and talking to the press all day. Late that night I speak to a socialist meeting at the school. I've done a lot of public speaking, and it's always draining, the same way that acting for two hours in a play is a full day's work. Tonight is particularly hard. I've been up late, getting up early, on the run, and I was already tired when I got to Genoa. I'm feeling my 53 years. But it is an enormous joy to talk about the American power I fought 30 years ago to a whole new generation (in this case 50 people in an old school gymnasium that echoes so badly I have to shout to be heard) at a great European demonstration. That exhilaration exhausts me too.

I leave the school at 10, and stop outside to munch the bananas I've been carrying around in my bag. Rafaela Bolini catches me up. She's from ARCI, the old cultural organisation of the Communist Party. The party's gone, but ARCI hangs on. She was the main person who hammered together the compromise at that long meeting I went to a month ago. Rafaela has been the person in charge of the international meetings for the GSF. I admire her enormously. I'd very much like to be somebody like her. She's also a good-looking woman 20 years younger than me. Earlier that day I'd watched her speaking to 300 foreigners down at the Convergence Centre, explaining to them the GSF policy on non-violence. I watched her confidence, her Italian dark glasses, her blue skirt blowing in the breeze off the sea. She wants to talk, and we wander through the empty streets.

We're both very tired. I urge her to get some sleep; I can see she's moving in a fog. She asks what I think will happen to our movement.

'I don't know,' I say. 'I know Saturday will be very big. The movement's growing now. For a while nothing can stop us. That doesn't mean we'll win in the end. I was part of the movement of the 60s, and we were smashed.'

She says that we have to learn from the South. We have to change.

'Yes,' I say, 'we have to learn all the time', I say. Then I talk about the old sectarianism, the way we rant. I say we have to change all that.

'Yes,' she says, 'oh yes.'

So I know Italy must be the same as Britain.

I say that I keep thinking about a quote from William Morris, the 19th century British socialist. Morris said people make their own history, fight for their dream, and then they win, but what they get is not what they meant at all. And then new people have to fight again, for the same dream, only they have to fight for it under another name. I say, that's what this new movement is groping towards, fighting for the old dream of socialism under another name.

It's astonishing how empty the streets are at this time of night. I'm lost.

'Those of us from the old socialism,' I say, 'we have to change and learn from this new movement. But we have to hold on to the good things from the old too, or the new movement will be lost without them.'

'How do you know?' Rafaela says.

'That's the problem,' I say. 'The hard part. How to know what are the bad parts you need to discard and the good parts you need to keep.'

'That's the problem,' she says. 'I think the old idea of a party has to go.'

I don't agree with her, so I say nothing. I'm trying to listen. I was a counsellor for 14 years. Sometimes when you're listening right, you know you're waiting for somebody to say the one thing they want to say. When you hear it, you know that's it. I knew it when Rafaela said: 'We are making history.'

'Yes,' I say, and wait.

We walk along, side by side, and she doesn't say the next thing. So I say it.

'It scares me,' I say. 'Making history. Two months ago I was nothing. I've been nothing all my life.'

'Yes,' she says happily, 'two months ago I was nothing also.'

'It's frightening,' I say.

'Yes,' she says, relieved to hear me say it.

We get to where I have to head up the hill, and she back to town. I say: 'It's all scary, but I've never been as happy in all my life as the last two months.'

'Me too,' she says, surprised, the words bursting out of her, because of course like me she looks worried all the time. She throws her arms around me, hugs me and leaves. I go up the hill.

We were staying with a Christian pacifist, Maria, a volunteer for the GSF. She spent her days checking ID on the door at the school that served as the GSF headquarters, and energetically cleaning up. It was astonishing how much crap the foreigners left behind them on the floor, on the school playground, at the Convergence Centre, as if they'd all been raised by servants. Maria cleaned up heroically, muttering a bit, always smiling.

Maria put up three of us from Britain, me, Chris Nineham and Martin. She made us wonderful breakfasts every morning, omelettes and sliced sausage and cheeses and breads. We felt guilty eating it.

Maria is my age. Chris is about 15 years younger than Maria and me, the grey just beginning to show in streaks above his ears. He was really offended at one point in Genoa when I referred to 'people our age'. He's tall, thin and lanky, and says 'you know' a lot. Chris works full time for the SWP, and is our point man for Globalise Resistance. He's a kind man, sociable, asks after you. It's a politician's manner, but genuine too. He's also a subtle thinker.

Martin was along to coordinate the SWP's recruiting and meetings at Genoa. He's about 30, a computer worker. He'd also been at Prague and Nice. Martin has a working-class accent, a big kind face and short, reddish, thinning hair. He always wears a baseball cap.

I got home Tuesday night just before midnight. I sat at the foot of Martin's bed in the room he was sharing with Chris. We talked quietly. The room was full of the stuffed animals that belonged to the little girl who had moved out to a friend's so we could use the room.

Chris told us about going to Sudan when he was 20 on a trip with some other friends from college. They went up the Nile from Egypt, then took the railway to the coast. They came to Kassala, a desperately poor town full of Ethiopian refugees; it was the early 80s. Chris couldn't bear what he was seeing. The worst, he said, was that the people were so friendly. He'd get a sandwich at a roadside stall, and eat it in front of all these hungry people, politely staring. While he was eating, somebody in the crowd would secretly pay for his sandwich, because he was a guest in their country. When he came to pay, he'd find this out, but the man had already walked away. Chris would run down the road, trying to find the man, shouting after him that he should take the money.

I tell Martin and Chris about walking home with Rafaela, and how pleased I was that she wanted to talk to me.

'She's been good,' Chris says. He's been in a lot more meetings with the GSF today than me. 'But she's in denial about the police. The rest of them are too. They keep saying that the police have promised us they won't go too far.'

Uh-oh, I think. Chris probably thinks I'm in denial too. I trust his judgment on these things more than my own.

'Do you think they're going to shoot people?' Martin asks Chris.

'I don't know,' Chris says. 'How would I know?'

Martin spasms on his bed into a sort of ball. 'I was hoping you wouldn't say that,' he says. Chris has been so calm through the last three days, wisecracking, encouraging us, telling us not to lose our nerve. Martin and I were kind of assuming it was because he knew something we didn't that made us safe.

'How would I know?' Chris says again.

Martin does a theatrical little moan on his bed, making a joke of it, but not really.

'Maybe they will, maybe they won't,' Chris says. He is a bit annoyed, like 'I'm not your mother, I can't solve this one for you.'

'It's all right for you,' I say. 'Nancy's back home. Her son Ruard, my stepson Ruard, is going to be here. She has to worry about both of us. Either one of us dies, the relationship's over.'

They both laugh at that, relieved at the joke, also knowing it's true.

Martin sits up. 'It depends how you put it, Jonathan,' he says. 'The relationship can survive if you do it right.'

'Yeh?' I say. I want to know.

Martin says, 'You say which do you want first, the good news or the bad news?'

We collapse in giggles, relieved because we've admitted to each other how afraid we are. Now that I'm showing more of my fear, I'm feeling less afraid inside.

The next day, down at the Convergence Centre by the shore, I seek out John from New Cross after lunch. John is 18 or 19, a student from London. He's thin, young enough that his chest has not filled out yet. His light hair is cut very short, and he too wears a baseball cap. He seems full of a contained tension since he came back from Gothenburg; anger, I think. John and I both spoke at a Globalise Resistance meeting in London a couple of weeks before. He spoke without flourish or affectation, just saying what he had seen. He ended his talk by saying quietly, 'We are winning.'

Now I find him standing by a table and say, 'Can I ask you a personal question?'

He's a young Englishman. A hairy American 10 years older than his father suddenly wants to ask a personal question. He says, 'Yes, maybe, well, certainly, it depends, OK.'

'You must be frightened here,' I said, 'after being so close to the shooting in Gothenburg. What do you do with your fear?' I see on his face that this is too personal, so I say quickly, 'I'm asking because I'm afraid.'

John sees I need help. 'Mainly what I do is I don't think about it.'

'So you wish I hadn't asked,' I say.

'When I think about it, I see those pictures of the faces of people in Seattle who were hit by rubber bullets,' John says.

'I'm sorry,' I say.

'It's all right,' he says. 'Then I tell myself there are an awful lot of people here. The odds are very small that it's going to be me.'

'Right,' I say. 'A hundred thousand people, it probably won't be me. I'll try that.'

It does help. But a little voice says: 'You're pretending to be a leader. You gave a speech at the Globalise Resistance people urging people to come and 50 people bought tickets for the train right afterwards. You were very proud of that. What if it's one of them?'

Our fear was what our enemies wanted. That is why they had shot somebody in Gothenburg. It's why the bombs had gone off in Genoa. It was working. The question was whether it was working well enough to stop us.

An American journalist interviewed me at the Convergence Centre Wednesday afternoon. He was my age, in a suit, with the handsome, reliable look of an anchor man. 'Frank' said he had heard rumours of a shadowy group, outside the control of the GSF, who were coming to town. They were bent on violence. What were we going to do about that?

I said I hadn't heard about any such people. I'd been to a lot of meetings in Genoa. I should have at least met somebody who'd talked about them. I thought it was probably all spin from the government, designed to put people off coming to Genoa.

I was right about the spin. But there were people coming bent on violence. I should have listened to Frank.

We talked some after the interview, two middle-aged men together. I ran into him again that evening. He told me he'd been at Chicago in 1968, for the protests at the Democratic convention. He bent forward so I could see the little white scar above his right eyebrow, from Chicago. 'I was in Paris in May 68 too,' he said. 'Just luck, really. I was doing my junior year abroad at the Sorbonne. I've been going around Genoa, having flashbacks all day.'

At Chicago, I knew, the demonstrators had chanted 'The Whole World is Watching' as the police beat them in front of the TV cameras. Senator Abraham Ribicoff, from the convention floor, had called the Chicago police 'Gestapo'.

And yet, in the end, the protesters had won. America left Vietnam. Clearly Frank thought this was history too.

Day by day the Convergence Centre fills up. People come from all over Europe. There are a group of Israelis too, looking for at least one Palestinian so they can hold a joint meeting. There aren't many people here from the third world, except for immigrants already living in Europe. It's too expensive, too far, and too difficult to get a visa.

We have stalls for both Globalise Resistance and the Socialist

Workers Party at the Convergence Centre. The SWP is working with our sister organisations from other countries in the International Socialists here. We're all Trotskyists, of a kind. Where we differ from the rest of the left is that we have always said that the old communist dictatorships of Russia and China had nothing to do with socialism. They were 'state capitalist', we say, by which we mean that the USSR or Cuba worked just like one giant company competing in the world market. To be a worker there was fundamentally no different from being one in the US or India.

The International Socialists in Genoa seem to have come out of the years of defeat better than the rest of the European revolutionary left, who are not much in evidence here. It's very nice being together here. We hold meetings at the Convergence Centre every day, yelling into the wind through a megaphone, trying to recruit people. We have one recruitment leaflet in, I think, seven languages, like they do with the instructions for a washing machine these days. But people don't really want to talk about ideas and alternatives yet. Every conversation turns to tactics, to what will happen on Friday and Saturday. This is fear, mesmerising us.

As people come in from other countries, they report on opinion polls in the papers from home. A German magazine asked people if they supported the aims of the protest in Genoa: 63 per cent say yes. In former East Germany, it's 71 per cent. The same question was asked in a poll for a Greek paper: 67 per cent said yes. Then the paper asked 'If you could go to Genoa, would you?' and 31.5 per cent of Greeks said yes. It's hard to tell what that means. Probably the question means if you had the money and could get the time off work. And not all those people who say yes would go even then. But it's a statement of strong sympathy, and it means if the G8 was in Athens the protest would be enormous. The next day a French paper asks about Genoa. Again, over 60 per cent say yes, they support us.

There are no polls asking these questions in Italy, Britain or the US. I am pretty sure the results would be the same.

This is amazing. We are the opposition, supported by no mainstream political party in Europe or North America. When the people who represent our views run in elections they get three per cent in the US, or five per cent in Italy. We are the margins. When people think about us in power, they draw back. But we are also the majority. On the issues, they agree with us. On privatisation, AIDS drugs, Star Wars and the like we have the support of something like three out of four, or four out of five, people. There is an enormous gap between the official parties and what people want. Ordinary people are not necessarily in favour of what we are in favour of. But they are against what we are against, namely what the G8 wants.

This puts the G8 on the defensive.

I'm speaking to a lot of journalists. Before the last two months I never spoke to them as a public figure. Now I'm a spokesman for Globalise Resistance. But I have worked in journalism, as a free-lance sub-editor in London doing shifts on magazines to replace people who are sick or on holiday. This means I know that journalists are human beings. I also know that what they think privately is often quite different from what they write. They do what they're told, like other workers. When I edit copy, I do what I'm told too. Knowing all this helps in talking to them.

The English language journalists in Genoa clearly have an agenda set by their editors. They are supposed to ask about violence. This gives me three options. I can condemn any violence, and join the official chorus. I can support violence, and occupy the monster role. I can say there won't be any violence, and not be believed.

Instead, I try to keep saying that non-violence and violence are not the issue. The politicians and the media, I say, are trying the make us all talk about violence and non-violence instead of about the issues. (As I say this, the media person interviewing me nods encouragingly just off camera.) I say this is because on almost all the issues, we have the support of the overwhelming majority in every country on earth. 'Thank you,' the journalist says at the end.

I start to get the feeling they are coming to me so I will say this. I think maybe they're telling each other. One broadcast team interview me and are clearly pleased. Later the same day they ring my mobile to say the tape they made has auto-buggered itself. They really, really want me to do another interview the next morning. We meet up, shake hands and run the interview again. I'm babbling about the issues, they're nodding, we're having a really good time. They have clearly been getting into the spirit of Genoa the last two days. At the end the reporter thanks me and they turn off the camera. I say to the reporter 'You forgot to ask me about the threat of violence. Could you please ask me again?'

The producer says to the reporter, laughing, 'How could you forget to ask that?' The producer is happy as she laughs, she does know why the reporter forgot.

But I tell her anyway, for his sake. I say: 'He forgot to ask it because he doesn't want to be the person who has to ask that question any more.'

She nods. Looking at the ground, holding his microphone, the reporter nods too. The expression on his face seems to me a combination of professional shame and personal pride. Then he raises the mike and asks me about violence.

I say piously, for the record, that violence is not the issue here.

Tomorrow is the first protest.

The march on Thursday is for the immigrants. We know it will be small. Publicly, the GSF has said we expect 15,000 today, 30,000 for the direct action on Friday, and 100,000 for the big march on Saturday.

We have said, very loudly, that there will be no direct action today, nothing even non-violent. We have tried to get immigrants from all over Europe on this march. Many of them won't have papers. Many others will be in danger of deportation if they are arrested. We want no possibility of arrests today.

Today is important because there has not been a national march about immigration in Italy before. Across Europe, the right is organising against immigrants. The driving force are the 'neo-fascists' and 'post-fascists': Haider in Austria, Fini and the National Alliance in Italy, the Motherland Party in Turkey, the BNP in Britain, the National Front in France, and many more. Racism is the guts of their politics, and speeches against asylum seekers and immigrants are the public face of their racism. But it goes far wider than the hard right. In Britain the Conservative opposition has been relentless in their attacks on asylum seekers, and so have most of the press. New Labour has fallen into line, denying most applications for asylum, building more detention centres and announcing how tough they are. Underneath all this official racism, there are rising numbers of racial attacks in many places in Britain. In the week we demonstrate in Genoa, in Glasgow a Kurdish asylum seeker who had fled a Turkish prison is knifed to death by two men shouting racist slogans. In Hull, England, 200 miles south, another Kurd almost dies of knife wounds the same week.

In Italy, the National Alliance and the Northern League, the two extreme right organisations in the government, are collaborating on a new anti-immigrant bill. So this march matters.

But it's only a taster. We don't expect it be that big.

I'm scared now, the most scared I'll be until Sunday morning. Maria and I try to talk over breakfast. We're both very frustrated by sharing the house and not being able to talk. She can speak a little Spanish, and so can I, but not enough. We try hand signals too. Chris and Martin and I all feel guilty too, eating all her food and cluttering up her house and not being able to talk to her. Also, every night she really wants to tell us the political events of the day, and we want to hear, and can't understand.

This morning she shows me a picture on the wall, next to one of the religious pictures, of herself and a middle-aged man. She says it's her husband. He died two years ago, of melanoma of the back and the legs. It was a long death, difficult to watch. He spent all his life, she says, fighting for justice for the workers. He spent years representing his fellow workers, wherever he worked, in one long case before the tribunal. And then she says something I don't understand.

Maria tries again. She makes her first and second fingers walk across the table toward me. He's dead, she says. But during these days he will be walking, like this, in the streets with us.

We both cry quietly, smiling at each other. Now I don't feel guilty about her putting us up. I know why she's doing it.

I go down to a meeting at the GSF headquarters in a school. I find the committee arranging the order of march for the afternoon. I'm late, everything has pretty much been arranged, and the meeting is in Italian. A Kurd from the PKK translates for me. He says they have decided to put Globalise Resistance almost at the back. I say OK. I'm not pushy enough for this sort of meeting. Also, I think it will be a small march, so it won't matter.

The march is supposed to start at four. In every country I've ever been in, protest marches always start late. You wait, hoping more people will turn up, and sometimes they do. The Italians say they are the same. We'll probably actually start about an hour late.

I meet up with the other people at the Convergence Centre at three. We're going to march together from there to the start of the march. In our place at the back of the march, we will have Globalise Resistance in front, and then behind us the Socialist Workers Party and the other groups from the International Socialists.

We walk up the hill toward the start of the march in fine order, yelling and shouting slogans. For me, the relief is enormous. In all those committees, I was aware of trying desperately hard to do my best alongside professional full-time activists. All the time, there has been the uncertainty of how it would turn out. Now I'm back, a face in the crowd. I'm no expert on street tactics, and I know it. The speeches and the meetings are done. I can just be part of it all, yell with the rest.

The sun is shining. We skirt round the police headquarters on the shore next to the Convergence Centre. Then we start on a road that sweeps uphill a bit, overlooking the port and the G8 meeting. Chris and I walked all this part yesterday, looking for how to get to the Red Zone on Friday. The police were moving giant ship containers in then, using trucks and cranes. Now the ship containers, two high, line the edge of the shore road so we can't look down on where the G8 are meeting.

The papers say the police and army down there have surface to air missiles. For what?

We swing along, singing 'Bandiera Rossa,' the old Italian communist song. It means 'Red Flag', though not the same as the British anthem. It's a great tune, and I'm learning the words. We get to the start of the march, in a broad piazza below a church with a spectacular green dome. The steep stone steps that sweep down from the church are covered with people. We go through the piazza, out the other side and down a side road.

Then we wait. The march starts moving off at ten past four because the piazza is already full. We're stuck down a side lane. But we're happy there, yelling 'Our World is Not For Sale' in Italian and 'One Solution, Revolution' in English.

After half an hour we still haven't moved. I walk up the lane a bit to see what's happening. It's all packed. I can't even get back to the school. I see an Italian feminist I know. We wave at each other in delight. The march is big. Really big.

I count back to 1974, the year the miners won a national strike, the last year the movements of the 60s and the unions were still winning. There have been 27 years of defeat since then. Hanging in there, telling each other some day the upturn will come, making ourselves believe it, people dropping out of political activity all the time. More than half my life. Most of my adult life. And it's over. The long, cold, fucking winter is over.

I see Maria on the side of the road, and I can see in her face, she knows it too. We hug.

Police are visible from one place, in the distance, behind a fence. Some French people are chanting something. I can usually get the chants, but not this one. It sounds great, though. I ask one of the French what it means. It's slang, he says. More or less it means 'The cash, the cops, they're both the same thing.'

I think about that walking back down the hill. The cash, the cops, they're both the same thing. The more you think about it, the more it means. This is my introduction to something new about the chants of the movement. For years we've been chanting 'Maggie, Maggie, Maggie, Out, Out, Out' about Margaret Thatcher, or 'No This' or 'Stop That.' But in Genoa, each of the chants is an idea. The cash, the cops, they're both the same thing.

I go back down the road. Chris Bambery is there. He flew in yesterday. Bambery is a full timer for the SWP. He's organisation in human form, always pushing people to do more, always trying to hold people together. His accent is working-class Scots, that gentle voice with marbles in the mouth. I respect him, but I'm also scared of his disapproval. He's a hard man, and he's angry now. 'Why are we stuck here?' Bambery wants to know. He can't bear just standing around. He's energy personified. I tell him we were put at the back of the march. I don't tell him I negotiated that. Particularly as he's staying with us at Maria's, and last night we took an hour and a half to get home from the Convergence Centre in a car because I was too stupid to figure out the one-way system. I'd only ever walked it. It was raining that night, and Bambery was making a heroic effort not to scream at me.

It's ten past five. We've been here an hour. The march must be huge. Bambery decides to sneak us all up the road on the pavement, past the anarchists with the black flag who are just standing there. At half past five we get to the point the march started from. An hour and a quarter, just to start.

I march with the others for 10 minutes, shouting with joy. I think this must be the most spirited part of the march. I'm proud of us. Then I have to run on ahead. I have arranged for a Kurdish comrade to speak at the rally at the end of the march. She's worked on a short speech in Turkish, and had it translated into English and from there into Italian. She'll read her speech from the platform and Carmela, who's Italian but lives in London, will read out the translation. I'm the one who knows the man from the PKK who's helping coordinate speakers, so I have to go with them.

We run, threading our way through the crowd, stopping to walk quickly and then running again. I'm faster than both the other comrades. They're both much younger than me, beautiful and thin. They're struggling to keep up. I'm so pleased. Maybe it's because they smoke and I don't. Actually I've been begging cigarettes all morning. I smoke when I'm afraid.

The crowd is a riot of colour. Every picture of the crowds in the next three days will show this. Lots of red: red flags, red shirts, red bandannas, right through the demonstration. But yellows too, not flags but shirts and caps. The yellows and blues are bright, primary, the colours a little kid would pick out on the colour chart and say 'That's blue!'

It's part of the new style. The crowds of my youth were counter-culture, full of tie-dyes and the like. It was a rebellion against a grey world, but we carried a lot of that grey with us. Not this confident colour, everybody dressed in their 'hey, look at me!' clothes, swirling round each other.

The street's packed, but there's space along the pavements for us to weave in and out past people. And the shouting. It wasn't just us. All the way through the demonstration, groups are shouting.

We come down past the rows of ship containers blocking off the view. Anarchists dressed as pink fairies are sitting on top of the containers, waving wands. I wave back at Venus from London, the head fairy, who has been making fairy tutus all week down at the Convention Centre. As people go by they bang on the empty ship containers with their hands, making a great echoing roar.

I'm watching for what groups are big, confident and shouting. The young communists, part of Communist Refoundation, are going at it with a will. So are COBAS, the union group. They even have a truck with a great driving sound system. Then we're up with ATTAC, and I know we're getting close to the front. We go into a tunnel under the railway line with ATTAC. They have banners all over the place, big thin ones on sticks, with a red per cent sign on them. I can't make out what they're chanting, but the sound in the tunnel is enormous, and I shout nonsense syllables with them at the top of my voice. Our numbers give us joy. Finally, we know we are not alone.

We're out of the tunnel. I'm mostly walking now, not running, but going forward. Right at the front we're in among the immigrants, but there are a lot of Italians here too. Everybody is chanting another idea: 'Siamo tutti clandestini (We are All Clandestines)'. The word means illegal immigrants, but also hidden people, hunted, underground. It also means: immigrants are no different from us. We will not say we are separate. Like when the Nazi occupation ordered the Jews of Denmark to sew a yellow star on their clothes, many Danes and the Danish king wore a yellow star too. But it also means: we are all oppressed.

We swing down along the shore and into the Convergence Centre, shouting one last time 'We are All Clandestines.' There's a big stage from the pop concert the night before. I get my two comrades through the bouncers, up with the speakers. Then I beg a cigarette from somebody I don't know and sit on the tarmac by myself, happy.

On the stage one of the organisers announces that the police estimate of the march is 50,000. He thinks it's 80,000. Later it turns out that the final police estimate is 30,000. The papers say 50,000. So probably 80,000 is about right. This was the curtain raiser. It's bigger than Seattle, four or five times the size of Prague. I know now, we all know, the direct action day tomorrow will be big. The march Saturday will be enormous: hundreds of thousands of people.

The police, and the government, must have known it too. Looking back, I think this was the moment they decided on real violence.

We cannot know the details of how the G8 and the Italian government decided to police Genoa. Such matters are never discussed in public. One always has to guess, on the basis of what evidence there is to hand.

Even with individuals, motivations are hard to judge. The best guide to motivations is usually to assume that people intended the consequences of their actions. So it is with governments. The best way is to assume that they wanted the consequences of their actions. The consequences of the way the police behaved in Genoa was to scare the people who went there very badly. We have to assume that's what they wanted to do.

On a big demonstration, the decisions about policing are taken from the top. They are not taken by the police acting on their own. The Genoa protest was the biggest political event in Italy that month, if not that year. Berlusconi and his interior minister must have given the police orders. There may well have been people in the police who wanted to go much further than Berlusconi. But they could not begin to do so without his encouragement for hard policing, and his backing afterwards. And Berlusconi could not have acted without consulting George W. Bush, or more likely the people with the brains around him.

Bush, Berlusconi, and the G8 knew Thursday evening that the demonstration on Saturday would be enormous. A march of that size would legitimise and strengthen the movement throughout Europe and around the world. In Italy it would give confidence to every group of workers in every workplace, and every community group fighting the local city authorities. It would also bleed confidence from every Italian foreman, supervisor and employer. The impact would go far beyond the anti-capitalist movement as such, and affect the details of daily life. On a world scale, it would greatly increase the size of the demonstrations against the IMF and World Bank in Washington planned for September.

Berlusconi and the G8 leaders must have wanted, badly, to stop the anti-capitalist movement in its tracks. If they didn't stop it now, they couldn't know what would happen next.

Remember, the opinion polls were saying that the protests had the support of the majority of people in every country in Europe. On most of the issues, we had the support of the major-ity of people in every country on earth. So the G8 could not argue with us over the issues. They had to highlight violence.

This was a two-pronged strategy. One prong was to make us out as violent. We will see later how they did this. The other prong was to use violence to frighten us.

But the turn to hard violence was not a simple decision for the G8. The very forces that made them want to stop the anti-capitalist movement also made violence a high risk strategy for Berlusconi and the G8. The degree of public support for the protests might mean that if people were killed, if police violence was very strong and very public, then people in Italy would be outraged. Support for the protests would increase and Berlusconi's Government could fall.

This had happened to him before, and recently. In 1994 Berlusconi had been elected prime minister at the head of the same coalition: Forza Italia, the Northern League and the National Alliance. Every year since the fall of fascism, there was a small march in Milan to commemorate the risings against Mussolini in 1943. In 1994 the ritual march came right after Berlusconi's election. A few thousand were expected. Such was the outrage on the left at the fascist presence in government that roughly 200,000 turned up on the day. A few months later

Berlusconi's coalition had tried to cut pensions. A million and a half pensioners and trade unionists demonstrated in Rome. The Northern League bolted from the wounded government, elections were held and Berlusconi lost. The same could happen to him again. He knew it, and do did everybody else in Italy.

If Berlusconi had reasons to fear going too far, so did the rest of the G8. A failed attempt to put the boot in would strengthen the movement all over the world.

But there was another pressure on the G8. All the newspapers and all the statistics were saying that the world economy was heading into recession. The G8 leaders had been trying to pump up the world economy by lowering interest rates. It wasn't working and they didn't know what else to do.

They were politicians who had to worry about elections. But the worry went far beyond the politicians. The corporate leaders knew that economic decline could provoke worker revolt. In a recession, two things occur in workers' heads. They are furious about what is happening to them, and they are afraid of speaking out for fear of losing their jobs. If the anger is stronger, people fight. If the fear is stronger, they back down, knuckle under, and get more frightened.

It can go either way. The political ideas in people's heads are crucial. During the last recession, from 1989 on, the communist dictatorships of Eastern Europe had just collapsed. The ideas of the free market seemed to reign supreme. Now, as the world headed into recession, the ideas of anti-capitalism were everywhere.

It wasn't simply that the G8 had to stop our movement. They, and the corporations, were also losing control of the one thing they were supposed to control: the world market. The G8 had been set up to talk about the world economy. At Genoa, all their public statements were silent on that. They didn't know what to do. What do people do when they are losing control of the things most important to them? They retreat and go to pieces, or they hit out.

Friday morning Fini, the deputy prime minister and leader of the 'post-fascist' party, went to the police headquarters in Genoa. He stayed there for the next two days. Later he claimed he had offered no direct advice to the police while he sat there. He had only told them, Fini said, to strike first before they were attacked.

5 | **AIDS**

Another reason we went to Genoa was that the high cost of AIDS drugs was causing millions of unnecessary deaths in the third world.

From 1990 to 1994 I was a counsellor in an HIV unit in a North London hospital. We did same-day HIV testing. My job was to see people in the morning to make sure that they wanted a test and that they understood what it meant. In the late afternoon I told them the result. About one person in 60 was positive. On the days that happened, I went to the pool after work and swam for an hour and a half. Then I bought a half bottle of whisky on the way home and drank all of it by myself.

My anxiety was trivial compared to the feelings of the people who had HIV. Our problem in North London was tiny compared with the international epidemic. What got to me though, was that there was really nothing we could do. We had drugs that treated the various infections people with HIV got, and so could keep them alive a bit longer. But basically we were helpless.

A Nigerian working in the unit had given up being a doctor to work on AIDS awareness training. One day I told her how I dreamed of new drugs that would provide a cure for HIV. She said 'Yes, that would be good, but the corporations would make sure they were too expensive for Africans.'

People went into shock when I told them the result was positive. After that, they didn't hear much of what I said. I always had to remember to explain the disease in the morning before the test, when they were listening. Once they knew they had it, the main thing they worried about was who to tell. Who had given it to them, and who had they given it to? There are a lot of fatal diseases in the world. AIDS is the one that moves along the roads of love, between lovers and from a mother to the baby in her womb.

I quit that job in 1994. Later that year doctors in the West began using the new combination therapies for HIV. Death and hospitalisation rates plummeted with new treatments.

These new drugs were not a cure. They stopped the spread of HIV in the body, rather than wiping it out. The drugs were pretty toxic, and some people found the side effects life-threatening. Many people had to stop taking them, and no one knew how long the drugs would be effective. Maybe they would keep people alive for five years, and perhaps 10 or 20. Maybe a new treatment or a cure would come along in those years. For the moment they were alive.

But not in Africa. In 2000, over three-quarters of people with HIV lived in Africa, and something like 90 per cent lived in the third world. (All statistics about HIV are pretty rough estimates. No one knows exact numbers.) The pharmaceutical multinationals ('Big Pharma') rapidly developed over 20 different drugs that could be used in various combinations of three. The patients took three drugs, every day, for the rest of their lives. Three drugs were needed because the HIV virus mutates rapidly. In any one person, it can change into a strain that was resistant to one drug, and so survive and spread to other people. There is a very small chance of the virus mutating simultaneously into a strain that is resistant to all three drugs. This combination regime sold in the United States for $12,000 to $15,000 a year per person, and in Europe for around $10,000. This was out of the reach of almost all individual Africans and all public health systems in Africa.

Pharmaceutical companies in India could make the same drugs and sell them for $300 a year. But African people and governments were forbidden to buy the Indian drugs. This was because of what was happening to the international patent system.

Patent rights to drugs in the third world are a new thing. Traditionally, local companies in poor countries like India, South Africa, China, Brazil and Bangladesh made exact copies of drugs developed in the rich countries. These copies are called 'generic' drugs. You can still go down to a shop in the bazaar in any town in India and buy antibiotics, malaria pills, and medicines for other common diseases. This was crucial to the fall in infant mortality in the third world after 1950.

In the 1990s this began to change. The driving forces were Big Pharma, the US government under Bill Clinton, and the World Trade Organisation. The WTO was founded in 1995, as the latest incarnation of the negotiations between governments about world trade. The WTO was designed to do four things. First, it would push through general liberalisation of trade rules. Second, it would push to end legal controls on the movement of capital and the behaviour of corporations. Third, it would open up public services (education, health, social services, libraries, garbage collection, water, electricity, and the like) to privatisation. The plan was that, after 2005, if there were any private companies in any service sector in a country, all services would be put out to compulsory bids from private corporations. For instance, because England has private schools, all education authorities would have to allow private companies to bid to replace state schools. The same would apply to hospitals, and so on. Fourthly, the WTO would try to ensure that patents and copyrights in the West were respected across the world.

In all cases (trade, patents, copyrights, services, capital movements) no one country would be able to restrict the operations of foreign corporations. Where there were disputes, these would be solved, not by votes or by courts, but by committees of the WTO, meeting in secret far from the place affected, and effectively dominated by the large multinationals.

This was a programme for the take-over of the world economy by American corporations, and for corporations of all countries taking over the public sector. Most, but not all, countries belong to the WTO. (Nepal and North Korea, for instance, have not joined yet.) However, the vision of free trade behind the WTO has not been fully realised. The Seattle protests, after all, took place outside a crucial international conference of the WTO. They closed it down for the first day. More important, they gave heart to the finance ministers from many poor countries who attended. If Bill Clinton can't even control his own people, they said to themselves, why should we sign up to US plans to wreck our economies? So the Seattle meetings ended with almost nothing agreed.

That slowed, but did not stop, the advance of globalising capital. The WTO was still committed to one world system of patents and copyright (called 'TRIPS') by 2006. All national legal systems would have to fall into line. The governments of many third world countries, including many in Africa, have already changed their laws. Some still have not, including India, China and Thailand, but those three have promised the WTO that they will fall into line by 2006. The old patent regime was underwritten by a very widespread feeling that there was not much money to be made out of third world pharmaceuticals, and billions of lives could be saved by cheap generic drugs. Under the new WTO regime, though, most people with HIV would die.

The current UN guess is that there are about 35 million people with HIV. After I quit my job, I used to lie awake at night thinking about all those people, feeling a helpless anger.

Then in late 1999 Zaki Achmat founded the Treatment Action Campaign in South Africa. Achmat, a South African of Malay ancestry, had been raised by his mother and his aunt, both textile workers and union shop stewards. In the 1980s he was an activist in Mandela's African National Congress struggle against Apartheid. Achmat was gay, and caught HIV from sex while a political prisoner under apartheid in the late 1980s.

South Africa was the country in the world with the largest

number of people with HIV: 4 to 5 million, about 20 per cent of the adult population. The great majority were adults who got the virus through heterosexual sex, or children who got it from their mothers.

Ordinary South Africans could not afford the $12,000 a year for individual treatment. However, South Africa is the richest country on the continent. It has great mineral reserves and rich corporations. The new elected government headed by Nelson Mandela certainly could afford $300 a year per person. They refused to supply Indian-made drugs. South Africans were increasingly desperate, full of anger, grief and fear. Many had buried someone they loved, and were wondering when they might die themselves. The government came under increasing pressure to do something.

In 1997 the South African parliament passed a law saying that the government could, if it wished, declare a national state of health emergency with regard to any particular epidemic. It could then import generic drugs cheaply without patents, or have them made cheaply in South Africa. Thirty-nine pharmaceutical corporations, including all of Big Pharma, brought a court case in South Africa to have this law declared in violation of WTO rules. The corporations did not intend to press the case. It was a blocking move to prevent any government action.

The South African government continued to make regular noises about importing drugs. Every time they did so, the Clinton administration threatened them privately, and sometimes publicly, with trade sanctions. Each time this happened the South African government retreated.

This was of a piece with their more general politics. When freedom came, black South Africa had expected much of Nelson Mandela's new government. They wanted more trade union rights, education and health services. Above all, they were promised a massive new government housing programme. The people got none of this. Blacks ran the government and some got places on corporate boards. But Mandela's ANC saw no alternative to implementing the neo-liberal global agenda. Under his more right-wing successor, Thabo Mbeki, there was official enthusiasm for globalisation. Across the board, Mbeki did what the corporations said. His AIDS drug policy was part of this.

Still, Mbeki had to be seen to be doing something about AIDS. He went for a left-wing cover for a right-wing policy. He tried saying that AIDS was not caused by HIV. That was a Western lie. It was caused by poverty and deprivation. Therefore, Mbeki said, he didn't have to let people have the drugs for HIV. He also said there was an indigenous African drug that would work, so he didn't need to import any. Both these stances infuriated people in South Africa. In any case, Mbeki's government was also refusing to import cheap generic drugs for all the other diseases South Africans had. Mbeki never said the scientists were wrong about the causes and cures of tuberculosis and dysentery.

From early 2000 on Zaki Achmat's Treatment Action Campaign challenged Mbeki in three ways. First they imported generic copies of Flucanazole to treat the thrush that can kill people with HIV. They did so publicly, in defiance of the law. Second, they began a campaign to get the Government to give pregnant women with HIV short courses of AZT. In western countries this drug, in combination with powdered milk instead of breast milk, reduces the incidence of HIV in babies by 80 per cent. Third, the Treatment Action Campaign pressed the courts to actually hear Big Pharma's blocking court case.

The Treatment Action Campaign modelled itself on the old struggle against apartheid. At workshops and meetings, they sang the old freedom songs with new words about AIDS. They went for support to the unions, and got it. They staged mass demonstrations. In a country riven with shame, they marched in thousands wearing T-shirts that said 'HIV Positive'. Everyone knew that Achmat himself had HIV, that he was a professional who could afford the drugs, and that he had promised not to take them until every South African could get them.

Mbeki's government was forced to let the court case go

ahead. Now Big Pharma had to make their case in public, and the Campaign turned to the world for support. The anti-capitalist movement responded. As the case came to its first court hearing there were small demonstrations across Europe and North America. The court postponed the full case for a few weeks.

On one protest in Britain I met Mitch, an 18-year-old student at Imperial College, the scientific school of the University of London. The rector at Imperial, the highest official of the college, sat on the board of GlaxoSmithKline, a Big Pharma company that owned several AIDS drugs and was part of the South African court case. Mitch wrote out a petition asking the rector to resign from the GlaxoSmithKline board over this issue. He had been going from one lecture to another, most with 300 or 400 students. Mitch asked the teacher for permission to address the class briefly. Then he explained the issue and the petition. About 90 per cent of the students would sign it, he said, and 100 per cent of the teachers. Imperial students had always been conservative, Mitch said, but there were limits.

Similar things happened all over the US. African-American politicians and ministers started talking, and there were demonstrations on many college campuses. One of the AIDS drugs involved had been developed with public money in laboratories at Yale University. Yale had then licensed it, for a royalty, to Pfizer, a Big Pharma company. The drug companies claimed they had to defend their patents because of the costs of research. Their critics said they spent far more on advertising than research. But in this case, as in many others, the corporation itself had spent nothing on research. Many Yale students were outraged. They protested, petitioned and demonstrated. The scientist who had developed the drug said he wanted generic copies imported into South Africa.

Yale was not just any place. In the 2000 American election the four main candidates for president and vice-president (Gore, Lieberman, Bush and Cheney) were all Yale men. So were the two previous presidents, Clinton and George Bush senior. Yale is a ruling-class institution. The challenge from the students there was deeply embarrassing. Pfizer announced it would pull out of the South African court case. The rest of Big Pharma followed. The case collapsed.

This would not have happened without Seattle. That protest discredited the WTO in many eyes. South Africans who had suffered helplessly for years now knew there was a chance to beat the WTO rules. The movement that followed Seattle made possible the worldwide protests in support of the South Africans. All over the world it put Big Pharma on the defensive.

Big Pharma had not given up, though. The collapse of the court case now allowed Mbeki's Government to declare a state of health emergency. It did not. The import of generic HIV drugs remained illegal. The Government still refused to give pregnant women AZT. It seems likely that Big Pharma and Washington had done a private deal with Mbeki before withdrawing from the court case.

Big Pharma and Washington also tried to hold the line in Latin America. Four countries there (Brazil, Argentina, Uruguay and Cuba) provided combination therapy to all their citizens who need it. Brazil had a law saying that any pharmaceutical corporation had to agree a price for each medicine with the Brazilian government. If the corporation was unreasonable, the government then had the right to insist that the drug be manufactured cheaply by a Brazilian company. Brazil had used this law to force down the cost of HIV combination therapy to $3,000 a year. They had thus halved the death rate and reduced hospitalisations by 80 per cent.

This was particularly threatening to Big Pharma because Brazil was much richer than any part of Africa. From their point of view, Brazil was a bad example that might spread. The United States, for instance, did not provide free treatment for all HIV patients. The US government took Brazil to the WTO over AIDS drugs.

Big Pharma fought back in other ways. Kofi Annan, the UN secretary-general, called for the rich countries to give $10 billion to a campaign against AIDS. This sounded good. The money, however, was going on prevention, not drugs. That didn't mean free condoms. It meant a lot of consultants and experts on large salaries. Real prevention doesn't cost much. It just needs an organised and coherent campaign by governments, doctors, churches, mosques, community groups and trade unions. Kofi Annan was covering for the drug companies. In any case, the rich governments came up with nowhere near $10 billion.

The corporations also offered some of the drugs to some African countries very cheaply or free. The one thing they would not budge on was allowing governments to buy generic drugs, or make their own. An exceptional gift by the company could be a one-off. Generic drugs were an attack on the very principle of patents.

Big Pharma worry that if drugs are available cheaply in Africa or Asia, then people will import generic copies from Mexico to the United States. For Big Pharma, however, the real issue was the world market for pharmaceuticals for all diseases. They could have given way on AIDS drugs. Their problem was that if they allowed the patent rules to change, they would lose the far larger markets for other drugs.

Africa accounts for only about 5 per cent of pharmaceutical sales, by price. South Asia (mainly India), East Asia and Latin America take about 8 per cent each. This begins to matter. But the big banana is the US market, with 41 per cent of sales by price. More important, the US market provides 60 per cent of all the profits of the pharmaceutical industry. This is because there is not really a world market in drugs. The prices in most industrialised countries are in effect negotiated, country by country, between Big Pharma and the various national health systems. In the US is there is no national health system. There, and there only in the rich world, Big Pharma can set its own prices. That is why they make 41 per cent of their sales but 60 per cent of their profits in the US.

The majority of Americans under 65 are covered by health insurance schemes run by their employer. A large minority, 43 million people, are not covered. Americans over 65 are covered by Medicare, a federal government programme that pays for most medical care but not for medicines. Old people, of course, are the age group most likely to need medicines and least able to afford them.

Most industrialised countries spend between 7 and 10 per cent of GNP on health. America, with worse health care on average, spends 14 per cent. This is a consequence of a system run for profit. It also means that health is the largest single industry in the largest economy on earth. So Big Pharma, and American capital, will go to considerable lengths to defend the principle of profit from health. That's what they were defending in South Africa.

This principle is under attack in the USA, however. Throughout the 1990s, the majority of big strikes there were about health benefits. The corporations were trying to cut back on the insurance they paid for their employees, and the unions were trying to defend it. Increasingly, corporations put their employees into Health Maintenance Organisations (HMOs), large private health companies which rationed the care available to patients and so would charge the corporations less. Every American you talk to has a horror story about their own or a relative's experience with an HMO. In the 2000 elections, one of the central issues was the cost of drugs to old people.

There is an important general political point here. The fight over AIDS drugs in South Africa comes from solidarity, not pity. Many people assume that the anti-capitalist movement in the rich countries is basically dedicated to helping poor countries. After all, they say, the rich countries benefit from the poverty in the third world. Western workers get what they have because workers in the third world don't. A minority in the anti-capitalist movement agree with this.

The majority of people on protests in Europe and North America, however, are there for two reasons. One is that they don't like what the system is doing to their own lives. The other is that they don't like what it is doing to in the third world. They can see these two are connected. The same system operates both north and south. The protesters in Seattle were a mixture of US workers furious about their jobs, and environmental and third world groups furious about the planet. All saw the WTO as their common enemy. In Genoa the majority of protestors were ordinary Italians who made the same links.

American workers don't benefit from the private health care system in the USA. They suffer. Infant mortality rates are higher and life expectancy is lower than in Canada, Britain, Italy or Japan. I went to Genoa to fight for South Africans. I also went for my mother. Her thyroid was damaged when her HMO in Providence rationed her treatment. Now that she's retired, she has to pay for her daily thyroid medicine out of her basic social security pension. She worries what will happen if she gets seriously ill.

The real divide in the world is not between countries. It is between those who dominate and those who pay the price. My mother, me, Zaki Achmat, 20 million South Africans, and over 200 million Americans are on one side. Thabo Mbeki, Bill Clinton, George Bush and Big Pharma are on the other.

So Big Pharma, the insurance companies, and the health care corporations are on the defensive in the USA. Their American profits really matter. But they also could not afford the political consequences at home of too large a campaign against their greed abroad. These conflicting pressures were why they first pressed the South African case, and then withdrew.

The court victory in South Africa was only symbolic. But the effects radiated across the world. Within a month, the Kenyan parliament had passed a bill allowing the import of generic drugs for HIV. As the bill was being debated in the parliament in Nairobi, the world's press watched as five-year-old Patrick, whose parents had died of AIDS, became the first Kenyan to take a spoonful of generic AZT. The priest who ran Patrick's orphanage was jumping the gun because he wanted to make sure there was no going back.

Then in June 2001, there was a UN world conference on AIDS in New York. As thousands of anti-capitalists and AIDS activists demonstrated outside, inside the conference the US government announced that they had withdrawn their WTO case against Brazil. The week before the Genoa protests, the South African unions called a one-day strike against the privatisation of public services, Mbeki's version of globalisation. In December 2001, the Treatment Action Campaign won another court case in South Africa and forced the government to provide drugs for pregnant women with HIV to protect their babies from catching HIV. In April 2002 the government was still refusing to obey the court ruling. There's a long way still to go. But protest had begun to save lives.

The epidemic need not have happened in the first place. HIV had spread to South Africa from central Africa. There was time for the South African government to know what was coming. By then, they also knew what had to be done to prevent it. Gay men in the United States had already invented the idea of safe sex.

The logic of safe sex can be simply explained. The HIV virus lives mainly in white blood cells. To infect someone, HIV has to get from one person's blood into another person's bloodstream. White blood cells are not found in saliva, urine or shit. So people don't get HIV from toilets or kissing. White blood cells are found in menstrual blood, semen and vaginal fluid. So the virus can be passed on in vaginal and anal sex. If a man comes inside the vagina or anus, and he has HIV, the virus can make its way into the bloodstream through the womb or the wall of the anal passage. If he is wearing a condom, it traps the semen and this does not happen. At the same time, the condom protects a man against any virus in a woman's vaginal fluid or menstrual blood working its way down through the urethra, the small hole in the tip of the penis.

There is also a slight risk in oral sex. Saliva and stomach acid kill the virus, so only a very small number of people get HIV this way. The danger arises if there are sores in the mouth or throat. But a condom eliminates the danger. There is no danger anyway if a man does not come in the other person's mouth. There is some risk in giving oral sex to a woman, but a 'dental dam' eliminates this.

The other danger besides sex comes from infected blood getting directly into another person's bloodstream. There are two ways this happens. One is blood transfusions, and the solution is testing donors and heat treating plasma. The other is when two people who inject drugs share a syringe. The danger is not the drug or the needle. It's the syringe. When someone injects drugs, he first draws back the plunger to make sure the needle is into the vein. That mixes his blood with the drug. Then he injects part of the mixture and passes the rest to the next person. The solution to this is for each injector to have his own syringe.

And that's it. Safe sex and safe drug-use work. Of course condoms sometimes break, even when you use lubrication. And couples who want a child have a problem using condoms. But HIV is not passed on every time someone has sex with an infected person. In the testing service I worked in, the majority of people who came to us because their partners had HIV tested negative. In poor countries the virus spreads more easily, because poor people tend to be sicker and their immune systems tend to be weaker. But even in poor countries, the use of safe sex by a substantial proportion of the population can stop the disease becoming an epidemic.

A massive safe sex campaign in South Africa could not have prevented HIV reaching there. But it could have meant 200,000 cases instead of five million. The apartheid regime mounted no such campaign. Nor did the ANC government that succeeded it. This was normal. The same neglect happened in all other African countries, India, China, Thailand, Russia, the United States and most of Europe. The reasons were political. To campaign for safe sex, governments and public leaders would have to explain sex clearly and simply. Worse, they would have to say that sex and drugs were not the problem. They have to say: Do whatever you want in bed, sleep with as many people as you like, just use condoms or a clean needle. The politicians cannot bring themselves to say these things in public. So they said use a condom, be careful who you sleep with, and abstain if possible. This confused people. If condoms work, people thought, why can't you sleep with anyone? If they're telling you to be careful who you have sex with, it means that secretly they know condoms don't work. The explanations people were getting made no sense. So they ignored them.

The politicians and media owners would rather have millions die than say in public that sex was OK. On the face of it, this is strange. Politicians have sex lives not that different from the rest of us. But in public the right wing, and politicians in general, have always been conservative in sexual matters.

The roots of this conservatism lie in the oppression of women. This is why gay men and lesbians are persecuted. What they do challenges the whole family system. Sexism sometimes means that women are supposed to be chaste. Other times it means that women are supposed to be sexually available to men who want them. What both these have in common is that women are not supposed to control their own bodies.

Public talk about safe sex would threaten this. Any encouragement of sexual liberation, such as a woman's right to choose what she does with her body or a man's right to make love to another man, challenges women's oppressions. It also opens the way for more general human liberation.

Capitalism needs the unpaid labour of women in the home. Corporations save money by paying women less than men. But the oppression of women also means that for most people inequality is part of their most intimate, their earliest, and their most loving relationships. That makes inequality of all sorts seem natural, to both men and women. Our rulers will not give up that advantage lightly. So they let AIDS rip.

Of course, the oppression of women creates a troubled sexuality in the heads and bodies of ordinary people too. It means we find it difficult to talk and think about our sex lives. That makes it easier for paralysed fear to replace safe sex. But we are not totally incapacitated. The women's liberation and the gay liberation movement have happened. Gay men in the US were able to invent safe sex. Drug users in many countries use separate needles if they can get them. People both accept inequality as natural and yearn for equality. The difference between ordinary people and our rulers is that we can be mobilised to campaign for safe sex. Our rulers have to be forced, and even then they lie.

The consequences of this neglect and lies now go far beyond Africa. South Africa is no longer the country in the world with the most cases of HIV. India too now has 5 million people with HIV. South Africa has a total population of 25 million. India has 1 billion. So far HIV is concentrated in two great Indian ports, Chennai (Madras) and Mumbai (Bombay). Delhi, Kolkota (Calcutta), and the other big cities are not badly affected yet. But India is a land of family values and sexual repression. This does not mean Indians behave differently sexually from anybody else. It only means that public life is full of shame and lies. And where people cannot talk about what they do, they cannot use safe sex. In India, as in many places, conservative family values produce a massive prostitution industry. The chastity of middle-class women is complemented by the helplessness of working-class women. Pimps and brothel owners allow poor women no choice to protect themselves. Bombay is the centre of Indian finance, industry, film and prostitution. The majority of the city's half a million prostitutes now have HIV. India's various conservative governments have done nothing. Government ministers deny the epidemic, mouth pieties about women, steal from the public purse, suppress public health campaigns, and go to prostitutes when their day's work is done.

The other deeply worrying country, with an even larger population, is China. Guesses about the number of people with HIV in China vary from 600,000 to 6 million. Here too, the government does nothing but blame the people with HIV, single out drug addicts, and provide no treatment. And, again, officially promoted sexism and repression make any public health campaign impossible.

Guesses vary as to how many people in the world will die before the epidemic runs its course. Maybe 100 million, maybe 300 or 400 million. A great horror is in the making. We must stop it.

6 | **Thursday night and Friday morning**

Thursday night in Genoa I ran through the rain, up the road along the shore 200 metres to the two big tents where the forum public meetings are held. We had a meeting of the Globalise Resistance and International Socialist contingents there. It was dark now, the rain pouring down as in the tropics, spray blowing in through the sides of the tent. There were maybe 300 people under the tent. God knows where the rest were. Probably looking for dry places to spend the night. There seemed to be at least some people from every country, so hopefully they'd get the word back to the rest.

Because this is it, where we actually get organised for the direct action. I can take a back seat. No one, including me, thinks I know anything about street tactics. Chris Bambery and Chris Nineham stand on a table and bellow into the gloom, partly lighted by a few street lights in the rain outside.

I sit next to John from New Cross, thinking, he's been in Gothenburg, he'll know what to do. I know we're going to form affinity groups. These are an American anarchist idea for demonstrations. You divide up into groups of six or eight or 10 friends. Then those people join arms and look after each other. So there is always somebody with you. I want to be in the affinity group John chooses.

Bambery shouts over the sound of the rain. What we were going to do, he says, is divide up into affinity groups of 12 to 15 people. Stay with those people all through the direct action tomorrow. Each group will be one line of the march. Always stay close to the line in front of you, and the one behind. Don't let a gap open up. Has everybody elected two stewards for each national group?

A ragged yes.

The stewards will meet in the morning. They'll control the demonstration on the day. Do whatever they say. If they say to go forward, go forward. If they say to retreat, retreat. And remember, you can't see what's going on from where you are. The stewards are talking to each other, moving around, using mobiles and radios. If they tell you to advance into the police, maybe it's because there's something much worse behind you. So don't argue. Do it.

OK, we say, although a lot of us aren't sure it is OK. I've known Bambery a long time. He knows what he's doing. I trust him to pull us out if it looks like somebody's going to get killed.

Divide up in affinity groups depending on what you want to do, Bambery says. If you feel like it's all right to go to the front and try to push in to the Red Zone, be in that group. But if you don't want to do that, join a group who aren't going to the front. Each affinity group should elect their own leader. Look at each other. Remember the faces. Don't lose each other. Join arms and keep arms joined. Now divide up into national groups.

Suddenly we're just Britain. Bambery is calling out areas of the country, saying Scotland over there, Birmingham over there.

John, who I know for a fact lives in South London, says 'I'm from Manchester', and he's gone over there. I was right. He's streetwise. Somehow he can see that the Manchester group looks safer and more competent.

I'm from London, but there are too many of us. Bambery is still yelling fast; the man is always in a hurry. He divides the Londoners into two parts. 'Everybody elect a steward for your affinity group,' Bambery yells, and then says to my group. 'Hannah is your steward.' When it was all over, I decided Bambery did that to stop them electing me steward. Since I'd been giving talks and sitting on committees, they could easily have made that mistake.

Hannah knows what she's doing. Our group stand around in a semi-circle in the cold. Hannah is short, thin-boned, with blonde hair cut short to the head. 'Tear gas is used to divide you,' she says. 'It makes you panic.'

'Nobody ever died of tear gas,' a big man named Sam says.

Hannah nods. She and Sam were both in Nice. 'Nobody ever died of tear gas,' she repeats. 'Has everybody got a bandanna?'

Yes, we all say. Most people held up red bandannas with a yellow fist on them they'd bought at the SWP stall during the day. I have one for Galatasaray, the Turkish football team, that I bought when Nancy was working in Istanbul.

'What you do for gas,' Hannah says, 'is you pull the bandanna up over your mouth.' She shows us how. She looks like Jesse James. 'There are two ways to cut down on the gas,' she says. 'One way is to rub lemon over it. The other is to soak it in vinegar, but lemon is better.'

'I heard vinegar is better,' John from Wood Green says.

'Some people say that,' Hannah says, 'but vinegar makes me sick.'

'Never touch your eyes,' Sam says.

'Why?' I ask.

'It makes it hurt much worse,' Hannah says. I can see her face remembering the pain. 'Do you want to do this?' she asks me.

'No. I'm scared out of my mind. But I'm going to try to do it.'

'I'm scared too,' she says, clearly reassuring me, also honest.

'I'm scared too,' says Lee. He's big.

Everybody else says they're scared. Susie says she doesn't want to be in the group that goes to the front. Just then somebody arrives from the Birmingham group to say they have some people who want to be at the back. Do we have anybody who wants to join them? Susie says yes, and she's gone.

'The important thing,' Sam says, 'is always keep hold of each other. Never drop the other person's hand.'

'Like this,' I say. I take the arm of the person on my left, fit it through my elbow, and then grab my left wrist with my right hand. 'See? That's strong. They can't break that.' I saw this in the non-violence training they were running outside the school yesterday.

'Yes,' Hannah says, nodding. She's like a good teacher, making every kid feel their contribution is valued. 'Everybody who got hurt in Nice,' she says, 'was somebody we lost hold of.' Hannah shows us how she was on the ground at Nice, and the people on either side kept their arms linked with hers, and they were half pulled down, but the people on either side of them stayed up.

We go round the circle, saying our names, then each other's names. I want to keep trying until I have everybody's name. Somebody, I can't remember their name, says it's not important to remember names. It's the faces you want. Let's look at each other's faces. And we do. It is strange, and reassuring. Nobody smiles. We really look at each other, slowly, memorising, not speaking. We come in all colours and sizes. I realise how small Hannah is. But Sam is big, and so is Lee. That's good.

A few more words, and we agree to meet in the morning. I'm off in the rain, running for somebody's car and a lift back to Maria's. As we leave, Bambery is still busy helping people find benches to sleep on out of the rain.

The original American affinity groups were groups of friends. That's what the name means. We're calling ours affinity groups, but we've divided people geographically. That way nobody's left out.

Lee from Vancouver tells us about picking affinity groups at the demonstrations against the IMF in Washington. He was in this big gym with all these people, and they said get into affinity groups. 'It was like picking teams,' Lee says. I nod. I too know that particular North American childhood hell. Lee explains to the others that the captains of each team in the playground take turns picking players. Some people are always left out.

After everybody got into affinity groups in Washington, Lee

says, there were still some people wandering around the gym looking lost. They'd go up to one group and ask if they could join, and be told no. Then some other person the affinity group knew would come up, and it would be all slapping backs and hands and 'hey, man!' and they'd be in. Then you'd notice the person who had been rejected was standing close enough to see this happen.

I'm carrying fear around inside me for several reasons. One is a memory of being gassed.

In November 1969 I was on a march in Washington, DC, against the Vietnam war. There were at least half a million people there, maybe a million. I was with my wife Liz, English, long red hair, short body, thin, freckled and determined. We marched past the White House, which was surrounded by buses parked nose to tail. Some people rocked the buses. We didn't. It was tense, but the crowd wasn't violent.

Then we went on to a demonstration called by the radicals outside the Justice Department. There were a few hundred of us. Liz and I were close to the front line. We didn't know what we were doing. A lot of the people round us were wearing army surplus gas masks, which irritated me. I thought they were posing.

Then suddenly Liz and I were in the front line. I know now how this happened. The people who knew what was coming melted back. In front of us, cop after cop came running down carrying great black weapons like ray guns in science fiction movies. The ray guns had a deep round bowl at the base, and a long black barrel with a silver coil wrapped round it. They were not firing the guns yet, but already they made a loud, eerie throbbing noise.

The stewards at the front seemed like Quakers. They formed a line in front of the police, facing towards us in the crowd, holding hands, shouting at us not to be violent. One of them, younger than me, his blond hair short, was wearing a blue button-down shirt. Then the gas guns started firing, and everything was smoke.

Liz and I were running. The crowd scattered. It wasn't tear gas. The police were using something else, something worse, like CS gas, pepper gas, something. I had been holding hands with Liz. Now she was gone, and everything was dark with the fog of gas. The police were running at us, and from then on I saw only in snapshots, when I had to open my eyes for a moment. I stopped, leaned over, looking at the ground, and there were strange colours coming up at my face. It took me a little while to understand I was vomiting. I straightened up and projectile-vomited forward, in a straight line.

It was a wide road, with high stone government buildings on either side, and no alleyways. I ran to a door at the bottom of one building. Through a broken window I could see soldiers inside, with guns. I begged them to open the door and let me in. They were young men with open faces. I felt they wanted to help, but they said no, they couldn't. I knew there were army snipers on the roofs of every building. I ran up to a policeman and begged him to arrest me. He said no, and raised his club and hit me. The strange thing was it didn't hurt. Then I was running forward, away from the Justice Department, through the gas. Men were lying on the ground all around, and I was running through them. I was round the corner, out of the gas. Somebody had water to wash our faces and eyes. I was next to a girl who was crying, saying 'Why, why, why, why?'

Then I went straight to the Washington Monument, in the midst of a grassy field, where Liz and I had agreed to meet if we lost each other. There were a lot of people there. We were half a million marchers, after all. For a long time I walked around, shouting, 'Liz, Liz, Liz,' and finally she was there.

While I was running and looking for her, she had been diving back into the gas again and again, pulling out men twice her weight lying helpless on the ground. I felt proud of her, and frightened, and a coward.

That's what I expected in Genoa. My biggest fear wasn't that I'd be hurt. It's that I'd be frightened and humiliated again. So I was very relieved to hear that nobody ever died of tear gas, and it was used to panic and scatter us. It fitted what I'd seen, and offered help.

Because of Washington, I never took COBAS and the White Overalls seriously when they talked about self-defence against the police. I thought it was political rhetoric. Looking back now, talking to Italians after Genoa, I understand that until 2001 the Italian police had been more like the British police than the American cops. Rough, but not that rough. The White Overalls could defend themselves against what they had seen before Genoa.

From the ages of 10 to 18 I lived in Texas and was beaten up a lot in school. Two weeks before we went to Genoa we were at home in London. Nancy was annoyed with me. I'd been going to meetings, coming home all distracted, and paying no attention to her. So she hit me on the back, not hard, but as if in play. I turned and roared at her, my face contorted in hate, first just a sound, and then 'Don't ever do that again.'

Nancy burst into tears and went up to our room. I followed her. I explained that I was afraid of her. I'm much bigger, but she was a high school athlete in St. Louis, and starting quarterback on her college women's football team. I knew if I ever hit her she'd hurt me bad.

So I said I was sorry, and how much I was afraid of being hit. Nancy, who had gone to high school too, said my anger was the kind that invited being hit. Boys like me, angry, obviously wanting to lash out but easily beaten, were the kind who got hit worst. You're in danger, Nancy said, when you go to Genoa. You have to be able to control that or the police will go for you. Your fear and anger will invite them to.

And don't lead people on the street if you have that inside you, she said.

★

95

So here I was in Genoa, a wimpy kid from Texas, trapped in the body of a 53-year-old man, trying to prove something to himself. But I don't think I was much more scared than anybody else. There seemed to be fear in the air.

When I thought about it, I knew my fear was out of place. I'd worked in HIV clinics, seen people's faces when their test results came back positive. This was trivial, compared to that. So why were we so scared?

The first answer is, there was a lot of playing at revolution and insurrection, a lot of Che Guevara T-shirts. Many of us had fantasies to match. But it wasn't only self-indulgence. We were hyping each other up. Tens of thousands of people, hundreds of thousands of conversations over the three days before, all speculating on what would happen, telling each other how to be safe. If we'd talked about why we came, what we were angry about and what we wanted for the people we loved, it would have grounded us. But most of our conversations wound us up.

The reasons this happened were political. On our side the main radicals were the White Overalls. They said they would break through using non-violence. The pacifists and the Christians were talking about how other protesters should not be too violent and provoke the police. Both the left and the moderates, almost all the people in Genoa on Friday morning, were treating what was about to happen on Friday afternoon as more important than the mass march on Saturday. The prevailing politics trained our eyes on danger.

The other side was throwing fear at us all the time. The media and the politicians kept saying the demonstrators would be violent. From this we understood, and were meant to understand, that the police were preparing to be violent to us. You couldn't avoid the papers and the television. The authorities were telling the papers that they had surface-to-air missiles to use against us.

So the media, and tens of thousands of people, wound each other up. The fear was a social fact. It was what the G8 wanted.

★

Friday morning I was up early for the film team. This was bizarre. There were documentary film teams all over Genoa. This one was making a video for Italian television, and an English language version. A camera would follow each of four people round town all day, from the moment they woke up till the moment they went to sleep. Then the director would cut the four stories into each other, following them through the day, until they had a one-hour documentary. In the Italian version they followed a policeman, a local priest, a protester and a record store owner in the Red Zone. For the English version they were using me as the protester, keeping the Italian cop, and adding a TV journalist for Sky News from Britain.

'Marco', the producer of the English version, told me why he picked me. They were not going to have a voice-over, just show what people did and said. But he wanted the video to be on our side. So he wanted somebody to make the political points, but not to camera, not pontificating. Marco wanted somebody whose job all day long would involve explaining things to people. He could film me doing that, and keep the good bits for the final edit.

He told me he also wanted the points I would make, and in the way I would make them. He had come to the Globalise Resistance meeting in London because he figured he'd find someone who wasn't raving about Molotov cocktails. But he did want someone who'd try to push into the Red Zone. The film required that scene.

When I left London Nancy said, 'Before you go on TV, get somebody to make sure you don't have any food on your face. It would be good if you washed your glasses too.'

So I had three reasons for going into the Red Zone. I wanted to. I had led people into this. And I'd promised the film team.

The film team turned up at Maria's at seven on the dot. I answered the door; everybody else was sleeping in. Then I went back into the bedroom. Daniel, the cameraman, filmed me crawling out of my sleeping bag on Maria's floor. I got up and made coffee and toast as he filmed. Maria had put out lemons for all of us to take that morning for the tear gas. A real Mom touch. I sliced up three lemons and wrapped them in cling film. Daniel kept filming. Bambery told me I hadn't zipped up my fly yet.

We sat down for coffee and I said we needed to talk about how we were going to work today. Daniel put the camera aside for half an hour. The only way I knew of to deal with this bizarre situation was to pretend the film team were real people, and part of our contingent. So I explained affinity groups to them, and everything about tear gas and linked arms I'd learned last night.

Daniel was Italian, originally from Padua but now living in Turin and going home every weekend. He was young, elfin, with a big nose and tousled long hair, and an instant sexy smile. A hippie and a pro. Fiona was young too, British, finishing an MA on environment and development at the School of Oriental and African Studies in London, where Nancy taught. She'd been to some GR meetings in London.

I said I wanted them to be part of my affinity group, I'd already told the other people in my group they would join us. That way they would be protected, with their arms linked.

Fiona said yes. Daniel said there was no way he could film with his arms held. He had to roam. We compromised. If things got heavy, he would stop filming and join on the end of our line.

Then I said there was a problem. I might be getting into a difficult situation, and I didn't want them to have to follow. 'Nobody dies for a job,' I said. They agreed fervently. 'If one of you really wants to drop back,' I said, 'we'll all drop back and we'll all tell your employer it was me who wanted to.'

They beamed at that, in the sunlight coming through Maria's window. I had solved their problem. Then they went off in the other room and called Marco. He told them that if things got rough they were to get right out of there, fast, and leave me to it.

'Don't die for your job,' Marco said.

Fiona came back in the kitchen and told me what Marco had said. But she added that she and Daniel had talked and they wanted to go into the Red Zone anyway. I asked, 'Is that political or personal?'

'For me it's political,' Fiona said. 'I don't know about Daniel.'

'It should be political,' I said.

'It's his choice,' she said.

Daniel remembers that at the kitchen table I said this might be my last day, but I would do my best. He thought to himself, if this guy is worried it may be his last day, what's going to happen to me?

I don't remember saying that. It's embarrassing to think I said anything that melodramatic and self-indulgent out loud. But maybe I was trying to hang on to what Nancy keeps saying to me for all kinds of situations I'm worried about. 'Just do your best,' she says. 'Don't try to succeed. Then at the end of the day, however things turn out, you know you did the best you could.'

She also says, 'Everybody's trying to do their best all the time. It may not be good enough for other people, but it is their best. Nobody intends to make the mess their lives turn into.'

We walked down the hill. The rain was over, the summer sun was out, the old city and the port was spread out below us. It was easy walking down the steep streets. I was on my way to the Convergence Centre.

When I got there I met my friends from home. Finally, people I loved had arrived. Richard Peacock, my flatmate for years, Rich Moth, still my flatmate, and Ruard, Nancy's son and my stepson. I hugged people. Rich Moth's girlfriend Nicola was there too. Short, thin-boned, lithe, with dark hair curling past her shoulders. Nicola was shy, with a smile that showed an almost constant sense of fun. After Rich Moth first brought her home, we all sat down with him and said this one's a goody, hang on tight. You can get scared, Rich, but don't fuck this one up. 'I know,' he said. 'I know. I'm trying.'

My friends had flown to Turin airport the night before. They had booked for Genoa originally, but the police had closed the airport. Ruard said they had been wandering around central Turin, trying to think how to get to Genoa. They went to the railway station to enquire, and like magic there was a special train hired by Communist Refoundation about to leave. So they hopped on.

Ruard was 27. After school he worked in Germany for a year as an au pair before he went to university. He married a Pole, and taught English in her home town for two years. Now he worked in the finance department of a company in London. Ruard liked the people he worked with, but tried to avoid telling anybody outside work that he was an accountant. He had just handed in his notice and wasn't at all sure what he wanted to do next. Sometimes Ruard thought about journalism. At other times he wanted to write a PhD thesis on the anti-capitalist movement in Poland.

Ruard told me that halfway between Turin and Genoa four cyclists were waiting for the train. They had cycled all the way from Poland for the protests. They had come over the Alps, and lost track of how many times different police forces had searched them and their bikes. Now they were exhausted, and still 100 kilometres from their goal. Rather than miss the protests, they decided to spend the money on a train. But all the little train stations along the route were full of cops who wouldn't let them in. Now, by luck, they had found an empty station and the GSF train had stopped. They got on with their bikes and looked around, worried. Slowly it hit them: every single person on the train was a rebel.

Ru was ever so pleased to see them. He always likes talking Polish. But it was mainly that they were here from Poland, that Poland was included, that this might be part of a new movement there. I think more than anything else Ruard wants a movement that will fucking do something about how people have to live in Poland.

Friday morning, after we all hugged, we stood round a table, the wind off the sea blowing our hair and words away. I explained about affinity groups. I said people should choose their groups according to what they wanted to do. Some groups would try to go into the Red Zone. If there was anybody who wanted to hang back, they could.

Nicola raised two fingers of her right hand to her shoulder, like a shy kid trying to tell the teacher she wanted to go to the toilet. I ignored her for the moment, and went on talking about tear gas and lemons. I was beginning to sound like somebody who had always known this stuff. Then I got a grip on myself and said to Nicola, 'I did see that.' We nodded at each other.

Thirty-eight hours later Nicola would be beaten, her wrist broken, a cop would pull a knife on her, she would be hospitalised, then arrested and charged with possessing a deadly weapon, and then disappear.

It turned out Richard Peacock wasn't going to be in an affinity group. In addition to the day job as a video editor, he's got an MA in art and makes films. He'd been in Prague and got great footage there. This time he was going to film. He would take two people with him. One was to watch his back at all times. The other was simply to follow him, one hand grabbing Richard's shirt. If Richard looked like getting into trouble, or the man watching their backs yelled, the person with a handful of shirt would pull Richard back and out of there. It sounded like a good system. Ruard was going to watch his back. Another friend of ours from home, Richard G, would be the puller.

It turns out there are two levels of media people at these things. One level is the reporters for TV and the big news organisations. They are often sympathetic to us, but they *are* the presence of the corporations. The police let them wander around amid the fog and the gas and the shouting, doing pretty much whatever they want. The other level is people like our

Richard Peacock. They don't look like the big boys, and they have a different kind of press pass. They're vulnerable. Both types of media are an immense protection for democratic protesters.

We got my friends, and their friends, divided up into affinity groups. Nicola and Rich Moth went into one that was hanging back. I gave the people I loved half lemons to smear on their bandannas. I had promised to meet some media people behind the big Doctors Without Borders truck, next to where the Turkish socialists had their mini-van. A woman came up to me and stopped me to ask how tear gas affected the baby if you were pregnant. The things people ask if you sound at all authoritative.

'How pregnant?' I asked. I used to be an abortion counsellor. It's reflex, stays with you forever: somebody says they're pregnant, you ask how pregnant.

'Four months.'

'I don't know,' I said, 'but in any situation where you're likely to get gassed you're likely to get hit in the stomach.'

'How?' she said.

'With clubs,' I said. 'Police.' I made a clubbing motion with my arm. She was English, but I had been talking to people with a mixture of languages for a week, now I helped out everything I did with gestures.

'Oh,' she said.

'I know some people who are going to be in one of the groups that won't go to the front,' I said. 'You should be all right with them.'

I told the media people I'd be right back. I went and found Rich and Nicola and introduced the pregnant woman to them. I can't imagine what I was thinking of, not telling her not to march.

My memory of that morning is that I spent most of it alone, waiting. Daniel says I was busy talking to people all the time, doing interviews, trying to help the young people.

At 10.30 I met up with my affinity group, and introduced

Daniel and Fiona to them. We looked at each other's faces again and memorised names. We told each other again not to be scared of tear gas and checked our lemons again. I fingered somebody else's SWP bandanna and it was thicker than my Galatasaray scarf. Thicker will be better, I thought, and got one of the red bandannas with the yellow fist.

There was still an hour before we had to leave. I needed to look at the ocean. I went out behind the portable toilets and sat on the rocks and watched the waves come in beneath my feet for 40 minutes. The toilets smelled, and there was a lot of garbage on the rocks. But the sea has always calmed me, made me feel at home. I didn't want to talk. Fiona sat silently a few yards away on other rocks. Daniel had gone off somewhere. Since there was no camera, I kept begging cigarettes from Fiona.

I was worried Nancy would see me smoking on the video they were making. Nancy and I were both trying not to, both wanting the other not to get lung cancer. Don't smoke at Genoa, Nancy had said to me. Nobody wants to think they're going into something dodgy led by somebody who chain-smokes all the way through.

She wasn't here. I had wanted her to come, and I missed her. But I was very glad she had decided not to come. The public reason she told people was that I was going to be a big cheese, and she would trail around in my shadow. She wanted to be her own person. The private reason was Nancy was quitting her job as a lecturer, taking early retirement to go to art school. She was worried sick something might go wrong with her pension at the last moment and she'd be trapped in her job. She was scared the college might fire her if she got arrested at Genoa. So she wasn't here. I was relieved because I didn't have to worry about her.

It was twenty to twelve. I put my umpteenth cigarette out and collected up the butts. I didn't want to leave the rocks any dirtier than they were. Then I went to meet my group.

7 | **Star Wars and global warming**

Everyone who looks at anti-capitalism is struck by how many issues we campaign about. From outside the movement, this can seem like a weakness. From inside, we can see that all these issues have their causes in the same system. The different campaigns don't compete: they reinforce each other. Two more reasons we went to Genoa were Star Wars and global warming.

Star Wars – officially the 'Strategic Defence Initiative' – was publicly presented as a plan for the defence of the United States against nuclear missiles. This programme had first been proposed under Presidents Reagan and Bush the father in 1981–92. It had gone into cold storage under Clinton. Then, in the later years of the Clinton administration, the idea had been revived. In 2001, under Bush the son, Star Wars was publicly going ahead.

There were two stages to the Star Wars plans. In the first stage, the Pentagon would develop a new missile defence system. Previous defences had relied upon ground-based radar. The new defences would rely upon satellites in space tracking any incoming missiles. The satellites would send information to ground stations, or even direct to anti-missile missiles. If this worked the United States would be protected from any nuclear attack. But the US would be the only country with such a system, so it could start a nuclear war without fear of being destroyed.

In 1972 the US and the USSR had signed a treaty limiting the development of missile defence systems. The thinking behind this was that if both countries knew they would suffer terribly in a nuclear war, neither would start one. But if either country developed a better defence system, they might be tempted to start a war. So the treaty was signed to prevent either side getting the upper hand. This missile defence treaty was part of more general arms control negotiations during the Cold War that had limited nuclear testing and tried to stop the spread of nuclear weapons to more countries.

In the later years of the Clinton administration, the US spent considerable sums investigating the possibility of new missile defence systems. When Bush came in, he wanted to make these new systems operational by 2002. This meant, in effect, tearing up the treaty with the Russians.

The US government faced a problem in selling this policy to its own people. Back in the Reagan years they had the Cold War. Russia and the US were enemies. So it was clear what a missile defence system was for. In 2001 there were no obvious enemies. This empty space was filled by the idea of 'rogue states'. The US government said they were threatened by Iraq and North Korea. To stop some madman in power sending nuclear missiles over, the US had to have new defences.

Many people saw through this argument. We all said that neither North Korea nor Iraq has missiles that can reach that far. Anyone with limited resources who wanted to hit the US would do better to carry a small nuclear device into the US in a suitcase and rent a small plane. Star Wars could not protect against this. On 11 September 2001, these arguments were proved right.

We also said that tearing up the missile defence treaty would begin a new arms race. Other countries, particularly Russia and China, will be tempted to mount similar projects. It will also rehabilitate nuclear weapons. These have already spread to India and Pakistan, two countries that have fought four wars since 1947. The cities of Lahore in Pakistan and Amritsar in India are 50 miles apart, perhaps a minute for a missile to be launched and strike. There would be no warning.

Israel has the bomb too, and has fought several wars with its neighbours. Israel only barely won the 1973 war. In 2000 they were finally driven out of Lebanon. If it looked like the Israelis were losing the next war, it is quite possible their government would drop a nuclear bomb on Cairo or Damascus.

Critics of Star Wars also said that the new missile defence systems would not work. The Pentagon's first two test missile firings failed. They claimed that the third, in the week of the Genoa protests, did work, although there is doubt about that one too.

All these criticisms seem overwhelming. But they didn't stop the Bush administration, because they missed the point. Bush and his team had other reasons for the project than missile defence. Behind the public face was stage two: massive lasers on satellites in space. Satellites can already take detailed pictures of the ground, highlighting a tank or a mud hut. Now lasers will be built on the satellites. They can be pointed at any spot on earth, and burn any thing or person there.

Lasers in space sound like science fiction written by a left wing paranoid. Stage two is not, however, a secret plan. The details are available on US Air Force Web sites and in official publications. Journalists publicised them extensively when Star Wars was first proposed in the 1980s.

These lasers would require immense power plants to work, but it is difficult to get enough fuel into space. With oil, and most other fuels, it would take more energy to get the fuel into space than it would provide. Solar power would have to use such large panels that it wouldn't work. The only technically feasible option is a nuclear power station in space. Engineers could probably get that up there and make it work.

The expense would be enormous, of course. Also, we all know that satellites sometimes blow up taking off or burn up coming back into the atmosphere. If this happened to a nuclear power station in space, let alone 50 miles above the earth, the long-term pollution of the earth would be terrible. If rockets carrying explosive material go up regularly, it probably will happen.

So Star Wars had to go hand in hand with rehabilitating nuclear power stations. Since the accident at Three Mile Island in Pennsylvania in 1979, and the much worse accident at Chernobyl in the Soviet Union in 1986, no new nuclear power stations had been built in the US. No one wants to live near one. As the old ones reached the end of their useful lives, they were shut down. This protected people from another accident.

Equally important, there is no way to get rid of nuclear waste. It piles up in storage sites, and leaks from them, or is dumped into the sea in containers that will one day decay and open. But as the new Bush announced his support for Star Wars, his administration announced plans for 30 new nuclear power stations in the US.

Recently the governments of Russia, China, Sri Lanka and Canada have publicly expressed deep concerns about the prospect of an arms race in space. So has UN General Secretary Kofi Annan. In November 1999 the UN general assembly passed a resolution saying that outer space should be reserved for peaceful purposes. 163 countries voted in favour. The United States and Israel abstained.

The worry is that it would not simply be US lasers in space, but that other powers would feel driven to put their weapons in space too. That could lead to laser and atomic wars in space, as the US tried to eliminate rival platforms in their early stages.

Laser platforms in space held several attractions for the US government. Most obviously, they would be able to attack anyone, anywhere, at will. There would be no shield against the attack. Unlike bombing, there would be no way of shooting down the satellite. It is a wet dream of global power.

There were other, less obvious attractions. Star Wars would be enormously expensive. During the Cold War the Soviet Union had tried to compete with American military expenditure. In the eyes of US strategists, the expense of that competition in the 1980s had been an important factor in ruining the Soviet economy, and the consequent implosion of the communist dictatorship.

Newly democratic Russia is still an economic basket case, and for the moment no threat to the United States. American strategists are, however, worried about China. If you include Hong Kong, China has the fourth largest gross national product in the world. At the moment the Chinese economy is growing much faster than the American, and many in Washington think it may already be the major power in Asia. But China is still much poorer than the US. A new arms race would be a major burden for the Chinese economy.

Star Wars would also help to solve a central problem of American power. In 1946, at the end of World War Two, the US was overwhelmingly the world's largest economy, with 45 per cent of the world's gross national product. By 1990 the US percentage of world GNP was down to 24 per cent. The US is still the largest economy in the world, and with the collapse of the Soviet Union became the lone super power. This will not last.

In the late 1980s it looked as if Japan might challenge the US economically. By 2000 Japan had been in a long recession. However, the European Union, led by Germany, was an increasingly strong economic competitor. The Europeans were flexing their financial muscles on more and more issues, from banana imports to global warming. In economic competition with Europe, the US no longer held the upper hand.

But in the military sphere they do. In 1999 the US accounted for 36 per cent of the world's military expenditure, more than the total of the next 9 military powers put together. The US is particularly dominant in military electronics and computer-driven weapons. This was made crystal clear in the Gulf War of 1990–91, where the US was overwhelmingly the dominant military power in the alliance. After that war, US power therefore appeared to reign supreme. During the 1990s, many governments that might have been tempted to stand up to US corporations, perhaps on behalf of their own corporations, were reluctant to assert themselves. So it benefited the US government and businesses to emphasise the military side of things.

In addition, there was a strong element of corporate welfare to Star Wars. Most of the expenditure would go to a very small number of US arms and aerospace corporations. For them, Star Wars would be a profits bonanza. Their ties with the Pentagon, and with Bush's Republican Party, were very close.

All of this said, however, the most appealing feature of Star Wars was still those lasers. This was because the major enemy US corporations were likely to face was not a competing super power. The real worry was popular movements, and particularly working-class movements against corporate power on the ground in other countries. Star Wars would give the US military the ability to target a hamlet in the Afghan mountains, a guerrilla band in the forests of Colombia, a crowd of 200,000 in Cairo heading for the US embassy, or factory occupations during a general strike in France. It is not just that any of these could be attacked. It is that selected showcase burnings would increase the general aura of US power, and make even mass movements hesitate.

It would be a mistake, however, for us to roll over and faint at the prospect of this ultimate power. Star Wars is vulnerable. Because satellites orbit the earth, listening and communication bases in the US are not enough. They must be sited around the world. Because of the particular curvature of the earth, two sta-tions in North Yorkshire, England – at Menwith Hill and Fylingdales – are crucial. A women's peace camp was set up outside Menwith Hill, and the British Campaign for Nuclear Disarmament (CND) started a campaign against Star Wars. Those bases can be blockaded, and with enough people they could be occupied. The movement necessary to do that could also make it impossible for the British Government to continue its support for Star Wars.

There are several other crucial bases dotted around the world, and they are similarly vulnerable. Then there are the bases in the US itself. Star Wars is not in the interests of ordinary Americans.

An increased arms race and the tearing up of nuclear treaties makes life more dangerous for Americans, not less. When US foreign policy makes enemies, it increases the risk that American soldiers will have to die facing them. The greater the risk of nuclear war, the more likely it is that Americans will be bombed, at home and abroad.

Preliminary estimates of the cost of Star Wars were a bit less than $200 billion. Everyone knows that the final cost of such projects will be far more than the preliminary estimates. The cost will be paid by working America.

The week of the Genoa protests the Pentagon did a test run of their missile defence system, launching a missile from Vandenbergh Air Force Base in California and shooting it down over the Pacific with a missile from Kwajalein, a coral atoll in Micronesia. (Kwajalein, incidentally, is the home of the islanders who had been forced to leave Bikini atoll for the first hydrogen bomb test 46 years ago.)

The day the missile was to be fired, 15 Greenpeace activists and two freelance journalists in inflatable rubber Zodiac boats attempted a non-violent invasion of the base north of Los Angeles. Five of them made it ashore and delayed the missile launch. If 17 people could do that, think what a crowd of 30,000 could do. With a growing anti-capitalist movement, this was perfectly possible. The US Government, well aware of this, is currently building their main base for the new missile defence system at Fort Greely in Alaska. Fort Greely is not on the Alaskan coast, or anywhere near the cities of Anchorage or Fairbanks. It is hundreds of miles inland, surrounded by arctic wastes. North Korean or Chinese missiles might be able to reach it. Ordinary Americans could not.

Missile defence was not the only treaty the US government was tearing up. They were withdrawing from international agreements of all sorts.

In 2000 over 100 governments met in Canada to finalise an

agreement on an international ban on the manufacture and use of land mines. The problem is that land mines seem to remain forever after the war is over. Cambodia, Afghanistan, Mozambique, Angola, Bosnia and Kosovo are littered with them. Farmers know the mines are there, but they have to make a living, so they get their legs blown off. The USA walked out of the land mines conference in Canada, saying they still needed to lay new mines in Korea. The proposed treaty died.

There was also a move for an international criminal court that could try people accused of war crimes. Enthusiasm had risen for this in some quarters as a result of the war crimes tribunal in the Hague that is prosecuting Milosevic and other Serb leaders from the Balkans War. There are limits to the Hague tribunal. It cannot prosecute people from other conflicts. It does not prosecute US, NATO, Bosnian Muslim and Kosovan troops and politicians. But people who like what the tribunal is doing feel the principle should be pursued more widely. In this, there seemed a broad consensus among many governments. A series of conferences met to agree a treaty for an international court to try war criminals.

Clinton's US government said they were prepared to allow an international criminal court to try American civilians for war crimes. But they insisted on a clause in the treaty saying that no one could be prosecuted for war crimes they had committed while wearing a US uniform. They were not seeking a clause exempting all soldiers, just American ones! The other countries could not see their way to agreeing to this clause, and the proposed international criminal court died.

That withdrawal, like the one over the land mine treaty, happened under Clinton. Under Bush, from January 2001 on, there was more of the same, faster. As we have seen, Bush threatened to tear up the missile defence treaty. And he decided to withdraw from the Kyoto treaty to control global warming.

By now the reasons for global warming are pretty well understood. The level of carbon dioxide in the atmosphere has been rising for the last 100 years. It is only now, however, that this is beginning to make a difference. The carbon dioxide traps heat that rises from the earth, providing a sort of thin blanket around the planet. The earth's atmosphere is very gradually getting warmer, leading to small changes in temperature and weather. There are more unpredictable storms, summers are hotter, the desert seems to be advancing in some places, and all the world's glaciers are shrinking. For the moment, this process seems containable. Scientists, however, are now pretty much agreed that at some point in the next 60 years we will run into real trouble. No one can be precise, of course. But the dangers are there.

The most obvious consequence of global warming is the melting of the polar ice caps, which in turn slowly raise sea levels. In time this will wipe out low-lying islands, coastal towns like New York and Mumbai (Bombay), and whole coastal strips like the Nile delta of Egypt, the eastern seaboard of the United States, and Holland.

Another danger is increasingly unpredictable and violent storms and droughts. Most plant and animal species are closely adapted to the climate of the place where they live, and often unable to deal with significant changes in temperature.

Some of this could be lived with in an equal world system. Many people would lose their homes, and see the places they love disappear. But they could move, be taken in somewhere else, and be given new houses and new jobs. If one part of the world was particularly badly affected by floods, storms, or drought, the rest could rally round and share. This is, however, not the world we live in. In ours, massive climate changes will lead to floods of refugees: the hungry and the dispossessed. That, in turn, is likely to lead to war.

So there is general agreement among scientists and the general public that something must be done. Environmentalists have worked out solutions. Rising levels of carbon dioxide have several causes. One is the increasing number of animals raised for food. They fart carbon dioxide. Cutting down the forests which soak up carbon dioxide is another cause. Particularly important are the tropical rain forests, because they contain so much more vegetation per square mile than the pine forests of the north. Here it is clear enough what needs to be done, and not beyond the wit of people. Trees need planting, north and south.

But meat animals and trees account for less than a third of the problem. The central source of rising carbon dioxide is in the burning of carbon fuels for energy: oil, gas and coal. These fuels all come from fossilised plants hundreds of millions of years ago. As they burn, fossil fuels release the carbon from these plants into the atmosphere. So we need to reduce the use of these fossil fuels.

This can be done in several ways. The first is simple energy conservation, particularly insulation of houses, offices and public buildings. The second is the use of alternative energies: wind power from windmill farms, wave power, the energy of sunlight from solar panels, and hydroelectric power from dams. Dams, it is true, have created serious environmental problems of their own. The other energy sources have not.

At the moment these clean energy sources all cost more than oil and gas; about two to three times. However, oil and gas are established fuels. There has been enormous research on them, and many engineering advances. If a fraction of what is spent on other energy sources went to research on alternative sources, they would come down in price. In any case, they should be subsidised, as nuclear energy is now. Unlike nuclear energy, windmills poison no one. The cost of these new energy sources is in the labour needed to make wind turbines, wave barrages and solar panels. The money is not thrown away. It is paid to people who work for it. More expensive energy would mean more jobs. It is not the case that there are already too many jobs in the world.

Finally, we need decent and extensive public transport. Cars produce much more carbon dioxide than industry. A public transport system to wean people away from cars would cost money. Again, this cost would really be human labour. Public transport would have to be free, come on time, come in numbers, and take you where you wanted to go. It would have to run on reserved bus lanes and new train routes.

Free public transport would be cheaper for society as a whole. When you buy a train ticket now, you pay for the labour of all the people who sell and check tickets. With free public transport, those people could be driving extra trains and buses instead. All this would also make childhood, and parenting, easier. The worst thing about raising a child in a big city now is that you cannot let them out to play in the street. Without cars in inner cities, the streets would be full of people walking, talking, and playing.

Of course none of this would be easy. A recent authoritative British report by the Royal Commission on Environmental Pollution estimates that a 60 per cent reduction in carbon dioxide emissions will be necessary to avoid global warming. That is why we need to implement all the possible solutions (trees, insulation, public transport and alternative fuels) on a very large scale.

The Kyoto treaty, signed at a UN conference in Japan in 1998, did almost none of this. Kyoto obliged the governments that signed up to attempt to hold down the rate of increase in their carbon dioxide emissions, and eventually reduce them by up to 4 per cent. Compared with what needed to be done, it was virtually nothing.

The US also insisted on a large loophole. This allowed countries with increasing carbon dioxide output, such as the United States, to pay money for the carbon dioxide reductions of those poor countries that were not increasing their emissions. In theory, everyone would gain. In practice, it would allow the US and other heavy polluters to go their own way and avoid the investment needed to clean up their act.

So Kyoto was deeply flawed, and the reductions were tiny compared to what was needed. There was in any case no mechanism for enforcing the agreement. By 2001 it was clear that the

US was running well over what it had agreed to, and nothing would be done.

Those moderate environmentalists who supported Kyoto admitted that all this was true. But, they said, at least Kyoto was a start. The principle of collective international action over the atmosphere had been established. In later agreements, the target numbers and limits can be pushed up in ways that would really make a difference. George W. Bush's new administration agreed with the moderate environmentalists and took fright. It quickly withdrew from Kyoto, and refused to negotiate any replacement.

Some liberals complained that this, and other US treaty trashing, were a form of 'isolationism', namely the US government turning its back on the world. The opposite was the case. Each US withdrawal from an international treaty represented a determination to dominate the world, not withdraw. Clinton spurned the land mines treaty because the US wanted to be free to plant further mines in other countries. Bush is tearing up the missile defence treaty because his government wants to dominate the world from space. Clinton boycotted an international war crimes court because the Pentagon wanted US soldiers to operate with impunity in other countries. Similarly, Bush's rejection of Kyoto was not an attempt to isolate American air. It was an attempt to dominate and pollute the atmosphere for corporate interests. Many of these corporations were not American.

The central problem was the global oil and auto industry. The two are linked. Oil is presently the most important fuel. The major oil companies are international powers. Car factories are at the heart of every major industrialised economy. One of the most used indexes of economic health is the number of new car sales in any month or quarter. The stakes are not just in the car factories themselves, but in the components manufacturers, steel plants and tyre factories that sell to them. A web of jobs spreads outwards from the car plants. Public transport would threaten all that.

Moreover, a fall in industrial production in the auto sector radiates right through the economy. As car workers and their

suppliers lose jobs, they buy less, and other people in quite unre-
lated industries lose their jobs.

There's another problem. The big auto companies, especially
the US ones, make quite small profits on small, energy-efficient
cars. The whacking great profits come from the big four-wheel
drive cars that have sold in increasing numbers over the last 10
years. These use twice as much gas, or more, than a compact car.
So profits push the car companies to increase oil consumption.
Profits also push the corporations to make cars that wear out
quickly. The technology to make cheap, energy-efficient cars
that last many years is there. The old Volkswagen Beetle, after all,
was designed 50 years ago. It has been taken out of production
now because it lasted too long.

Of course a fair world and a democratically controlled
economy could deal with a reduction in the number of cars and
car jobs. After all, alternative energy sources still cost more, which
means that they produce more jobs. In a fair world, people dis-
placed by technical change could be paid until they could find
jobs with equal pay. Most car workers hate their jobs, and would
quit pretty quickly if they could find another job that paid as well.

Again, though, we don't live in that world. Critically, a decline
in the auto industry would mean a collapse of profits for particular, real corporations. In a decent world, if there was less work to
do the leisure could be shared out. Under capitalism, the loss of
profit would not be shared out. So the car companies in particular fight like tooth and nail to protect themselves.

And cars are bound up with oil. There is an established struc-
ture of economic power around oil. There are the major world
oil companies, and the governments that control the major oil
reserves. These corporations, and these governments, are dominated by American economic and military power. A decline in
oil production would spell something close to economic collapse for Saudi Arabia, Indonesia, Nigeria, Russia, the Emirates,
Kuwait, Iran, Iraq, Libya and Venezuela. It would also be devas-
tating for the millions who work as migrant labour in Arabia and

the Gulf, and for countries like Pakistan and Nepal, which rely on income from their citizens working abroad. It would shift power from the US government and corporations to other countries. Wind, wave and solar power can all be produced closer to home.

Again, as with global warming, a fair world could make up for these losses. But, again, we don't live in that world. And the oil industry represents an enormous block of power.

That is why Kyoto was a weak compromise. The economic powers-that-be gutted it. Even that was not enough for Bush, himself an oilman, his administration packed with people who had worked for big oil. He was not defending the interests of ordinary Americans, or of working people in Europe. A large majority of Americans are in favour of doing something about global warming. The atmosphere that is being polluted is the one they breathe, and they know it.

I live in inner London. A main trunk road runs three blocks from my house. Trucks thunder down it all day long from the North, heading for the docks and the Channel Tunnel. My daughter has asthma. I spent thousands of nights in her childhood lying in bed while she coughed in the next room, gasping. There have been enough times she's ended up in hospital. I always know, and so does she, that people sometimes die of asthma. More common, though, are the constant lung problems and coughs that hold her back in life. I used to think it was because she got whooping cough when she was little, and that was my fault for not giving her the vaccine. Then I learned that a quarter of children in Britain have asthma now, and in my neighborhood in Islington the rates are far higher than that. It's the main road, everyone says.

8 | **Friday**

The police had blocked off the Red Zone with fences. The fences protected the long sweep of Via Antonio Gramsci along the edge of the port and the two main streets running up from it. But instead of blocking off the big roads, the police had mostly blocked off the small side streets. These were easier for them to defend. We could only bring a few people to bear in any one side street, and they could trap us from behind. So the map of the Red Zone looked like two trees coming out from the port, with many short cut-off branches sticking out. (See the map, px.)

The estimates of the numbers of police and soldiers kept changing, but there were somewhere between 16,000 and 20,000. They had a pretty big perimeter to defend.

We were coming at them in seven different columns. In Prague we had been three, and I thought that was a crazy division of forces. This was worse. Everybody expected the police to attack the radicals at some point. The leaders of the moderates didn't want their people run over and beaten when this happened. And they didn't want to be associated with a riot.

In our contingent, we had said that some affinity groups would go forward and some hang back. We weren't going to be macho about that. It was a personal thing, what you felt comfortable with. We were trying to combine people who wanted to have a go with those who didn't, standing behind them, morally supporting and cheering them on. This was because we wanted the whole movement to do the same. That way we could have all marched together.

The reality, though, was that the Genoa Social Forum was split on tactics. This was not about who wanted to do what, personally. It was about which leaders of political groups wanted to be responsible for what.

A month ago we were going to start Friday at five in the afternoon, when it was cool, as the G8 began to meet. A week ago the time had advanced to 2 o'clock, in the heat. Then we were all going to march separately, but at a certain moment we would all lie down on the street, all over Genoa, for two minutes to symbolise the dead from the G8 policies. Now we were going at noon, with no agreed action at all. Day by day, we had been getting more eager.

It's noon. We're off, moving out of the Convergence Centre, down the broad main road. We're going to try to take the fence down and get into the Red Zone. There must be 15,000 police inside the Red Zone. We won't get far once we get the fence down. But we can do that. They did it in Quebec.

The police are on our left. Our contingent is Globalise Resistance, the International Socialists, and a lot of individuals who have decided to join us. I'm up in front, in about the fifth row. The front line holds the GR banner, not in the air on poles, but across their chests, in the European manner. I have no way of telling how many people are behind me. We're moving quickly now.

The 300 people on the GR train from Britain have reached Genoa. But they're stuck on the other side of town, cut off by the police. I wish we had them. Without them, GR feels small. But I'm also glad we're with the socialists, that there are people I can rely on going into this. We go up the road, walking quickly, wanting to get to the Red Zone before the police realise what we're doing.

It isn't far. I know this. I walked the route two days ago with Chris Nineham. I know where we're going. Most of the people with me don't know, so the police don't know either. For most, used to long marches, it's a shock as we round the corner ten minutes after setting out and there, a hundred metres down a side street, is the fence.

Behind it are the police in black, with helmets and shields and an armoured car. I put up my red bandanna around my nose and mouth, like a bandit in the Wild West. We pause now, looking at the line of police. I rub more lemon on my bandanna. In 30 seconds we're off down the side street to the fence and the Red Zone, beginning to run. 'Don't run,' the stewards along the edges shout, 'don't run.' And we don't. But we're there, in no time, shaking the fence. I'm maybe four rows back now. I don't want to be anywhere near the front row. The fence is built across the road, bolted to the walls on either side, three times the height of a man. Behind the fence is the armoured car, with a man sitting on it with some sort of big gun. There are policemen around him, on the ground. Then there is another fence behind them, maybe 40 metres back. So if we get through one we have to get the next one down.

But the fences don't look sturdy. You can shake them. This is narrow wire, like the wire around New York city playgrounds but not as thick. The fence is made up of panels, each with a steel rectangular frame, bolted or tied together, I can't see which. I'm trying to take this in. The panels are big, which makes the fence unstable. The front row of demonstrators are pulling on the fence, rocking it, but not bringing it down. Somebody throws a rope up at the left top corner, where there's a smaller triangular panel. The small white rope doesn't catch on anything. They throw it up again, and it loops over an edge and gets stuck on the top panel. They start yanking the rope, trying to rock the top panel down and pull the fence away from the wall.

'Where's John?' Hannah shouts. She's our steward, in the middle of our line. She is carrying a red flag on a small pole, so we know where she is at all times. 'Where's John?' we all shout. 'Where's John?' Hannah has been counting all of us, all the time, like a teacher on a school trip. Her flag is like those banners old regiments had, and for the same reason. In case we get split up, we can find her. But this feels much safer than battle.

The tear gas starts in front of me. We breathe, hold our line. Some people are crying, but we're all saying to each other, 'don't panic, don't touch your eyes, hold the line.' And we hold. We're all right. It smells acrid.

This isn't pepper gas or CS gas, I think. This isn't a lot of gas. This is all right. But I am very aware that if the people in the front line had started to scream and run back, eyes streaming, calling for water, we would have split and been easy meat.

'I'm here!' John shouts. He's back on the end of the line. Who knows where he was? 'John's here,' we all shout to Hannah. Fiona the producer has my right arm. Daniel is off somewhere, filming.

In the row behind me Alison from Glasgow is shouting into a megaphone, 'We are Winning, Don't Forget'. Yesterday Alison gave a speech at the Convergence Centre through that megaphone. She said 'This is the time and place for all youse who never amounted to anything. All youse that sat at the back all through school, hoping the teacher wouldn't call on you, tomorrow is yours.'

Alison yells, and we yell back, 'We are Winning, Don't Forget'. It's the chant of Quebec three months ago, when the police attacked as they pulled down the fence there. It's another idea, this chant. It reminds us they are attacking because we are winning the war of ideas, out there in the whole world. That is why they have to attack. And 'Don't Forget,' because as they attack, it is so easy to forget our strength in the fear.

A fine spray comes arching out of the gun, up over the fence, falling down on us. I look up, and think, this is the real gas, not that toy stuff. The fine spray falls on us, cold and somehow sticking to us. I wait for the burning on my skin. Nothing. It's a hot day. This stuff is wet and cool and doesn't smell. It keeps coming. It's water. They are shooting water cannon at us. But they can't shoot it straight at us, because that would knock down their fence. So they're arching it up in the air, and showering us.

We all understand this, looking at each other, laughing, relieved. Tom Behan, the academic expert on the Mafia who got our train back, is on my left. He reaches back and grabs the mike from Alison, and starts 'Singing in the Rain' through the megaphone. We all sing along as the water falls down on us. Tom does a little dance as he sings, and then he's bent over, crouching over the mike, giving it all he's got, singing from the belly. People always make fun when I sing, but now I'm yelling louder than Gene Kelly, doing little dance steps in place.

Ruard is supposed to be with Richard Peacock, filming. But I see Ru right up at the front, on the right, alone. He's climbed up a Walk, Don't Walk sign. The sign is broken, and flashes madly back and forth every second, red and green. Ruard is standing on it somehow, holding on with one hand. He's leaning out, his body at 45 degrees, above all of us, waving the biggest red flag in Genoa. He's wearing a red bandanna around his neck, a black vest to show off his chest, and baggy green combat trousers with pockets. He looks like the painting of *Liberty on the Barricades* by Delacroix, but in an Englishman's body. For years he had ME, used to come home from college almost weeping with the pain in his head from reading four hours of books. He wouldn't say anything when he came in, just go sit at the piano and play Chopin. Always Chopin, who I didn't know but grew to love, so beautiful and melancholy, Ru's feelings about his illness flowing through his fingers and filling the house. Now he's fit, impossibly beautiful, and he knows it, a grin splitting his face as he waves his flag.

I'm too far away to call to Ruard. I pull the small rucksack off my back, fumble in it among the lemons and water for my little camera. I wasn't going to take pictures, but Nancy will want one of Ruard. It's still raining water cannon.

I think there are maybe 500 people behind me. Ruard, who is looking back from above, later said he counted roughly 2,000. The organisers at the back estimated 3,000, with people joining us all the time.

'Where's John?' Hannah shouts. 'Where's John?' Fiona and Tom shout. I have my little camera pouch out. 'Back,' the stewards are shouting. 'Walk back. Slowly. Walk back.' And my row does. I'm still trying to unzip the camera, arms locked. I look around to see why we're going back. On my right there's an archway over a little alley. Through that arch I can see riot police, in black, with shields and helmets and visors. A lot of them, running towards us slowly and in formation. That's why we're going back, so they don't divide us. I have one last try at getting the camera out. Nancy will want a picture of Ruard. I'm not thinking straight.

'Stop,' the stewards yell. 'Stop,' and we stop, right where the alley on the right comes in. I jam the camera pack in the bag, get the rucksack back on my back. There's a gap in front of our row now. Right in front of there's no one, but there are about three lines worth of people up at the fence. They are spread across the road there, ragged, pulling and shaking the fence and the rope, full of enthusiasm. The top corner of the fence starts coming down. The police are coming on my right, jogging. There seems no time. Chief stewards run up and down my line, yelling at the people in front to pull back. We're all shouting at the people by the fence: 'Come back, come back.'

We can see that the police are going to pour into our street and cut off the people by the fence, and probably beat holy shit out of them. The people by the fence look back at us, like maybe we're stupid, or we're following orders. As if we don't understand, or we're selling out. Can't we see they almost have the fence down. Don't we understand? And we're screaming. I'm pulling my right hand through the air above my head, scooping air like a commander or a football coach or a worried father trying to get his child to come back to a safer place.

This is all happening very fast, but it seems to take forever, like a car crash. Some people at the fence start to pull the others back. The police are in the little square in front of us, and the people at the fence are coming back to us, closing the gap, surging round the police on the far side of the street, where a gap is still open. I lose sight of Ru.

From behind me, people are ripping their placards off the sticks and throwing the sticks at the police. They arch over in the air. 'No sticks,' the stewards shout. 'No throwing.' We shout together, 'No sticks, no throwing.' In the relief of not being boxed in and cut off, we'll shout whatever they tell us to.

The police are patrolling the line along the fence, moving back and forth, black and bursting energy. Hyped. There are maybe 60, maybe 100. We stand there. They stand there. There's more gas. Then they come at us, in line, their shields down, clubs held in the air over their shoulders.

I'm in the third row. Why the fuck am I in the third row? I didn't start off in the third row. The police are battering people now. A solid line of police, inches from our front row. Their clubs are making short sharp overarm strokes, fast, and then back and then clubbing again. All the cops are in a line, moving rhythmically. I'm afraid for people's heads. Kevin Gately and Blair Peach, the two people the police have killed on demonstrations in Britain in the last 30 years, were both hit on the head. The human head is funny. Sometimes the police crack it and you bleed all over but you're fine. Other times they jar it a little and you're dead. I'm trying to see if the people two rows ahead are getting hit on the head.

I went to Blair Peach's funeral in Southall. He had been killed on an anti-Nazi march. Silent Sikhs, men and boys, stood around the flowers that had been laid where he died, an honour guard looking at us in solidarity as we passed. The head is so fragile.

'Walk back,' the stewards are yelling. 'Walk slowly,' we shout. 'Don't run.' No gaps. 'Don't run.'

Tom has my left arm, Fiona my right. The two lines in front are being forced back on us. We all know now: if we move too fast we'll open up a gap, then the police will be in the gap, we'll lose the front line and all our rows will come apart. So we retreat slowly, much slower than walking. I disassociate. It looks like an old European film in front of me, or a documentary. The colours are fantastic, reds and yellows and blues on our side, the cold black on theirs. The clubs rise and fall.

On my left there's a small tree, some six feet high, growing in the middle of the road. The city has put wire around it to protect it. A man is pulling at the tree, trying to arm himself so he can fight back. I lunge to help him, but as I start to pull I remember non-violence. So I grab him, pull him off the tree, and link arms with my row again. On my right an enraged guy charges forward. He has a big piece of wood raised above his head as a club to strike out at the police. The people on my left grab him, take his stick, throw him back into the crowd.

The person in the row in front of me starts to fall back, sitting on my knees. I fall backwards with the weight, sagging into a squat, but not yet flat on the ground. Tom and Fiona have my arms on either side, holding me up. Behind me, Alison and the woman next to her both grab the rucksack on my back and hold on to it to stop themselves going under.

We're moving back, holding formation, not letting gaps, right up against each other. I see Jimmy Ross's bald head in the front line. He's just retired as a teacher in Glasgow. I stayed with him and his wife last month, when I went up for a meeting. Nice man. Sixty or so. We're still moving back, slowly, chanting 'We are Winning, Don't Forget.'

And now we're back, away from the police. The cops let us go. They have too long a space behind them. We outnumber them. We could come back and through them.

We lost only one person, Margaret from Glasgow in the front line. The people on either side lost their grip on her arms and she went down under the police, where they could kick and club her. After that she was arrested.

I look around for Ruard and don't see him.

We're walking backward now. We're almost to the place where this small side street turned off from the bigger road. Now we turn around and face away from the police. We march out of the side street and across the main road. Great, I think. Chris Nineham and the senior stewards have pulled us back before somebody got killed. I guess that Chris must be thinking our people have had taste of action now, and feel we've done something. We can go home now. I can feel in the crowd round me that it hasn't been quite enough for them. They're buzzing. I'm buzzing. We're chanting: 'One Solution, Revolution.' It's drawn out long like a football chant, rising to a punch on the final 'shun'. And it's another idea too. There's a democracy in our chants. Anyone with a megaphone or a big voice can start a chant. It's the ones that capture our thoughts and feelings that the crowd keeps going.

One Solution, Revolution. It means there's no way to break the power we have just faced but revolution. But not armed struggle, not a coup. Instead democracy from below, strikes, demonstrations, votes, more strikes and mass uprisings by ordinary people. Until you build a movement so big that the police are scared off the streets. Then the powers will send the army in. But if the movement is big enough, when the soldiers are ordered to fire on a crowd, they know their lovers, brothers and mothers might be in that crowd, and they refuse to fight. That democracy from below is the only answer to the armed might we face. The chant also means that to all the chaos of capitalism, to all the kaleidoscope of suffering, there is a simple solution.

Once we cross the main street we turn and go up a hill. Oh fuck, I know where we're going.

I can feel from the crowd that we hadn't done enough yet. Chris Nineham, Bambery and the other senior stewards must feel that too. We're not satisfied. And the police are spread very thin. 16,000 to 20,000 cops is just about enough to defend the fences and garrison the Red Zone in depth. But all over Genoa the police are moving out from the Red Zone, sometimes miles out, attacking. I don't know this yet. But I do know we see hardly any police away from the fence.

★

Up ahead, Chris Nineham thinks we may still get into the Red Zone. The police and the White Overalls are fighting about a mile away from us, and the protestors may break through there. If they do, he wants very badly to join up with them. And if they don't, the police may yet leave us an opening. There's an element of theatre about all this, he thinks, but at any moment the theatre could turn very serious indeed. He keeps thinking: in Quebec they got the fence down.

Uphill my affinity group comes to a junction. If we turn left here, we will be leaving the area allotted to us by the GSF and going into the section of ATTAC and the Refoundation Communist party, around the Piazza Dante. If we turn right here, we go gently downhill to another fence around the Red Zone along a sloping street two lanes wide, with broad pavements. On the left of this street are solid old buildings. On the right is a waist-high iron fence. Over that fence is a cliff. I know. I walked down this street with Chris Nineham two days ago. After Prague I know one thing about routes for demonstrations: don't go on a bridge. I added to that: don't fall off a cliff.

'It's a lovely route, though,' Chris said. 'Right down there to the Red Zone. There's not that many routes in here, Jonathan.'

'Come here, Chris. See. Look.' He looked, saw the long drop to the ground eight or 10 storeys down.

'If you fall down there, you die,' I said.

'Yes,' Chris said, in the voice he uses when I'm right and he's not going to argue, but he's going to do what he wants anyway.

Now here we are. There are 25 police in riot gear at the cross-roads, standing on a corner, the cliff and the drop to their left, our right. We turn into them and walk down the road towards the Red Zone. They scramble, grabbing their clear plastic shields, making a line in front of us, walking backwards. We are suddenly confident. They scrabble to get right across the road in front of us. Their line is only one man deep, and not shoulder to shoulder. We drift down towards our left, the buildings, the gap their line has not cut off. But we have arms linked, staying in line. We know not to give that up now. 'Walk quickly,' the stewards are shouting, 'Don't run.' We all take up the shout, 'Walk quickly. No running.'

The police are worried that we will pass them on the left, by the buildings, and surround them. They are strung out in a single line across the road. They have to face us. They dare not turn round. So they're walking backward, fast, trying to hold their line. They are dressed in black, carrying heavy shields and clubs. Their black helmets have clear plastic visors, like storm troopers in a space movie, but you can see their faces. They're afraid. One cop glances from side to side, quickly, making sure the man on either side of him is holding the line.

The line of demonstrators in front of us is moving quickly. A gap has opened between us and them. We run to close it. Hannah is shouting 'No running, no running.' We pull up. The steward on the side of the lines in front shouts, 'Quicker, comrades. Walk fast. Fast. Don't run.'

There are spaces opening up between the cops here and there, a person or two wide. On their right, our left, the three police nearest the walls of the buildings are suddenly isolated. Our front line has split them. I watch one young cop walking backward next to the wall. I see the fear on his face. He can't use his club. He would have to stand still to do it. We could jump the police now, and pulverise them. We don't. But we do push forward that little bit faster. Our hearts are exulting. Literally pounding. I can feel my chest swelling outwards with joy. It's on their faces: we are many, they are few.

I have been so afraid all my life. We have all been afraid. Of the teachers, of the boss, of the police, of the snub in high school, of looking wrong, of getting fired, of your wife's face after you come home and say you lost your job, of the way a supervisor shouts at you at work and you have to stand there and take it. Now the police, of whom we are so afraid, are afraid themselves. We have a power. We aren't looking around at each other, I can't see anybody's face, but I know the whole crowd exults with me.

We're going faster, almost running. 'Don't run,' the stewards say again. We're up almost to the fence. The cops are back against the fence, pressed on it, close to each other. There's a gap in the fence, about two metres wide, that we could get through. The police are blocking that. Behind it is another armoured car, and another fence behind that. The front line has stopped, not pushing up against the police. I think this is instinctive, not an order from the steward. We are suddenly afraid of what going through that fence would mean. A senior policeman comes from somewhere and pushes out through the knot of riot policemen, erupts into the empty space between them and us. He slaps his thigh and struts, stomping his long black leather boots, a desperate parody of masculine confidence. He's a big man. He's showing us he dares stand there, alone, without a riot shield and a helmet. He's showing us he's in charge. And showing his men as well.

He walks up and down in front of his men. We stand there. The riot police stand there. They dare not charge us, nor we them.

A young man in a black balaclava, an Italian I think, just behind me, has a large stick in his hand to attack the police. 'Drop it,' a woman shouts at him. He doesn't know the English words, but understands the meaning. Many people have joined in our lines since we formed at noon. 'No,' the woman is shouting. I turn back towards him, twisting my body, holding up my line. 'No,' I'm shouting, 'No. Drop it.' The woman moves out of her line, walking after the Italian lad, still shouting at him. He is short, a boy really, and looks confused. Perhaps we looked like the revolutionaries, and this makes no sense to him. He's trying to walk away from the woman, but she follows him, keeping 10 feet away, but leaning towards him, shouting. This makes no sense to him either. We don't touch him. We're using moral force, the force of the crowd, and in a minute he drops the stick, looking disgusted.

Then we hear the stewards say, not shouting, that the police are behind us now. 'Start walking backwards.' We do. Arms linked, in lines. I know they can cut us off. They must be angry. 'Turn around,' the stewards say. Each row in turn drops arms. Each person turns round 180 degrees, and grabs arms again and we're moving together. Precision, as if we've practised it a thousand times. (We've done it once before, 30 minutes ago.)

My line is very near the back now. Up ahead we have numbers. If the police attacked us there, we could cause trouble. Where we are, they can just wait for the last few rows and cut us off. We don't want to let any gaps open. 'Don't run,' the stewards say now, and we don't; we don't want to panic. I hold on to Fiona tight for reassurance. 'Quickly,' the stewards say, because we have to get out of there.

'Break the lines in half,' the stewards say. 'There's a gap ahead. Make lines of six.' Hannah tells us quickly where to break. I am still in her smaller group, and grateful. I feel safer with Hannah.

This is the most dangerous it has been. But I am less scared than I was. I am learning. I have seen the police retreat. I am more, we are more, than we were this morning. My pride in our discipline is immense. Then we're stopped, and I'm afraid again. It's a traffic jam. The rows ahead of us are turning right round a corner, uphill. The police have closed in tight on this corner. We are pressing up against the wall of the buildings. At least we're not on the other side, where the cliff is. 'Keep Moving, Don't Run.'

The police are on our left, watching us. I am in the middle of my row of six. Some of our people have made a long protecting line, arms linked, facing the police, covering our lines of six. Without them the police could easily charge in from the side and scatter us. I am very glad the protecting line of people are there. They have arms linked, but there are too few of them. In places their arms are out straight, just gripping each other's hands. Right by me, two hands lose touch. They shout for more people to come into the line. We are about 10 or 12 short lines from the back of our contingent. I look at the opening gap, know I ought to step into it, and don't. The police are standing, watching us pass. You can see they can't decide whether to attack or not. Daniel has his press pass around his neck, and is standing in front of the police, looking down into his camera. He is filming me not stepping forward. I feel no shame. My face will show any viewers what fear looks like, I think. I don't look at Fiona next to me, nor she at me. The man on my left breaks off and fills the protecting line, and so do others.

'No masks,' the stewards are shouting, 'Masks down.'

Oh Jesus. We must have people in black masks somewhere, refusing to take them down. A fight is coming.

The line protecting us is opening up again, almost immediately. They shout for help. It has to be done. There's no one else doing it. I drop Fiona's arm, step into the line facing the police. Fiona does too, grabbing my arm again, me looping around the person on one side, she on the other, and the line is solid again.

I disassociate again. The police are in front of me. I tell myself: don't look at them. I can feel only a little something will push them over the edge. Direct eye contact would be madness. I can see the cops, the tension in their bodies, the urge to move filling them. 'Masks down,' the stewards scream. I pull my red bandanna down, round my neck. So does everybody else. If we're gassed, so be it. That's not what we're scared of. I don't know why the police don't attack. I don't know there are 2,000 or so people ahead of us.

We are walking sideways, holding on to each other, trying to move as fast as the lines of six we are protecting. They are walking forward. The people inside must not run. If they do, the police will chase. Everybody knows this. In our protecting line we walk sideways fast, like crabs. I can feel our line stretching out again. 'Masks down!' Carmela is shouting in Italian. She is a steward, suddenly in front of me. The big cop, the macho strut, is next to her.

I look back. Two young men are in a short line almost at the back. They look Italian, and wear black kerchiefs around their mouths and just below their eyes. They are in the middle of a row, walking with the rest, refusing to take their kerchiefs down. We understand, all of us, that if they don't the police will attack us all. We are at the end of the march, isolated. We are screaming at them. They refuse to lower the black masks, their bodies sullen. None of us touch them. Somehow we understand we must persuade them, not make them. We also all understand that if we start fighting each other, the police will pile right in, and we are lost.

On many demonstrations there are undercover cops, agent provocateurs who mingle with the crowd and start fights so people will get arrested. But these are not provocateurs. They are frightened young men, stubbornly holding their ground, but on the same side as the rest of us. I know people in Britain who wear masks on demonstrations there. They say the reason is simple: time and again the police give photos of demonstrators to the press; the papers run them with headlines saying 'If you know these thugs, turn them in.' Your family sees it, your boss sees it, you lose your job whether you've done anything or not. They look cool, too, those black kerchiefs and masks – like the SAS or the Zapatistas.

Daniel is standing just in front of the police, to one side of me, filming me. The situation is surreal. The senior policeman, the macho strutter, suddenly flips. He runs through our protecting line, pushes through several more people and grabs one of the masked young men. The people nearest close round the senior cop, shouting 'Non-violence. Don't do it. Let him go.' The other police don't know what to do. No senior police officer is supposed to ever expose himself in this way. Everyone, on both sides, feels the situation is on a knife-edge. Dozens of people surround the cop now, their hands in the air to show they mean no violence, shouting 'Peace, peace'. But they're pushing the cop too, jostling him as he wrestles with the young men. The cop drops the young man and retreats back to the police lines.

The short lines of marchers have gone faster up the hill than us in the line covering them. There are only a few lines behind us now. I walk sideways, grateful for Fiona on my arm, acutely conscious of my body. Of how bitterly tired I am, of the sweat soaking my body, of the adrenalin running through my blood. Feeling my age, the inappropriateness of my doing this. Feeling also the weight and fat in my broad-shouldered body, that means maybe I can hold my place for a little while if I have to. We are around the corner and going up a hill, away from the Red Zone, away from the police now behind us. We break our protecting line, fall in behind the rest, and breathe. We're believers, every one of us now, in collective discipline. Again, suddenly, there are no police around us.

We are marching up towards the Piazza Carignano, above the Piazza Dante where ATTAC and the Refoundation Communists are. There's not much choice. We can't go back. And we don't want to confront the police again.

Piazza Carignano is a large square at the foot of the massive old church, where the march for the refugees began on Thursday. Now we rest. We sit, sprawled around the square. I go round looking for Ruard. I find him, we hug. I have the mobile, and could call Nancy at home. But I decide to wait until we are out of all this for sure. I beg a cigarette, and then another. As we chat, an ambulance comes through, siren wailing, light flashing. We get up, make room. Then another. There is a hospital down the side street where we waited for the refugees march to begin. Somewhere else, other people must be getting hurt.

We all rest. It's lunch break time. We've been marching for hours, high on adrenalin. There's music and lots of people are dancing. Some people are stringing banners across the road. There's art work and sculpture. I'm too tired to pay attention to the fun.

After an hour's rest, Chris Nineham goes down the short, very steep street, one long block down, to Piazza Dante. There he asks the people from ATTAC and the Refoundation Communist Party if we can come down to join them. They say yes, enthusiastically.

★

ATTAC began as a campaign for the Tobin Tax founded by French socialist intellectuals in 1998. The Tobin Tax is a proposal for a tax of one half of one per cent on every international currency transaction. The idea is that enormous amounts of currency move around the world every day in speculation. The scale of this movement endangers the financial market in every third world country, and the money that arrived in a country over years can leave in days.

Of course, countries don't go into economic crisis simply because of speculation. The money floods out because something is wrong in the local economy. When banks panic, a tax of one half of one per cent won't stop them. No one, including ATTAC, thinks a Tobin Tax can stop global capitalism or world poverty. But it would slow down speculation. The money raised could be put towards the debt of poor countries. And a movement that could win the Tobin Tax would take heart and move on to do much more.

ATTAC grew swiftly. It now has 20,000 members in France and in the spring of 2001 grew rapidly all across Scandinavia. The founding conference of Italian ATTAC in June attracted 700 people. These new young people flooding in wanted far more than a Tobin Tax. ATTAC rapidly became the largest anti-capitalist movement in Europe.

ATTAC was the main anti-capitalist organisation at the Gothenburg protests. After the shootings there, the French leadership of ATTAC were worried. They had close links with the Socialist Party, the governing party in France. They didn't want to be associated with what the press would call riots. For Genoa, the leadership of ATTAC mobilised roughly 700 people from France. They supported the protests formally, but did not pull out all the stops. The new Italian ATTAC turned out in force.

Both ATTAC and the Italian Refoundation Communist Party were split about how to demonstrate on the direct action Friday. Refoundation dealt with this by officially splitting their forces. Their Young Communist organisation marched with the White Overalls, three miles or more away from the main body of Refoundation. That made sense, they said, because of course old people were more afraid and younger people wilder.

ATTAC decided they would go with the older Communists to Piazza Dante, where they planned to not challenge the Red Zone. This did not sit well with a lot of ATTAC members, who had been shouting joy and anger in the tunnel on the march the day before. Many of them decided to march with the Young Communists and White Overalls across town.

For a while I got very annoyed every time somebody in Genoa said that of course older people were more scared and should be protected. I was scared, sure, but a lot less scared than when I was 21. By the time you're 53 some things have happened to you that are a lot worse than getting hit by policeman, and you're less scared of dying. You've had a life. But after a while I understood that all this talk about old people was covering a political division.

The differences within ATTAC and Refoundation were not caused by age. It was a split between an established moderate leadership and new people who came in with passion and no habit of compromise. It's the same split you get in many strikes. Before the strike, union leaders seem like radicals, and rank and file members seem apathetic. Then many ordinary union members find the strike changes their whole idea of the world and themselves. The union leaders are stuck in the habit of negotiation and terrified of going too far. Now the rank and file want to stay until they win all their demands, and the union leaders are trying to get them back to work. When you get that kind of split between workers and union leaders, there is no age difference. In Genoa there was an age difference between the leaders and new activists, and to avoid a split everybody was talking about age.

The leadership of ATTAC had asked us not to join them, because they were worried that if their young people saw us, they would get all militant too. When Chris Nineham went down to Piazza Dante to ask if we could join them now, the leadership of ATTAC had already left. The younger people who had stayed said 'Sure.' Chris came back up to get us. We formed up with flags, holding arms, and marched down to Piazza Dante.

The fence of the Red Zone ran down one side of the Piazza. Here it was perhaps 400 metres long, maybe 6 metres high, and looked easier to pull down. There had been trouble here already, with the young people in ATTAC banging on the fence, and the police replying with tear gas. But nothing really heavy.

As we come down the steep street into the Piazza Dante, the people in the square cheer us, clapping in continuous slow rhythm, yelling. We and they are chanting, in French, 'Un, deux, internationale solidarite' ('One, two, international solidarity,' but it's better in French because each syllable is stressed and you really bang the final 'ay'.) It's like being in a liberating army. I look around, at our marching order and our red flags. We look like revolutionaries.

We join the crowd, happy, smiling. The hard stuff is over, and we're among friends. The ATTAC people spread out along the fence, shoulder to shoulder, and they bang on the fence with the flat of their palms, rhythmically. The noise is enormous. The fence shakes. There are police behind it, armoured cars, water cannon and gas. We hang back. We have promised their leaders we won't cause trouble.

I have to pee. The back of the square, on the side away from the fence, looks a likely place. There is a big archway here, with a modern office block above. I can see the marble entrance atrium to the building further in, breathing power. The street beyond the arch leads away from the square. ATTAC stewards under the arch bar the way. They tell us foreigners: 'Many police there. Bad place.'

I point to my fly. A woman smiles and lets me through. I walk 20 paces, round the corner of the arch, and pee in a corner. God knows what other people are doing. The whole day I saw only three other people peeing. I don't see any cops down the street, but I believe the ATTAC stewards. The Piazza Dante is a trap. The only way out is the steep narrow street we came down. That's at the far side of the piazza. If the fence comes down, the police will break through and trap many of us.

Two young men from ATTAC climb the fence in the middle. They pull at the top section of the fence. It sways back and forth. It will come down easily. Below them the others are pulling at the fence.

A group of ATTAC stewards come forward, holding narrow, tall, sausage-shaped balloons, four metres high. They are trying to defuse the tension. The balloons are decorated with the ATTAC symbol, a per cent sign in red for the Tobin tax. They run to the fence in a line and let a dozen giant balloons go. The balloons rise into the air, over the fence and the heads of the police. We all cheer. Then the people go back to pulling on the fence together. All this time people are playing music, and an acrobat on stilts dances through the crowd. The police are using water cannon on the people by the fence.

If the fence comes down all these people will be trapped. We promised the leaders of ATTAC and Communist Refoundation that we wouldn't create trouble in their area. It's their people shaking the fence, not us. But they wouldn't be doing it if we hadn't marched down here. And they're not ready for what comes next. They have no lines, no linked arms.

Our stewards move us out. We try to link arms, get in formation, make sure we leave no stragglers, protect the rear, like we've learned. Our chief stewards tell us not to regroup. Just move. 'Now,' Bambery says to me. 'Move, Jonathan. Now.'

'What about all these people?' I say.

'Now,' Bambery says.

I understand. If we don't leave right now the ATTAC people won't come. They're too wired. If they see us move off, they'll follow. The only way we can get them out of here is to start going ourselves. Vittorio Agnoletto of the GSF is on a microphone by a truck, urging everybody to leave, right now, in Italian. I'm off, into the steep street. A crowd fills the street, moving up, not running, but walking fast. I hear the sound of tear gas being fired behind us. I turn round and see the puffs of gas down in the square. Suddenly people around me are running. I grab a man on my left, telling him to link arms, walk backwards slowly up hill. The people around don't seem to understand my English, but they get my meaning. Soon we have a line, holding arms, faces towards the gas, walking backwards. One woman, temporarily blind from the gas, runs toward us, crying, with three friends pushing her through. With my free hand I am waving to the people below, calling them up the hill, shouting 'Slowly, slowly.' And then in Italian, 'Tranquillo, tranquillo.'

The people from Jubilee South go by. They're a group with a programme like Drop the Debt in Britain, but from the third world. Drop the Debt Britain chose not to come on the direct action day. Jubilee South have. They're from Africa and Latin America and the Philippines, serious people.

Now the crowd are streaming up the hill. The running and the panic have stopped. The gap has closed below us. The ATTAC people who were tempted to fight have come up to join us. Daniel and Fiona are here. They were close to the fence when the gas came. A grenade hit Daniel. He shows me the black burns, says it hurts a lot. He is surprised. 'We were leaving,' he says. 'Why did they gas us when we were leaving?'

'To show their power,' I say.

We get back up the hill, to the piazza below the church. The International Socialist stewards are there, moving us on down the other side of the hill, waving at us to walk out, not linger, not talk, just go down that street there. The socialists are stewarding us all now, no questions asked. We march out of the Piazza, down a street back towards the shore, thousands upon thousands strong, the different political tendencies all together now, one. Fiona and I are in a line that holds up a Globalise Resistance banner. The whole crowd is shouting, in English, 'One Solution, Revolution', with our right fists in the air. I'm shouting it. Fiona the video producer is shouting it. Daniel the cameraman, a pro, is in front of us, filming us, his right arm rock steady holding the camera, his left fist in the air as he shouts 'One Solution, Revolution.'

We march down the hill. The ship containers on our right cut off our view of the G8, but we know they're there. Our noise is enormous. We chant 'Our World is Not For Sale' in French, then Italian, 'We are Winning, Don't Forget' in English, 'So-So-Solidarite', a slogan of Quebec, in French. The street is packed, smiles and giggling everywhere.

We come down to the main thoroughfare, the Viale Delle Brigate Partigiane (the Street of the Partisan Brigades). We swing past the police headquarters toward the Convergence Centre, cheering ourselves in. We haven't taken the fence down. Nobody got into the Red Zone. We didn't stop the G8. But we feel we've won. We fought the police, we held our ground, we united with ATTAC and Communist Refoundation.

I call Nancy and tell her Ru's OK. Then I look for my affinity group. We all buy food in the big covered tent, sit down around a table, our little band of sisters and brothers. Later I sit on the ground for an International Socialist meeting in the open air. A speaker says news has just come through that a demonstrator on another march has been shot dead.

The whole demonstration had been split up into seven different marches. (See the map again.) In the north-west were CUP, one of the two radical union groups. They were about 5,000 strong, almost all workers, and planned to march peacefully without going anywhere near the Red Zone. In the north were the mainly Catholic pacifists, also several thousand. They planned to march down towards the Red Zone, but to turn round before they reached it and not challenge the police.

In the north-east were the largest single group, the White

Overalls and those who marched with them. They would try to get to the Red Zone, would not attack the police, but they would wear a lot of padding to protect themselves from police beatings. In the south-east were COBAS, the other radical union group. They were going to try to get into the Red Zone, and would defend themselves if attacked.

In the south were three separate groups: the mostly foreign gentle anarchist Pink March, Globalise Resistance and the International Socialists, and ATTAC and Communist Refoundation. Several kilometres to the east the Drop the Debt group were holding a prayer vigil rather than a march.

Finally, there were several hundred anarchists in the Black Block of anarchists. They had no one place of their own, but moved between the other groups. They had not announced their intentions, but everyone assumed they would try to get in the Red Zone and fight the police.

One protestor, Kalpana Lal, marched first with the pacifists and then with the White Overalls. Kalpana is a geneticist in London. She had been in Prague, loved the feeling and the buzz of the Convergence Centre there. Kalpana is a person of strong opinions, but open to argument, and has little time for people who are dogmatically sure. She came from London on the Globalise Resistance train that the French railway unions had saved for us. There were about 300 people on the train, and Kalpana insisted on running a non-violent resistance workshop while they sped through France. She'd been to one in Prague run by the American pacifist Starhawk. The GR organisers weren't sure it was a good idea. There were two things we didn't like about the pacifist model of non-violent resistance. One was the emphasis on courageous suffering, just sitting and getting beaten, instead of retreating. The other was that it's often an elitist model. A minority of brave people volunteer to be beaten, and the rest watch. That said, we had taken over their tactics of linked arms and affinity groups, and they worked. Kalpana wasn't into passive suffering either, and she was certain the people on her train needed some preparation for Genoa. She ran the workshop.

The train was delayed at the Italian border Friday morning. Then they got into buses for the last leg to Genoa. As Kalpana and the rest of the passengers were getting off the buses in the north of Genoa at 12, we were already swinging down towards the Red Zone.

Kalpana and the rest tried to walk down to the shore and the Convergence Centre. A wall of police and gas stopped them. Kalpana and her immediate friends turned back up hill and joined the pacifist group who were marching down toward, but not all the way to, the Red Zone. Kalpana later wrote a diary of Genoa. She called the pacifists the 'White Block.'

In the square there was a band playing some samba. People swaying, kids chasing, old people laughing. Everyone friendly and relaxed ...

Crucially, there was a stall selling some pasta, which quickly disappeared. We shared what we had. Ever-resource-ful Andy had acquired some beer ... At this point some Black Block arrive in the square. Dressed in black. They looked young, skinny, masked up in black. A group of about 10 were trying to go across the square down the hill towards the action. Just where we had been considering going moments earlier. About 30 White Block stood in front of them with their arms raised showing them their palms painted white. The Black Block waited. Then around 50 more Black Block arrived followed by lots of police. The police helicopter marked the spot. The police started to surround the square. The situation was starting to get tense. We were trying to get our group together so we could move out. Not sure which way, just out!

The Black Block threw a couple of missiles at the police and then ran away. The police attacked us.

Note – it's very important – the Black Block ran away and then the police attacked the pacifist crowd, not the Black Block. Back to Kalpana:

> The police attacked us. Running at us, letting off tear gas. We tried to get out of their way. I ended up on the ground, pushed up against a stone wall bordering the square. Then the batons came. My hand was protecting my head. I was hit on my fingers and my head. My fingers hurt more so my instinct was to withdraw my hand exposing my head, but I kept it there. I was aware that Issy had fallen on top of me and was protecting me from more beating. The beating continued for several minutes. It was not just a couple of lashes as they went past. It was systematic beating of women lying on the ground trying to protect themselves. I remember hearing 'Don't hit, BBC.' When they did move on, we rose and managed to hold on to each other. We were still in tear gas. I was paranoid about tear gas because I wear contact lenses and so thought my eyes were going to drop out cartoon style. My instinct was to run blindly. Nick called out to walk calmly. We did. We walked out of the tear gas and down some steps.
>
> A woman in front had her head split open. Blood caking her hair. A man with her asked for water and poured it over her head. The gushes ran red. She fainted. He picked her up and carried her down the steps. We weren't in the clear yet.
>
> Issy was in a lot of pain and in shock. We weren't sure if her hand was broken and her shoulder dislocated. Issy, Nick and Sam had an impressive amount of bruising. I escaped unscathed. I felt guilty that Issy had ended up protecting me.

They got clear to one side of the main Catholic pacifist march. Most of the pacifist marchers, including our host Maria, were driven two kilometres back up the hill to their starting point, gassed and beaten all the way. Kalpana and her friends found themselves to one side, between the pacifist march and the White Overalls:

We could see the police helicopter hovering in the direction we were going in. We could hear dogs. We decided to go back up the steps we had escaped down. We joined back up with the GR lot from the train. We were confused, bedraggled and shit scared. Trying to be supportive of each other. Me and Issy started dreaming about getting the hell out and sipping beer in some bar, being waited on by gorgeous Italian men. Slight drawback, we had no idea which way to go to be safe. The shops were all shut.

We had no clear strategy but to avoid the police and thus were moved on a few times. We rested up in a square on some grass ... I watched from our vantage point from the top of the hill. In the distance, the other side of the train station, was the White Overalls demo. I couldn't see all of it but it was certainly some thousands strong. They faced police onslaught. I saw repeated tear gas and water cannon. But they stood their ground for over an hour. So either they had a sizeable number of people together or the police had hemmed them in, meting out torture. I managed to score a cheese sandwich off some women who were very generous with the last of their food.

Some GR people had been out scouting and returned. They said there was a choice. Those who were tired and had had enough could go one way towards the square where we were supposed to sleep, OR going through a little bit of tear gas it was possible to get to the Ya Basta demo which was 10,000 strong. I was wired. I hadn't suffered like the others and I wanted to be part of a demo making a difference, not just running away from police. With big hugs to my people I said goodbye.

I acquired a new affinity group, Anna and Suzy. We were clear that we wanted to join the demo. We would stay at the back and not stick around for any heavy stuff. We marched up the road, chanting, past a burning car, past traffic and pedestrians. It was scary but we were loud and gaining confidence. We approached up the steps to the demo, cautiously because something was happening up the top. When we got to the top people were running, panic and mayhem. Police coming at us. We went down the steps not running but with linked arms. We hesitated at the other side of the road. I wanted to get the hell out but Anna and Suzy hesitated, waiting to see if they came after us. The police came at us with tear gas, batoning people. They went past us. I had prepared with my goggles and a bandanna soaked in lemon juice. Also, having already experienced the tear gas I was less scared of it. I wasn't too badly affected. The tear gas was more intense this time. We walk a fair way to get out of it. Anna and Suzy had not prepared. They were really suffering. Choking, eyes streaming and starting to falter. We had arms linked and I was dragging them, shouting at them to keep moving. A guy was shouting in pain. His head was split open with blood pouring down his face. I couldn't help him. I had to get us out of the tear gas. When we were out of the tear gas round the corner, Anny and Suzy started spitting and recovering. That guy came round. I got people to stop and pay attention to him. An ambulance pulled up and he started heading in the opposite direction. In Italy the police routinely go to the hospitals and arrest people. Apparently, the paramedics could have patched him up without taking him to the hospital, but he wasn't going anywhere near them. The ambulance left and I don't know what happened to him. We were still only round the corner from where we had just run from. We were not in a safe place. We collected people and moved up.

Not far we found a place selling beer. It felt like an oasis. There's something about beer which makes you feel normality has returned. Andy arrived with news that the police had shot someone! Fuck! Serious shit!

What had happened was this. The White Overalls had set out from the Carlini stadium earlier that morning. The police met and stopped the march before it got to the Brignole station, well before the Red Zone.

The activists from the social centres in the White Overalls had planned to both lead and protect the marchers. They wore extensive padding themselves, like American football players, and had homemade clear plastic riot shields. They would push into the police lines with their shields, standing shoulder to shoulder, and try to get to the Red Zone. If the police attacked the crowd, they would stand between the cops and the rest of the demonstrators with their shields and padding.

Two things went wrong. First, too many demonstrators joined in with the White Overalls. Their methods had been worked out for small groups. There was no way a few hundred padded activists could protect a crowd of 20,000 from the police.

The other thing was that the police attacked far harder than the White Overalls expected. Every Italian I talked to afterwards who was there said they had never seen the police like that. The tactics the White Overalls had used for so long were no protection. On previous demonstrations, the White Overalls had led the crowd up to the police, and then the police and the Overalls had pushed and shoved. This time the police went round the White Overalls. Also, the Italian activists were used to a situation where the police attacked those who defied them. This is normal in Britain too. It is the people who shout at the police, or come close to them, or look at them with insolence, who get attacked. This time the police attacked the people who shrank back as strongly as the others.

The White Overalls reacted bravely. They tried to put themselves between the crowd and the cops. They looked round for something, anything, to make barricades to hold the police back. They found the large green plastic bins that the city of Genoa leaves out for people to put their garbage in. The bins had wheels, and people pushed them into the middle of the road. But most people were scattered, running, stopping to throw tear gas canisters back at the police, angry, chaotic and scared.

The tactic that most disorganised the White Overalls, and that they least expected, was that the police drove vehicles into the crowd. They used police buses and jeeps, and they drove at 50 miles an hour. People scattered for their lives. The buses and jeeps would then pull back and drive into the crowd again and again.

One of the jeeps overshot, and ended up almost against a wall. It stalled, and a few demonstrators approached the jeep, angry but scared as well. A soldier, a young conscript, was sitting in the back, the jeep open behind him. He threw out a fire extinguisher at an approaching demonstrator, Carlo Giuliani. Giuliani was 23 years old and did casual work when he could get it. He had been born in Rome, but had lived in Genoa most of his life. His father was a full-time official with the trade unions in Genoa, and Carlo had learned his parents' love for social justice. Now he was wearing a black mask to hide his identity, though he wasn't part of the Black Block. He stooped and picked up the fire extinguisher. On the video of the event, it looks as if he is considering throwing the fire extinguisher back at the jeep. Then he lowers the fire extinguisher, apparently deciding not to, and the soldier shoots him in the head with a handgun.

Giuliani fell. The jeep driver reversed back over his body, stopped, and then drove forward again over the body. The protesters fell back, and a wall of police came running up and surrounded Giuliani's body. They took his mask off. He looked young, and very thin.

At least eight other shots were fired by the police that day, although no one else died. The police drove the White Overalls all the way back to the Carlini stadium, gas and batons all the way for two or three miles.

Down in the south-east, the radical trade unionists from COBAS had said they would march to the Red Zone. The police attacked them as they gathered, before they even began marching. The force was such that COBAS were unable to hold the square they had gathered in.

COBAS and the White Overalls had got nowhere near the fence. They were beaten back and scattered, one dead and many injured. Globalise Resistance and the International Socialists got to the fence and almost into the Red Zone, with only one person injured or arrested. The Pink March did the same.

The main reason for this was that the police attacked the White Overalls, COBAS and the Italian pacifists much harder than they did the foreigners. In the eyes of the police those groups were the real political opposition, the people they needed to frighten and break. And they attacked the pacifists who were not confronting them as strongly as they did the White Overalls and COBAS.

For the Italian police the international groups were less important. They had to stop us getting into the Red Zone, but they didn't need to break or punish us. Also, they had never seen us before. The way Tom Behan put it later was that to the Italian police we looked like Teletubbies: strangely dressed, talking incomprehensibly, and all holding hands. We also looked disciplined, collective, and possibly violent, but above all unpredictable. And there were thousands of us. It wasn't worth really taking us on, and they didn't have to.

But although the police attack was the crucial variable, I also think that linked arms, rows, and elected stewards were better tactics on the day. They would not have saved us from what the White Overalls faced. But they would have lessened the chaos. The White Overalls tactic of a minority protecting the majority did not work, and nor did the COBAS strategy of self-defence.

In a similar situation next time, I would want to use the same tactics. It would also be very important for the crowd to control any who wanted to attack the police, as we did. But the most important weakness in every march was that we were divided.

If the division into three groups in Prague was stupid, the division into seven in Genoa was tactical madness. Had we marched together, we would have been 40 or 50,000 people. There is safety in numbers. The police could not have attacked a march of that size in the same way. This is partly because they would have faced far more people. But it is also because there is a moral authority in numbers. The more moderate among the crowd would have restrained the more radical. And the more moderate would also have gone to the aid of those attacked.

This is why the Italian left and the unions usually demonstrate in one united march, as we do in Britain. The division in Genoa was the flip side of the strengths of the GSF. We had agreed at the meetings that we would all respect each other's actions. That unity had been hard to achieve. But the price of even that unity had been the acceptance of an actual division on the day.

Next time (if we can): linked arms, elected stewards, advance and retreat as a block, and all together.

That night Carmela, Daniel, Fiona and I drove back to Maria's across Genoa. Smoke hung in many places. Burned-out cars, smashed windows and debris lay in the road. We turned a corner and fire engines blocked a one-way road. We stopped, caught. Carmela leaned out the window to talk to the fire fighters. They said there were a lot more fires in the city. The protesters had set fire to banks, which were at the bottom of blocks of flats, the fire fighters said. All day they had been evacuating people from those flats. Old people, they said, and people in wheelchairs. The fire fighters said they had all been going to come on the great march tomorrow. Now they couldn't. They all had to be on duty, waiting for more fires. Stupid, they said, and worse than stupid.

Carmela was leaning out the window, asking more. One of the fire engines blocking the road was pulling out. I was edgy; afraid we might be picked up by the police at any moment. Carmela wanted to ask more. She was still leaning out the window, talking, as we drove off.

The city was dark, the streets empty. As we drove an American reporter called my mobile and interviewed me then and there.

Daniel was next to me, the red light on his camera winking in the dark. I was desperately tired, angry at all the trashing which made us look violent and played into their hands. But I was angrier at the killing. I had talked easily to this reporter that morning, and the day before. Now I was parrying him. He wanted me to condemn the rioters. I didn't know yet how Carlo had died. I did know I mustn't say anything to provide ammunition for the hue and cry that would come from the media. And I was frightened that I was so tired I'd somehow say the wrong thing. So I said, over and over, that the vast majority of us had been non-violent, that my section of the crowd had been completely non-violent, and yet the police had gassed and beaten us.

At Maria's we watched TV. They showed the same shots over and over. First there was Carlo Giuliani standing behind the jeep, holding something that looked like a fire extinguisher, his hands raised as if to throw it. He was wearing a white tank top. A black balaclava covered his face. In the same photo there was a policeman in the jeep, his face hidden, a gun in his hand pointed at Carlo. The TV technicians had drawn a red circle round the gun so you could pick it out.

The next picture was from a slightly different angle. It showed, very clearly, the license plate number of the jeep. The TV reporters were telling us the police knew who had done the shooting.

The next picture was Carlo Giuliani's body under the jeep, after the driver had backed it over Carlo's head. His legs were sticking out from under the car.

Then they showed Carlo lying on the road, surrounded by police. He was still, a pool of blood around his head. His balaclava had been pulled off so his face showed.

On the TV we saw an ambulance arrive to treat Carlo. It seemed there was a doctor in the ambulance, or at any rate some one more middle class and official than a paramedic. The police wouldn't let him through. The TV cameras were filming all this, the cameramen getting up close, clearly trying to support the doctor by showing what was happening. And then the black hand of a cop covered the lens and pushed it back.

Maria had been on the pacifist march. She sat next to me in front of the television, shouting her anger at the screen, anger at the Black Block, and then her body bending and straightening as she shouted at pictures of the police.

One television station broadcast a discussion live from the Convergence Centre in Genoa. Vittorio Agnoletto, the main spokesperson of the GSF, was allowed to speak straight to camera. Agnoletto is a doctor, and the director of the government-sponsored organisation that tries to help people with HIV. He called upon the G8 to cancel the rest of their meeting out of respect for Carlo Giuliani's death. Then he said, live to the Italian people: 'You have seen what has happened here. I ask you to forget about what you were planning to do tomorrow. Get in your car, get on a train, get a bus. Come to Genoa tomorrow. March with us.'

Everything now depended on how many people came tomorrow.

9 | **Oil, dictatorship and war**

We return to the issues. This chapter is about war and dictatorship in the Middle East. The causes here are the same as for global warming: US support for the oil industry.

The story I tell here is complicated. From the point of view of Washington, the history of the Middle East has been one damn thing after another. As soon as one threat to oil was stamped on, another sprang up. This was because US control relied on dictatorship, war and inequality. All of these produced bitterness and instability. That's why the story is so involved. The important thing to keep track of is how each US victory produced another threat.

At the end of World War Two, in 1945, the US found itself the dominant economic and military power in the world. The most important commodity in that world, then and now, was oil. The majority of the world's known oil reserves were in the Middle East, most of it in Saudi Arabia, Iraq, Kuwait, and Iran. All the countries of the Arab world had been colonies or clients of European powers. But by 1948 the Arab countries and Iran were all independent. They were, however, now dominated by the United States. American policy in these countries had had three main thrusts. One was to support the power of the major oil corporations. The second was to keep the price of oil low, for the sake of US and world industry. The third objective follows from the first two. It was to support, and where necessary create, dictatorships in the Middle East in order to keep control of the oil out of the hands of the people who live there.

Let's take Saudi Arabia as an example. Since 1918 Saudi Arabia had been an independent kingdom dominated by Britain. In 1945 the US-owned Arab American Oil Company and the US government took over patronage of Saudi Arabia. For the last 50 years, Saudi Arabia has been the largest oil producer in the world. It also has the largest oil reserves; for most of the last 50 years about 20 per cent of known reserves. Whenever they want to, the Saudi government can increase production rapidly enough to flood the world market and hold down the price of oil. This they have done at several crucial moments. These policies are not in the interests of the Saudi people, who would benefit from a high price of oil.

Effective power in Saudi Arabia lies collectively in the hands of the thousands of princes in the royal family. Because they are ruling so clearly against the interests of their people, the Saudi dictatorship has been brutal. There are no democratic rights and no trade unions. No one knows where the public purse ends and the bank accounts of the princes begin, and the princes make fortunes from bribes.

The royal family's claim to legitimacy comes from their role as guardians of Islam's holy cities, Mecca and Medina. The official ideology of the state is Wahhabism, an 18th century reform movement in Islam. Wahhabism emphasises the seclusion and oppression of women and brutal punishments like the cutting off of hands. Most other Muslims regard Wahhabism as backward and cruel. However, Saudi Arabia is not now a backwater of the global system. It is at the centre. This deeply sexist dictatorship is not in need of modernisation. It is the modern form of control of world oil.

The princes go on about the purity of Islam. Then they go on holiday to Beirut and London. There they gamble, losing hundreds of thousands of dollars, or millions, in a single night. They forbid liquor at home and drink themselves into stupors abroad. They thieve from the country endlessly, and yet every Saudi prince still has both hands. This hypocrisy is obvious to all in

Saudi Arabia. The Saudi princes are also hated across the Arab world. Hotel porters and waiters may scrape in hopes of a tip in Cairo, but they too hold the princes in contempt.

The dictatorship has been able to kill or torture all nationalist opposition into helplessness. They have not, however, been able to shut down the mosques. Given the religious justification for their rule, they can't. So the hatred of the Saudi people for their rulers has found its way into the mosques. This puts more pressure on the princes to be more brutal and puritanical in their interpretation of Islam. The more puritanical they become, the more their hypocrisy stands out.

The Saudi regime also has little military protection against its own people. The princes have noticed the military coups in the rest of the Arab world, and kept their army small and weak. In short, the Saudi regime is brutal, hated and fragile. Throughout the last 50 years, the main concern of US policy, and of the Saudi princes, has been preventing a rising from below in Saudi Arabia.

The first main challenge to this policy came from Arab nationalism in the 1950s. The leading Arab nationalist was Gamal Abdul Nasser, an Egyptian. Egypt had no oil, but it did have the largest population in the Middle East. Nasser came to power in a military coup that overthrew the British-backed king. His regime was a dictatorship, but it took the land from the old landlords and handed it out to poor Egyptian farmers. That gave Nasser popular support in Egypt that remained fervent for 20 years. Nasser also nationalised the British and French owned Suez Canal, the major foreign corporation in Egypt. In reply, the armies of Britain, France and Israel invaded Egypt in 1956. President Eisenhower of the US came down on Nasser's side, and told the invaders to withdraw. They did. The US at this point was hoping to live with Arab nationalism, and did not want British and French power in the Middle East.

Quite soon the US government decided they could not live with the nationalist threat to oil. All over the Arab world, nationalists looked to the Egyptian example of deposing the king, handing out the land and nationalising the foreign companies. Nationalist governments took power in Syria, Iraq and Libya. A civil war broke out in Yemen, the other large country besides Saudi Arabia in the Arabian peninsula. Yemen has no oil, but it does have hundreds of thousands of migrant workers in Saudi Arabia. The Saudi government backed the Yemeni royal family in the civil war, and Nasser's Egypt sent soldiers to fight alongside the nationalists. If the nationalists won, it was widely thought the Saudi royal family would be next to go.

The US looked round for some way to smash the nationalist threat to oil. In Farsi-speaking Iran, a democratically elected government had moved to nationalise the oil. In 1953 the CIA organised a coup that installed the Shah, who left the oil alone. In 1958, in Iraq, a mass popular revolution led by communists in the streets overthrew the king. The CIA then helped army officers to see off the mass movement in a series of coups and factions fights. But there was still the example of Nasser and Egypt.

The solution to that, it turned out, was Israel.

We have to backtrack a little here, to explain how Israel came into being. Since about 1900 the Zionist movement in Europe had agitated for a Jewish homeland in Palestine. Until 1939, however, Zionism was a minority movement among European Jews. The majority supported either the socialist or the communist parties, and saw their fate as linked to other European workers. In any case, Palestine was already full of other people: the Palestinians.

The holocaust changed all that. It was not just what the Nazis did to the Jews. It was also that the governments of Britain and the United States had refused entry, on racist grounds, to most of the Jewish refugees fleeing Nazi Germany. The Soviet Union, too, discriminated against Russian Jews. So many survivors of the Holocaust decided that the Zionists were right. No one would stand by the Jews. They must have their own homeland to be safe.

The majority of Jewish refugees did not go to Israel. But enough went to make Zionism a credible proposition. Britain, the colonial power in Palestine, was no longer strong enough to hold on to the colony. In 1948 Britain departed. Palestine was divided into a Jewish Israel and an Arab Jordan. The Zionists, however, received a small and divided Israel. They went to war with their neighbours to expand their borders and create what they saw as a viable state. This necessitated what is now called ethnic cleansing. There were simply too many Arabs living in their proposed new state. Zionist paramilitaries massacred over 100 men, women and children in the village of Deir Yassein. In other villages, too, the paramilitaries and the Israeli army killed enough to persuade most other Palestinians to flee.

This created large refugee camps in all the neighbouring Arab countries, many of which are still there 54 years later. A minority of Palestinian Arabs were able to stay within the new borders of Israel, although many had their land taken for Jewish settlements. The Arabs who stayed are now about one-sixth of the Israeli population.

There was strong sympathy for the Palestinian refuges among ordinary Arabs in all the neighbouring countries. It was also very widely felt, quite correctly, that the Arab kingdoms had not fought properly to defend the Palestinians. A strong Arab nationalism, people felt, would build modern armies that could return the Palestinians to their homes.

This made Arab nationalism the central enemy for the new Israeli government. Then the Palestinians in the refugee camps themselves began to organise, under the leadership of Yassir Arafat and the Palestine Liberation Organisation. The PLO launched small guerrilla raids into Israel. To stop them, and the larger threat of Arab nationalism, Israel launched a war on three of its neighbours (Egypt, Jordan and Syria) in 1967. The Israeli armed forces destroyed the Egyptian air force, humiliated the Egyptian army, and won in six days.

It was a decisive blow against the prestige of Arab nationalism in the eyes of Arab workers. The defeated Arab regimes cracked down on the PLO in their own countries. Nasser died in 1970, a defeated and demoralised man. His successor, Sadat, launched a war against Israel in 1973. This was a much closer run thing than the 1967 war, but again Israel emerged triumphant, taking over territory from Egypt, Jordan, Syria and Lebanon. In response, the Arab oil countries all agreed to cut off oil to the United States, as Israel's sponsor. The world price of oil went through the roof, threatening the US economy. Under US pressure, the Saudi government broke the embargo and turned the taps back on. The price of oil came down.

The 1967 and 1973 wars broke Arab nationalism. The US government noticed. They had found their hammer in the Middle East. The US had supported Israel in 1948, of course, as had the Soviet Union. However, this support played a minor role in US policy. Foreign aid was limited, and the US supported Egypt against Israel in the 1956 war. After the triumph of 1967, all this changed. The alliance with Israel became the cornerstone of US policy in the region and Israel became the leading recipient of American foreign aid. By 1996 Israel, a country with a per capita income of $19,000, received 25 per cent of all US foreign aid. Without this support, the Israeli economy could not have survived.

So by 1979 it seemed that nationalism was exhausted in the Arab world. US power, the oil companies and the dictatorships were safe. Then Iran went into revolution, and suddenly Islamism replaced nationalism as the threat to American power.

Islamism is a form of right-wing political Islam. Islamic politics can, and has, taken many other forms. There is nothing automatic about the support of Muslims for Islamist parties. Fifty years ago most Arab Muslims supported either the nationalists or the communists. In the course of the 20th century millions of Muslims, world wide, became active socialists or communists, and hundreds of millions supported those parties.

They saw no more contradiction between their religion and their politics than a British Catholic does in voting Labour, or an American Protestant does in voting for a liberal Democrat. In fact, to these Muslims their support for socialism fitted with the equality they felt was central to Islam.

Many of the grandchildren of these people now support Islamist parties. These parties are not one monolithic whole. There is as much variation as there was in socialism and communism. Some Islamist parties, as in Turkey, are basically parliamentary. Some look to terrorism. Sometimes Islamists join mass popular uprisings. All of them, however, are modern movements.

It is true that Islamists say they look back to the pure Islam of the time of the prophet. But they hold the Islam of the villages in the 19th and 20th centuries in contempt. They look back to their own mythologised version of ancient time, not to actual Muslim tradition. Islamism, as an ideology, developed in the late 19th and early 20th century in reaction to Western colonialism and imperialism. It was an attempt to change the Islamic world to confront a new reality. The social base was the middle class: civil servants, teachers, students and traders in the bazaar. This was an urban movement. It remained a minority movement until people decided that communism and nationalism would not solve their problems.

This Islamism was both anti-imperialist and right-wing. In this, it reflected its middle-class base: opposed to the colonialists, the old kings and the landlords, but also fearing the working class. The Islamist emphasis on the modesty of women was part of their right-wing politics. Like the nationalist parties, the Islamists tend to oppose imperial power when they are out of power. In power, or offered a piece of power, they are pulled to compromise with capitalism and the imperial system. Their recent popular support has come from their anti-imperialism. Where they have gained power, as in Afghanistan and Iran, their right-wing policies have eroded that support.

The turning point in the rise of Islamism was the Iranian

revolution. In 1953 the CIA had replaced a democratically elected government in Iran and put the Shah in place. The oil wealth had produced a large upper class, but most people stayed poor. In 1979 they began a revolution against the Shah. Demonstrators marched in the cities and were shot down by the police and army. They marched again, 40 days later, in religious commemoration of the dead from the first march, and were shot again. Forty days after that, they would march again. People began to march in the winding sheets they would be buried in, to show the police how they felt.

Along with the demonstrations went strikes. The crucial ones were in the oil fields and the banks. Finally, after months, there was a mass demonstration in Tehran. The air force was ordered to strafe the crowd. The broad main avenue was full. The planes flew over. The people looked up and waited. The planes did not fire. The pilots only buzzed the crowd, and went back to base. Left-wing revolutionaries went to the main air base and said 'Give us arms.' The airmen did, and the Shah fled on a US Air Force plane. The bank workers stopped the rich moving their money out of the country. The revolution had won.

It was by no means clear, however, what power would replace the Shah. The strongest force among the crowds and the strikers were the Islamists, led by Ayatollah Khomeini. Until the 1970s, Islamists had been very much a minority in Iran. The nationalists and the communists had been stronger in the 1950s. But the nationalists had been broken by the Shah, and the communists had collaborated with his government.

Islamist domination in the Iranian revolution was still not a foregone conclusion. The far left, influenced by the Palestinians, Maoism and Castro, had considerable support. They could muster 100,000 people to march through Tehran against the Islamists and for women's liberation. In factories and workplaces all over Iran the strikes had created workers' councils. The Islamists had to consolidate their power.

They did it by a dramatic blow against the US. Islamists

students seized the American embassy. The women and African-American staff were allowed to leave, on the grounds that they were oppressed in the US. The men were kept as prisoners, on the grounds that many of them were CIA operatives, which of course some of them were. This electrified Iran. The CIA had put the Shah in power. The US government had kept him there. The oil companies were American. Finally, someone was challenging US power.

From Washington's point of view, this was a humiliation. In the short term, there was nothing they could do. Retaking the embassy would have required a major war, something which, in the wake of the Vietnam War, the US government knew that the American people would not accept.

The threat went far beyond Iran. The Iranian example enthused people all over the Arab world, and beyond. Mass Islamist movements grew in Lebanon, Palestine, Syria, Saudi Arabia, Egypt, and Algeria.

The US government and ruling class reacted to this new threat to oil in several ways. First, they launched a campaign of demonisation of Islamism, and of Islam itself. For 20 years, the Western media have depicted Muslims as backward, sexist, irrational fanatics and terrorists. To see the effect of this, read any American or British newspaper article about 'Islamic fundamentalism'. Substitute the word 'Jew' or the word 'black' for 'fundamentalist', and the racism will leap off the page at you. Anti-Muslim prejudice is now the only respectable form of racism in the West.

The US government also encouraged two wars to break the Islamists. In 1980 Israel, with American support, invaded Lebanon. There was already a civil war in Lebanon. The insurgents were a coalition of Islamists and Palestinian refugees, and they were winning. The Israeli army invaded to drive the PLO out of Lebanon. The US supported them to break the Islamists. Civilian neighbourhoods were heavily bombed, both by Israeli planes and American naval artillery. Right-wing Lebanese militias, with

Israeli support, massacred Palestinians in the refugee camps. The Islamists were not beaten, but they were cornered.

When the Israelis withdrew from the Lebanese capital, Beirut, American and French soldiers occupied part of the city. One suicide bomber in a truck full of explosives killed over 200 US marines. The American troops were withdrawn. The American people were still very clear they would not die for US foreign policy.

The civil war, however, continued until 2000. The Israeli occupation of southern Lebanon lasted 20 years, with torture and bombing regular events, until the Islamist Hezbollah finally drove the Israeli army out. The long civil war was cruel. Beirut, which had been a byword for wealth and tranquility in the Middle East, became a byword for horror.

The main American-supported assault on Islamism, however, was against Iran by proxy. Saddam Hussein was the military dictator of Iraq, Iran's neighbour. Saddam had come to power as a nationalist, and had been allied with Russia for several years. He was now threatened by Islamists in his own country. When the US offered support, Saddam switched sides and declared war on Iran. The ostensible cause was a dispute over access to sea routes for oil.

Islamist rule in Iran was still fragile. The Iranian government welcomed a war with Iraq, as a chance to consolidate their power by uniting against a common enemy. The war lasted seven years. It was an odd replay of the trench warfare of World War One. The Iraqis had the guns. The Iranian government had more popular support, and more people. So their tactic was human wave assaults across minefields into machine guns. A million people died.

The US adopted a position of public neutrality while arming both sides. What they wanted was a war that would weaken both sides. Saudi Arabia, Kuwait and the Gulf States, all threatened by Islamism at home, funded the Iraqi army. In 1998 the Iranian army was about to win the war. At this point, the US government sent the Sixth Fleet into the Persian Gulf, towards the theatre of war. This was seen by all as a threat to Iran. A US naval ship shot down an Iranian airliner, killing all of the 290 passengers on board. This may have been a mistake. But the US government refused to apologise or discipline the captain of the ship. The point was clear to all.

Iran made peace. Saddam was now in a difficult position. The US had saved him, but his army had been defeated. All those Iraqi boys had died for nothing. His dictatorship was deeply unpopular and the economy was collapsing. The war had been expensive. Saudi and Kuwaiti aid had helped. But now the Kuwaiti government refused to pay him what they had promised.

Kuwait had great oil wealth. It had been created as a country in 1920, when the British colonial rulers had split Kuwait off from Iraq in order to control the oil more easily. Iraq had always maintained an official claim to Kuwait, much in the same way that Argentina had always claimed the Falklands. Now Saddam decided to move on this claim to solve his political and economic problems at home. The Iraqi invasion was swift and successful.

Suddenly the US and Saudi governments had a problem. If Iraq got away with taking Kuwait, they could do the same to Saudi Arabia. The precedent of seizing an oil country had to be stopped. The US began to put together a coalition with European and Arab governments for a war with Iraq.

Saddam could not retreat without serious domestic consequences. He wrapped himself in the flag of Islam. Until this point there had been no evidence he was even a believer, and Iraq was a solidly secular country. Now he invoked the name of God in all his television broadcasts, just as US presidents do. He called for a holy war by Arabs against the Americans. And he announced his support for the Palestinians. His calculation was that the hatred for US imperialism and solidarity with the Palestinians among Arab workers would prevent their governments from making war on him.

The US response was to label Saddam a new Hitler. It was

pointed out that his government was cruel. He had used poison gas against rebellious Iraqi Kurds and Iranian troops. He had biological and chemical weapons. All this was true. None of it had been a problem, however, when Saddam was a US ally.

Saddam was also accused of having 'weapons of mass destruction'. The words were carefully chosen to imply that he had nuclear weapons. He did not, although the US and Israel did, and the US remains the only state to have used nuclear weapons. Saddam did, however, have chemical, and some biological, weapons. So did the United States, Britain and Russia. The US had used the chemical weapon Agent Orange extensively in Vietnam.

The US-led coalition against Iraq held together. Most workers in Egypt and Saudi Arabia did not support their dictatorships going to war with Iraq. But everyone in the Middle East also knew what Saddam was, and had little sympathy for him. American troops and planes were stationed in Saudi Arabia, and did most of the fighting against Iraq. US B-52s blanket-bombed the Iraqi conscript army. The Iraqi government has issued no statistics, but the best guess is that some 100,000 Iraqi soldiers died. It may have been as high as 200,000. The US army shot large numbers of prisoners. There was also intensive bombing of Iraqi cities. This was targeted particularly on military and government installations, factories and water and sewage treatment facilities. Although civilians were not the main target, roughly 17,000 were killed.

The Iraqi conscript army had no love for Saddam. They broke. The US retook Kuwait, slaughtering the Iraqi army from the air as they fled to the border. Then the US army stopped at the border. President Bush had encouraged Iraqis in radio broadcasts to rise up against Saddam. Now, seeing his defeat and weakness, the Kurds in the north revolted. So did the Shia Muslims in the south, led by Islamists. The US did nothing to help. Saddam's elite, non-conscript, Republican Guard, restored order in blood. The rebels felt helpless without the expected US support.

President Bush and Chief of Staff Colin Powell held back for two reasons. Powell had done two tours of duty in Vietnam. He dreaded a repeat of that experience. Defeating Iraq in the desert was one thing. Occupying great cities would be another.

The other reason was that the US did not want the Iraqi rebels to win. A Kurdish victory would encourage the ongoing Kurdish revolt just over the border in Turkey, America's ally. An Islamist-led victory in southern Iraq would only give heart to Islamic movements elsewhere. After the American bombing, it was unlikely that any democratic government would be friendly to the US. Bush and Powell had been hoping not for a popular revolt, but for an army coup that replaced Saddam with a dictator they could work with.

The end result of the war, however, was to leave Saddam in power. This meant that the US had only half-broken the threat to its power. The US, with British help, began a decade of regular small scale bombing of Iraq. They also instituted UN sanctions against Iraq, preventing essential imports and the sale of most of Iraqi oil. Iraq had been a rich, overwhelmingly urban, country. Saddam and the rich did not suffer from sanctions. They got richer on smuggling. But average incomes fell to less than a quarter of what they had been. Medicines were largely unobtainable. Child malnutrition became common, and the weight of babies fell drastically. A particular problem was that the bombing had destroyed the sewage and clean water distribution systems. With the sanctions, these could not be repaired. Children began to die of infectious diseases.

Doctors and scientists from the Harvard School of Public Health made regular trips to Iraq to monitor what was happening to the children. Throughout the 1990s, they published their results in the *New England Journal of Medicine*, the leading US medical journal. Based in part on their findings, the UN has estimated that during the 1990s half a million more Iraqis under the age of five died than in the 1980s. If one includes older children and the elderly, roughly a million died from sanctions.

On US television, an Arab journalist asked Clinton's foreign minister, Secretary of State Madeleine Albright, whether she could justify the dead children in Iraq. She said that there sometimes there was a price one had to pay. This response is widely known in the Arab world, but not in the US.

US troops and planes remained in Saudi Arabia after the war with Iraq. This was an emotive issue in that kingdom. Saudi Arabia was the guardian of the Holy Places. It now looked as if there was, in effect, a Christian army of occupation. The Saudi government, however, was feeling increasingly insecure and could not rely on their own army. They wanted the US troops available in the event of a popular revolt.

For the moment, though, US power over oil had been restored. But, again, the war had created a new problem. The US had not included Israel in their coalition. When Saddam landed a few missiles on Israel, the US prevented Israel retaliating. If Israel entered the war, it was likely that popular revolt would prevent the Arab regimes from continuing their US alliance. The US also had to promise their Arab allies that after the war, they would do something to give the Palestinians their own state.

We need to double back again to what had been happening in Palestine. In the wars of 1967 and 1973 Israel had seized substantial territories from Syria, Jordan and Egypt. The most important of these were the city of Gaza and the towns and villages of the West Bank. The people in these two regions were Palestinians, and many of them were already refugees from 1948. After the 1948 war, the Arabs who remained in Israel had the right to vote in Israeli elections. Israel's new Palestinian subjects in the West Bank and Gaza could not be allowed the same rights. Arabs would then have had about 40 per cent of the vote. In coalition with the Israeli Jews who wanted a lasting peace, they would have been a majority. So Israel ceased to be a democracy. The Palestinians were integrated into the Israeli economy as low paid workers commuting from the territories. The Israeli occupation was, of necessity, brutal. There was no other way to keep down a resentful and conquered underclass.

During the 1980s the Palestinian resistance moved from the refugee camps abroad to the occupied territories of the West Bank and Gaza. This new resistance, called the Intifada (Uprising), was not based on guerilla war or terrorism. Instead, schoolboys demonstrated and threw stones at Israeli soldiers. The Israeli soldiers shot the schoolboys. This went on for years, and the television pictures had electrified Arab workers across the region. The Arab rulers felt something had to be done.

At the same time, Arafat's PLO was in a weak position. They had sided with Iraq in the war. In retaliation, the other Arab regimes had withdrawn their funding for the PLO. Arafat had always depended on that money to run his operation. He could not imagine continuing without it, although the Intifada schoolboys had needed no cash to do what they did. Now Arafat was willing to make any deal the US told him to, in exchange for US and European cash.

Agreement was reached, in a series of negotiations brokered by the US government. Arafat and the PLO were allowed back to the West Bank and Gaza, and given considerable US and European aid. In the short term, the PLO had control of parts of a few towns. In the long term, there would be a separate Palestinian state in the West Bank and Gaza. Palestinians dared to hope. Hundreds of thousands of Israelis demonstrated for peace.

In practice the Israeli government was unwilling to allow a real Palestinian state. Palestine would have armed police, but no army. Defence remained an Israeli sphere. The Israeli army reserved the right to send the tanks in, and periodically did so. Since 1973 hundreds of Jewish settlements had been built in the West Bank and Gaza since Israel took them over. The settlers came from the hard racist right in Israel. Most Israeli Jews wanted some sort of peace and would not live there. The settlers were opposed to any peace: that was the point of the settlements.

So the settlers periodically shot their Palestinian neighbours. If the Palestinians retaliated, the Israeli army backed the settlers with guns. These settlements now had much of the best land. They would remain in any Palestinian state. Israeli army garrisons would defend them. The main roads would remain part of Israel, with Palestine thus divided up into dozens of isolated enclaves. The Palestinians would find work in Israel, at low wages in unattractive jobs. Whenever they protested about anything, the checkpoints from their homes into Israel would be closed and their income stopped. This happened repeatedly.

This was the agreement on offer, in theory, from the Israeli government. It was not an independent state. Palestinians compared it to the Bantustans in apartheid South Africa, or the Native American reservations. There remained also several million Palestinian refugees in exile. Under this agreement, they would not be allowed to return to their homes in Israel. They would not even be allowed to return to the West Bank.

Arafat was willing, however, to accept the Israeli offer. On the Israeli side there was always a reason for delay. During the delays, the Israeli government supported many new Jewish settlements in the West Bank.

In the limited areas it did control in the 1990s, Arafat's government was a dictatorship, and corrupt in ways that made Palestinians ashamed. In Gaza the police arrested rich businessmen and tortured them until their families brought large cash ransoms to the police station. When the Israeli army wanted someone arrested in the areas Arafat controlled, his police went in and arrested them.

The Palestinian movement had always been led by secular nationalists. A substantial minority of Palestinians are Christians. Any national movement has to include people of both religions. But during the 1990s Hamas, the main Islamist party in Palestine, were the only serious opposition to Arafat's deal with the US and Israeli government.

In 1998 I sat in on a day of classes in the English department of Bir Zeit University, the centre of militancy on the West Bank. As so often in English departments, all but one of the students were women. One seminar was devoted to Zora Neale Hurston, an African-American writer of the 1930s. The teacher and the students discussed how Hurston had tried to combine her communism, her feminism, and her commitment to the struggle of her people. The resonances for women in Palestinian society were obvious to everyone in the room. Half of the women wore headscarves, as a sign of their support for Hamas. The other half did not, as a sign of their secular values. All of them were of the generation that had come to political life through the revolt of school children against Israeli rule in the 1980s. In the discussion of Hurston, there was general agreement that the fight for feminism had to be combined with the national struggle. The women in headscarves said this more eloquently, and at greater length, than the women with bare heads. These women were not wearing headscarves because they wanted to be oppressed but because they saw Hamas as the only people fighting the Israelis.

Israel proper in 1998 was a land of fear. Everywhere there were armed soldiers, on the buses, standing guard on the street corners, kissing their girlfriends with automatic weapons slung over their shoulders. Nancy and I stayed in a hotel in East Jerusalem, the Arab quarter, near the Temple Mount and the Wailing Wall. Three soldiers stood at the street corner. Arabs passed, moving hurriedly, eyes down, no one daring to look the soldiers in the face. Then one old man, with a neatly trimmed white beard, looked at them as he passed. His face was full of judgment and silent hate. I guessed he felt that at his age he was safe. Half an hour before dark all the Arabs shops were closed, and all Arabs were off the street. Two hours after dark gangs of young Jewish men appeared. Nancy and I watched from the hotel balcony as they swaggered through the old cobble stoned streets, looking for Arabs. The soldiers watched them pass, and did nothing. Two nights later a gang found an Arab street cleaner, employed by the city, doing his job in the early hours of the morning. They beat him to death.

This is no way for Palestinians to live, or for Jews. It is not what the fighters of the Warsaw Ghetto died for.

Throughout the 1990s there was constant debate within the US government over Israel. Some in Washington argued for a settlement that the Palestinians could live with. If not, feelings for the Palestinians would remain a constant problem for any US control of oil in the region. So the US pushed the Israeli government into negotiations, which Israel then stalled. Others in Washington argued that the bottom line had to be support for Israel. The only alternative was humiliating the Israeli government and handing the PLO and Hamas a very public victory. That would hearten every movement of opposition in the Arab world.

The hard-liners won the argument in Washington. The argument rumbled on, however, because Israel was now a liability but a Palestinian victory would be too.

By 2000, the US had stalled the Islamists. The price had been high. If you add up the dead in the Iraq-Iran war, the Iraq-US war, the Iraqi children who died from sanctions, and the dead in Lebanon, Palestine and Israel, you have more than three million people.

There were still continuing threats to American power. The Saudi economy has always relied on a workforce of short-term immigrants, low paid and without rights. Until 1990 the Saudi government was able to keep the incomes of Saudi citizens, however, at respectable levels. Between 1990 and 2002 the per capita income of native Saudis fell from roughly $15,000 (£10,000) to roughly $5,000 (£3,300). The Islamists gained increasing support among the Saudi people. The leader of one wing of the Saudi Islamists was Osama Bin Laden. In the 1980s Bin Laden had been funded by the CIA and Saudi intelligence to organise foreign volunteers to fight with the Islamist resistance to the Soviet invasion of Afghanistan. When the Russians withdrew from Afghanistan, the CIA ceased funding the Islamists and Bin Laden went home to Saudi Arabia. There he initially supported the Saudi and US alliance against Iraq. But the permanent stationing of US troops in Saudi Arabia turned him against the US and the Saudi regime.

Egypt under Nasser's successors had become part of the US fold, and opened up to American corporations. Until 2001 Egypt was the second largest recipient of American aid, after Israel. (That year Colombia took over second place.) In 1998 the Egyptian regime even began to take back the land Nasser had given to the peasants and return it the old landlords. One index of the hatred felt towards that regime was that Egypt, a country of 80 million people, has 500,000 full-time riot and secret police.

And then in Palestine a new Intifada began.

None of this was in the interests of ordinary Americans. Remember global warming. All these wars and dictatorships had been instead of building windmills and saving the planet. And now the Middle East war came home to America in three ways: 'Gulf War syndrome', the Oklahoma City bombings, and September 11.

In the war against Iraq the US used large numbers of shells and bombs coated with depleted uranium. This very heavy metal makes a strong casing, but is radioactive. After the war, the radioactivity created an epidemic of cancer, respiratory diseases and skin conditions in the parts of southern Iraq that had been most heavily bombed. The sanctions made it impossible for Iraqi doctors to treat most of the sick and dying. Back in the US and Britain, many veterans also suffered the same symptoms. There these were called 'Gulf War syndrome', as the US government wanted to continue using depleted uranium in other wars.

Timothy McVeigh was a sergeant in the US armed forces in the Gulf War. Like many other US soldiers, he was ordered to kill prisoners and did so. It sickened him. When the war finished, he went home to civilian life. He had been a believer in the

American Way. Now, angry and betrayed, he looked for an explanation. The one he found was among right-wing militias who blame the US federal government for everything. Then the FBI attacked a small right-wing religious sect in Waco, Texas. The FBI shot and shelled their headquarters, and set it on fire. Dozens, including many children, died in the fire.

McVeigh, watching on television, decided that the US government was now killing Americans in the same way he had been made to kill Iraqis. He turned to counter-bombing. It is unclear if he acted with one confederate, as the FBI says, or if he was part of a wider militia conspiracy. In any case, McVeigh put a bomb in the federal office building in Oklahoma City. One hundred and sixty-eight people, including 19 children in the nursery there, died.

On 11 September 2001 the long Middle Eastern wars came home to the US on a far larger scale. It is difficult to be sure where the hijackers came from, as some of them may have been using false passports. But as far as the FBI can tell, they came from Egypt, Saudi Arabia and the small Gulf kingdoms. There is not yet any convincing evidence that Osama Bin Laden organised the bombings. This does not mean he is innocent. It just means we don't know. But we do know that Bin Laden approved of the attack on New York, and is widely regarded as a spokesman for it. The reason for the attack was clearly opposition to US policy in Saudi Arabia, Egypt, Palestine and Iraq.

The general reaction of most people in the Middle East to September 11 was complex. There was pity, sympathy, a feeling that 'now they are suffering what we have suffered', and a fear of who would pay for US revenge. The terrorist organisation involved was small. We have been told that Bin Laden controlled thousands of operatives in 60 countries. This is demonstrably untrue. During all the bombing that followed in Afghanistan, the 'Al-Qaeda network' was only able to mount one attempted bombing of an American airliner by an Englishman who was unable to set light to the explosives in his shoes. For a worldwide terrorist organisation, this is nothing.

But if most people in the Middle East did not support either the attack on New York or Al-Qaeda, the US revenge that followed began to change things. By April 2002 a newspaper poll *in Kuwait* revealed that the majority of people there now said they supported Bin Laden.

In the US itself, people were seeing, for the first time, what the consequences of bombing look like. For those airplanes were, in effect, bombs. The TV showed ordinary working people speaking, in a language Americans could understand, in states of fear, grief and confusion. Those shots of people jumping from the burning buildings brought home the terror bombing creates. And this time everyone was asked to identify and sympathise with the dead and bereaved.

The bombing was wrong, as the bombings in Iraq and Oklahoma had been wrong. The political logic of the bombers on September 11 was almost the same as the logic of the bombing of Iraq. The US government had punished the soldiers and children of Iraq as a way of attacking their government.

Most Americans, however, didn't know what their rulers were doing in the Middle East. The US media lied to them systematically, mostly by simply not telling them what was going on. These lies are greatly to the credit of most Americans: the media have to lie because there is a moral gulf between the ruling class and working America. The media and the politicians lie because they assume that if they told the truth about what the US does in the world, most Americans would be outraged.

The plane crashes created both a problem and an opportunity for the ruling class and the politicians in Washington. The problem was that in much of the Middle East, US power depended mainly on fear and the idea that the USA was invincible. September 11 reduced that fear and made the US look vulnerable.

The opportunity for the American ruling class was that a war in Afghanistan might give them control of Central Asian oil. The horror of New York might persuade American people, all these years after Vietnam, to be willing to die again for American foreign policy. Victory in Afghanistan and the Middle East might also increase US power across the world, as the Gulf War had done in 1991.

Events are still unfolding, and much will have happened by the time you read this. Only two things are certain. One is that the forces at play will be the same as for the last 50 years: the desire of the US government and corporations to control oil, the collaboration of the regimes in the Middle East, and the resentment of ordinary people there. The other is that ordinary Afghans, Iranians, Arabs, Jews and Americans will suffer.

Saturday dawned beautiful, the light flooding through Maria's high windows, the hills of Genoa spread out before us. There was a morning meeting. Afterwards I found my friends from home, Rich Peacock, Rich Moth, Nicola and Ruard. They were off to a café for breakfast. I said I'd catch them later, I wanted to get up the road to the start of the march. It was supposed to start three miles down the coast and march towards the city centre along the sea. Then, just before the Convergence Centre, we would turn right towards the Brignole station, well before we got anywhere near the Red Zone. There would be no confrontation with the police, we had all agreed. This would be completely peaceful. We would march up through the city centre to the main football stadium. Then there would be speeches and we would disperse.

It was just after 11. Already, the broad pavement along the coast road was full. A mass of people was moving out towards the starting point. We were supposed to begin gathering at 12, and march off at 2. If the pavements were already full, this was going to be big.

The G8 had held their morning press conference. Berlusconi, Bush and Blair had backed the Italian police all the way. Chirac of France and Putin of Russia, it was said later, made private noises to the press about the level of police brutality. But there were no public statements. The G8 was in agreement. Their show would go on.

The fascists and the police were pushing the envelope.

Berlusconi and the G8 were signalling that they were free to do so. Nobody intervened to speak to the police. Nobody tried to get Fini and the post-fascists out of police headquarters. That told the police Fini had the stamp of authority.

None of the great and good from the third world who had been invited to mediate said anything. Nelson Mandela and the rest kept their mouths shut, but no one noticed.

A mile and a half down the road I met the march coming towards me. The GR banner was almost at the front. I fell in. They told me that the crush at the gathering point was already so great by 12 that they had to move off two hours early.

Later I asked every journalist and film crew I could how many they thought marched. They'd been to more big marches than me. They all said it was hard to tell. Marches of over 150,000 are simply too big, and too rare, to count accurately. Today, they said, something in the order of 250,000 or 300,000 was as good a guess as any. I settled on 300,000. We covered four lanes of the coast road, and the broad pavements on either side, marching close together. Four hours after the front of the march set off, the back was still forming up.

The summer sun was hot. We drank a lot of water. On our left the sea was blue, and cool. Directly in front of us were 50 or so Kurds of the PKK, marching with big pictures of Ocalan, their imprisoned leader. On our left, on the other two lanes, were ATTAC. Behind GR were the International Socialists.

Drop the Debt was supposed to be marching in front of us. They had brought as many people as GR had from Britain, maybe even more. They had planned to go on this demonstration only, avoiding possible trouble on the Friday. Now they had decided to pull out, and stay back at a church by the seaside and pray. Some people said this was only understandable. After the trouble the previous day they were frightened. They were old, after all, people said, mostly middle-aged Christians.

But some of them were there, at the front, with us. More

were scattered further back on the march. Not all older people are afraid. The idea that Christian activists will not participate in a peaceful march insults them. They worship a man who gave his life for other people's sins. Christian activists were central to the civil rights movement in the USA. I had been on enough marches with Quakers against the Vietnam war. The liberation theology Catholic friars and nuns I stayed with in Venezuela were serious, dedicated people. This withdrawal from the march was not cowardice. It was a political decision by their leaders, who did not want to be seen to be going too far.

There were so many of the rest of us it didn't matter. We chanted together, all taking up each other's chants. There was no feeling today that 'you are ATTAC and I am GR and he is a Kurd'. Soon we passed some anarchists on the pavement, silently holding a large black flag with one word newly painted in white: 'Assassini'. They were calling the police who killed Carlo Giuliani assassins. As we passed, we all chanted, 'Assassini, Assassini,' our voices thundering.

There were no police marching with us. They were waiting, up ahead, in the centre of town. We passed a police station, at the top of a cliff above us. We could see the police outside in riot gear, looking down. 'Assassini, Assassini,' we yelled at them, in defiance. There was also a pleasure that we could do it, that everybody in the crowd felt the same.

Yesterday we had been determined. Today we were angry. This was a crowd the police should not attack, I thought, these people might fight back. Yet it was also clear that this crowd was not looking for a fight. People wanted a peaceful march. You could feel it.

We started getting reports on what the march looked like behind us. It looked like all Italy was there, they said. The majority of the marchers were young, but there were all ages in the crowd. Communist Refoundation had turned out all their people, almost 100,000. The union groups were here. This march was mostly working class, white collar and blue collar. And it was a sea of red flags. They'd gone up to the attic, I thought, and got down Mom and Dad's old communist flag.

All day, I saw only one parent with a child on the march. That meant people had decided to come, but they didn't think it was safe for children.

At the front of the march we came to the Convergence Centre. There were a line of riot police at the corner where we were to turn. In front of them were the stewards of Communist Refoundation, arms linked, backs to the police, faces to us. They were there to stop the police charging, but mainly to stop any of us provoking the police. We didn't want to. We turned up towards the Brignole station and marched on.

Half a mile further on we stopped. The word came up the march: at the corner near the Convergence Centre the police had charged and split the march. We would stop and wait for the march to reform. We sat, sprawled on the pavement, not nervous, just waiting. Fifteen minutes later the word came down the line: the march had reformed. We moved off.

A police helicopter flew over the crowd, and back again, intimidating us. As one, we chanted 'Assassini, Assassini,' the words rumbling up into the sky. We had our right hands in the air, giving the helicopter the finger as we chanted. All of us, Kurds, Christians, ATTAC, socialists, Italians and foreigners. The helicopter pilot, shamed or intimidated, flew away.

There were high blocks of flats on either side. From one balcony an older woman was pouring buckets of water on the crowd. We danced toward the water, grateful for the cool in the heat, cheering her on. On another balcony a couple had let down a giant white flag saying 'Citizens of the World Welcome to Genoa'.

But there were almost no people watching the demonstrators. On every other march I have been on, people line the pavements, interested, gawking, wary or sympathetic. This time they didn't. Few people looked out the windows.

Unsympathetic Genoese from the city centre, it seemed, had left town for the summer holiday. Sympathetic Genoa was on the street, with us. The strongest chant of all was 'Genova Libera (Free Genoa)'.

We yelled in every language. 'One Solution, Revolution,' we chanted, and it seemed like everybody took it up. I had been a revolutionary a long time, one of a few serious and tired people in a room above a pub, keeping the flag flying, rehashing the Russian revolution, selling newspapers Saturday morning outside the local Safeways. Now a great demonstration was chanting for revolution, and I was one small speck in it.

Many in that crowd must have been thinking: 'What revolution? Who makes it? How? What do we make?' On the 2001 Mayday march in London a home made banner had said: 'Overthrow Capitalism and Replace It with Something Nicer.' It was a joke, but also serious. It expressed what many people in the movement say: 'We don't want what they had in the Soviet Union or China. What do we want? What would it look like?'

Somebody started the chant of Seattle: 'This is What Democracy Looks Like'. The Americans had chanted that in Seattle as the police attacked them. The chant in Seattle expressed outrage at the hypocrisy of American liberalism. On the streets of Genoa, we heard the chant and looked round for the police. They weren't there. The chant went ragged, began to die away. And then we understood. This is what democracy looks like. Us. Here. We are what democracy looks like. And we all shouted together, 'THIS is What Democracy Looks Like'.

We were glimpsing a possible future for the first time. Our movement would have to be far bigger, broader, more rooted, more confident, angrier and kinder, before we could really imagine the shape of that future. But we knew now that it would be democratic, as the old communist dictatorships had not been. And it would feel something like this, but much greater. Great revolutions have never taken their shape from somebody's plan, but always from the new world that long frightened people have been able imagine when they find themselves among enough of their own kind, fighting together.

The word spread through the crowd: the G8 meeting was cancelled. It went fast, a mouth over my shoulder, just louder than a whisper, and me grabbing the person next to me, passing it on, the word moving through us like a wind. I hugged Guy from GR full crush, then the woman behind who had been sharing her water with me, then people I didn't know. I was crying. We danced. I was wiggling, my head thrown back, and all around me was joy. 'We are Winning, Don't Forget,' we yelled, not chanting together now, just each of us yelling. I have never been happier.

A woman said she was listening to the BBC and they had just denied the G8 was cancelled. I decided the BBC was wrong. We marched on, still happy, still congratulating each other, but doubt seeping in. In a few minutes we all knew, no, the meetings had not been cancelled. But there was a reason we had believed the rumour. It wasn't just hope and wanting. We were 300,000. We could feel our power. It was possible. Our joy reflected our confidence.

Twenty minutes later we came to a small piazza just before the stadium, the end of the march. The final rally began in the piazza. I was exhausted. Three days of smoking, a week without enough sleep, adrenalin, fear and joy, and now it was all over. The Kurds made a circle and began to dance. Only Kurdish men had been marching with us, but now Kurdish women appeared from somewhere and joined in. It was a sedate dance. Every one held hands moving clockwise, then counterclockwise, raising their hands together every once in a while and going 'Huh!' It was one of those dances for people who don't want to be too exuberant in public. Give me the *atan*, I thought, the circle dance in the Afghanistan of my youth, with its restrained but fevered sexuality, the wild tossing of head and hair. But the Kurds were happy, it was their custom, and I lay down in the shade of their banner with a splitting headache.

The last thing I saw before my eyes closed was Ruard, standing with a packed crowd on top of a newspaper kiosk in the middle of the square. He still had the largest red flag in Genoa, a city of red flags. Below the flag, fastened to the flagpole, was a handwritten cardboard sign in Polish about the Tobin Tax. He waved the flag from side to side, tirelessly, welcoming in the marching crowds. I slept, my work done.

I woke up an hour or so later and lay there. Then I walked round, met Rich Moth and Nicola, and we found a bit of shade against one wall of the small piazza. The crush was too great there, though, as people came into the square. I said I'd meet them back by Ruard's kiosk. He was still up there with his flag. I said 'hi' to people here and there. There were speeches, but the square was too packed for the sound system to penetrate. Now I heard Rafaela Bolini's voice in Italian on the microphone, loud, worried, controlled, and I knew something was wrong. People were starting to move out of the square, up towards the stadium. I pushed up through them. The International Socialists were leaving. So I turned back, towards the kiosk where I had left Ruard, Rich and Nicola. Over the heads of the crowd now, looking back down the road, I could see the blue of the police uniforms, the flashing lights and the jeeps. The police were sweeping up the end of the march.

I learned later that about 30 minutes before the police had attacked at the point by the Convergence Centre where the march turned to go up from the shore to the stadium. By then about two thirds of the march had passed, 150,000 to 200,000 people. The last third was still to come.

One American TV journalist was moving along the shore road when it started. He was with the Black Block, expecting trouble and pictures of violence there. The Black Block were clearly provoking the police, breaking car windows, setting fire to vehicles. It didn't make sense to the journalist. There were police around. They could see what the Black Block were doing.

Why didn't they just arrest them?

Fifteen or so people in black balaclavas went up to the bank across the road from the Convergence Centre that had been set on fire the night before. They set fire to it again, while the police watched and did nothing.

Well up ahead the police waded into the people from FIOM, the metal workers' union, and started attacking. The TV journalist left the Black Block and ran forward to the fighting.

FIOM's strongest base is in the car plants; they're an old communist union, and they've been at the heart of opposition in Italy since 1919. FIOM had not come for the direct action day. Now here they were, with their flags, marching branch by branch. In and around them were the marchers of Communist Refoundation. Refoundation had representatives in parliament, and five per cent of the vote.

Now the police attacked them as they had attacked us the day before, with gas and clubs. This time the crowd had no linked arms, no agreed plan of defence. They had not been expecting this. In the food and drink tent of the Convergence Centre, the staff at the beer stall pulled on their gas masks and kept serving beer.

A journalist was with a contingent from Irish Globalise Resistance, marching just behind Refoundation. He had booked a ticket on the GR train from Calais undercover, without saying he was a journalist, presumably hoping to catch people making Molotovs or rolling spliffs. Now, as he sat on a wall in the sun, watching the march go by, a cop hit him over the head from behind. Several other cops pulled him down. They beat him as he lay on the ground, then took him to a nearby railway track and laid his body across the line.

The other journalists watched as the police beat people in the sunlight, on the pavement. A British television cameraman and an American TV journalist told me later it was unlike anything they had seen in Europe before. Not worse than South Africa, or Israel, but different from there too.

A Scottish photographer told me that in most countries the police beat their prisoners behind corners or in doorways. You know they're doing it. In a doorway, you can see the person's arms and legs jerking in and out, and you know they're being hurt. But here the police arrested people and beat them on the pavement until they lay still. After a short time another police-man would come along, and beat the fallen person for a while, and then move on. The cop could wander off and the prisoner stayed there, too frightened to move. The Scots photographer had never seen anything like it. In Israel, he said, you knew that if you photographed the police or army beating someone, they would beat you too. There were rules. Here there seemed to be no rules. Maybe the police wanted him to take photographs. He wanted to, and did so, waiting for the attack at any moment. The uncertainty scared him.

After they split the march, the police drove the marchers back in two directions. The metal workers union and Communist Refoundation were driven up the road toward the stadium and the front of the march. The police beat them from behind, and fired tear gas grenades over their heads in front of them, so that for a mile or so they walked into the gas. People pleaded with the police to stop, telling them the organisations of disabled people were marching with Refoundation. There was a group of blind people, and many in wheelchairs. Don't make them walk into the gas, people begged. The police officer in charge relented, and ordered his men to stop firing gas grenades over the head of the crowd. A few minutes later, for no reason anybody knew, the tear gas grenades started coming over again.

The police violence was hardest against the metal workers and Communist Refoundation. But they struck strongly against the tail of the march too, where the White Overalls were. The White Overalls and the rest of the 100,000 were driven back two miles along the shore road to their starting point, the stragglers clubbed and gassed all the way. Many groups had buses waiting back at the starting point of the march to take them home. The police surrounded some of the buses, and beat people as they got on to go home.

This level of violence was extraordinary. There was nothing Italian about it, nothing traditional, nothing normal. For 50 years no police force in Europe had attacked a crowd of anything like this size. The great demonstrations in Leipzig in 1989, when 100,000 people marched night after night in the weeks before the East German dictatorship fell, had not been attacked. The mass demonstrations that brought down the Czech regime had not been attacked. Nor had the great Rumanian crowd that gathered in Bucharest and booed Ceaucescu.

The only partial exception was London in 1990, when the British police fought with a quarter of a million protesters against the poll tax. That crowd had been non-violent before they were attacked, and had the support of the majority of the population. Trouble began there when some people attempted to sit down in the road across from the prime minister's residence. The police charged into them, and the larger crowd reacted by fighting with the police.

After the 'poll tax riot', 14 million people refused to pay the tax, it was abolished, and Margaret Thatcher was removed from office by her own party. And even in this case, the police had not set out to attack the march as a whole. Nor did they try to split the march.

The police had never attempted anything like this in North America either. The marches of this size (Martin Luther King's civil rights march on Washington, the marches in New York and Washington against the Vietnam war, the great gay and lesbian marches in the 1980s, the Million Man march) had not been attacked. Gas and clubs were used against a militant section of the November 1970 anti-war march in Washington. When many in an anti-war crowd of 100,000 attempted civil disobedience in Washington in 1971, they were arrested and held in the main football stadium in the city. But never had the governments of the USA or Canada approved an attack on a whole march of this size in their own country.

What was happening in Genoa was new. The police could have charged any part of the demonstration. They did not choose to target the White Overalls or the International Socialists, who had defied them the day before. They left the Black Block alone. They chose two quite different targets: the largest union present, which had not even been in on the direct action, and the one parliamentary party present.

They were sending a message, loud and clear. Nobody was going to be allowed to demonstrate against capitalism. Non-violence would not save us. Avoiding any direct action would not save us. Respectability would make no difference. Anyone who demonstrated would be attacked and broken.

This was an escalation since yesterday. Then they had attacked people on the direct action protest. Now they were rewriting the rules of European protest.

Again, we cannot know exactly what was going on in the corridors of power. But the day before the police had pushed the limits of what they could do. They had killed a man. That evening they had the support of the media, Berlusconi, Bush and Blair. There had been, we can now be sure, no angry phone calls from senior government officials to police headquarters. In any case, the deputy prime minister, Fini, had been sitting in police headquarters in Genoa, encouraging them. He, and the police, had received approval for what they had done. So now, Saturday, they were pushing the envelope again.

Again, there would be no official criticism that evening, and no angry phone calls. In response, late Saturday evening the police would push the boundaries further.

In the days afterwards, people would tell stories of prisoners forced to sing fascist songs in the police stations. They told of the police holding knives to people's throats, and making them kiss a picture of Mussolini, or shout 'Viva il Duce'. As Norman Blair, a British anarchist, stood in custody after being badly beaten, his arms and legs spread against the wall, the policeman asked over his shoulder, into his ear, 'Who is your government?' Norman had heard the man beside him answer, and so knew to say 'Polizia.'

Some of these stories may be urban legends. Norman's is true. These things certainly happened to some people. But the Genoese told these stories to each other over and over to make a point they could not quite bring themselves to put directly into words: the police have become fascists.

Fini had company in police headquarters: with him were three other MPs from his party, the National Alliance. He said that he gave no specific operational orders to the police, and merely told them to attack before they were attacked. Fini was not only the leader of what had once, long ago, been Mussolini's fascist party. He was also the deputy prime minister, the number two man in the government. Everyone must have assumed that he was there representing Berlusconi, as indeed he must have been.

But there was also a further worry, connected with the fascist tradition. 'Fascist' is often used as a word of insult for right-wing politicians. This is a mistake, as it is important to remember that the fascism that grew up in Europe in the 1920s and 30s was different from other right-wing parties in three ways. First, they were a mass movement on the streets. Traditional right-wing parties had relied on conservative politicians, the police, and sometimes military coups. Mussolini and Hitler's movements, by contrast, built large organisations of street fighters. Mussolini's organisation, for instance, attacked socialist party offices, union offices and cooperative stores. Hitler's brown shirts attacked communists, socialists, and union officials, both in their offices and on the streets. They also organised mass marches. Traditional conservative parties distrusted the crowd. The fascists organised the hatreds of the small businessmen.

The second way in which fascist parties were, and are, different is that they organise separately in the state machine, particularly in the police and the army. They build their own party in, and partly against, the officers in charge, because they plan to take over the police and the army.

The third way in which they differ from many conservative parties is that in power they move to smash not just the revolutionaries and communists, but all union representatives. Under a fascist government in Britain, I would go to prison alongside Bill Morris of the TUC and Tony Blair of New Labour. That is what happened in both Italy and Germany in the 1920s and 30s. The fascist project is about breaking all working-class organisation.

So fascist parties pose a different, and worse, danger than other repressive or conservative movements. Fini and his National Alliance came from this tradition. But there is some doubt that they were trying to organise separately in Genoa. Fini has been trying to give his party a new public image for 20 years. He wears a suit and speaks in a moderate tone. Berlusconi speaks in more extreme tones, and Bossi of the Northern Alliance is more frankly racist. Unlike Mussolini's party, or the British National Party, Fini does not organise gangs to beat up people on the streets or in their homes.

There certainly is a strong fascist tradition in the Italian police. This is not only the result of recent organisation by the National Alliance. At the end of World War Two, there was no clearing out of fascists in the Italian police, in the way there was in Germany. The fascist police commanders remained in post, and have handed on the tradition to their successors.

Some people say that Fini is a traditional fascist, hiding his colours for the moment, but organising in the police. Others say his party has changed, and are now only right-wing authoritarian racists. I don't know the Italian situation well enough to be sure.

However, if Fini was not organising separately, then he was there just as the deputy prime minister, simply Berlusconi's mouthpiece. In that case, the author of the violence was the prime minister himself.

I would guess that the truth was somewhere in between. Fini and the senior police were trying to push the envelope; Berlusconi was allowing them to do it. At each point that the police escalated, Berlusconi could have reacted. So could Bush, Blair and Chirac. What they did instead was to publicly back the police. That gave Fini and the police the confidence to escalate again and see what happened. So on Friday the police killed a man. They were supported afterwards from the top. So on Saturday afternoon they attacked a mass demonstration in a way that had not been done in Europe or the United States for 50 years. They were supported from the top. So Saturday night they would go further.

I was at the top end of the small square when I heard Rafaela over the sound system telling people to leave. I turned and walked through the square, looking for Ruard, Rich and Nicola. Over the heads of the crowd, about 600 metres away, I could see the riot police. They looked blue in this distance, with many flashing lights, and they came on slowly but inexorably. I didn't know it yet, but they were driving the last of Refoundation and the metal workers uphill before them. I did know something was wrong.

Ruard was gone from the kiosk. I couldn't find Rich and Nicola in the crowd. I decided all three had seen enough yesterday to know to move out when the crowd started to leave. I hoped that was right. Two Turkish socialists grabbed me and asked what was happening. I said there were police behind us, and we had to move on out.

They said some of their people were missing.

'Find them quick,' I said. 'Hold hands and go uphill out of the square, on that road.'

An Irish contingent were next to them. I said the same thing. Half of them stood by the Turks while the rest ran to gather up stragglers. 'Move your people out as soon as you have them,' I said. 'Is there anybody else from the socialists?'

'Manchester are up those steps,' an Irish woman said.

I went up the narrow stone steps leading out one side of the square. They were packed with people resting. I found some Scots, and then the GR groups from Manchester. I made myself sound authoritative, and tried to explain the situation as simply as I could. I had learned an awful lot in the last 28 hours. We all had.

Back down by the kiosk the Irish and the Turks had all their people. We moved out, holding hands. At a fork in the road, I told people to go up the road on the left. They did so. A hundred metres on somebody who had just joined us said the socialists had taken the other fork. I told everyone to turn around and go down the other fork.

All around us people were moving urgently, walking not running. I wanted to catch up to the socialist contingent, and not get caught at the back. I didn't know what was happening behind us. I did know from British demonstrations, and from Prague, what the police can do to small groups of people they find isolated at the end of marches.

We reached the stadium. A GR steward, a big man, was standing on a grassy knoll, waving his hands to direct the socialists left, around the stadium, and out to a piazza on the other side. We moved as fast as we could.

'I have to pee, Jonathan!' somebody yelled, just like on a school trip. 'Forty-five second pee stop!' I said. The men went every which way. The women squatted in an alley while I stood in front of them. It took 90 seconds and we were moving again.

There in front of us was the glorious big banner of the Greek socialists. Relieved, we ran to catch up. The socialists were all stopped together, waiting while Tom Behan scouted the situation ahead of us.

In a few minutes Tom reported back that there was a way open back to the Convergence Centre now. It might not stay open for long, the stewards said. We were going to try it. They also said anyone who wanted could try to get to where they were staying. But don't go alone, or in a small group.

Every one around me wanted to stick with the big group.

We walked back down into town, moving quickly, not running, arms not linked, but staying together. At times gaps opened up between us and the people in front of us, and we had to run briefly to close up. We were going back two blocks west of where we had come up, closer to the Red Zone than we had been all day. We went under the railway bridge and came out by Brignole Station. Now we moved down the Street of the Partisan Bands, perhaps 200 metres wide. There were police here, in small groups. In front of us would be the police station and the main concentration. There were ship containers across the road, with only two gaps in them, each maybe 10 metres wide. Stewards stood in front of the gaps, telling us to split up, some to go through one gap, some the other, and then join up on the other side. 'Quickly,' they said, 'don't run.' We didn't link arms, we wanted to look unthreatening, but we stayed together. We were through the gaps.

Just ahead of us Chris Bambery had been the first person through the gaps. Somebody told me later that right on the other side of the line of containers, the police officer in charge held up his arm, palm forward, in the universal cop's symbol for halt. Bambery held up his hand too, palm forward, smiling, as if it were a greeting or a salute, and walked round the officer. As people followed Bambery through the containers, the police officer stood there unsure what to do.

Clouds of smoke were rising from different parts of the city, billowing in the air higher than 10 storey buildings. The bank near the Convergence Centre and the flats above were still smoking.

We made it back to the Convergence Centre safely. There we held a hurried meeting. Bambery pointed at the smoke rising over Genoa and said nobody should go out into the city in small groups. But 300 British had to go back across town to meet the buses that would take them to the train. The buses would leave at 11. 'Wait here until 10,' Bambery said. 'Then go all together. If you walk, go in a group of at least 50. Here's the number for the radio taxi. The taxis are safe.'

The Greeks decided to stay in the Convergence Centre until the morning, and then find their buses to take them back to the ferry to Greece. I held a little meeting for the people who were going to fly out of various airports, or stay on in Italy for holidays. They divided up into groups, according to the part of Genoa they were staying in. Some groups decided to stay in the Convergence Centre until morning. Others said they would go back together to where they had stayed before.

I was most concerned for the four people who had been sleeping in the Carlini stadium with the White Overalls. Remembering Prague, I thought the police would pick on somebody tonight, and the most likely place was the Carlini. I asked the four how much the stuff in their backpacks in the stadium was worth. Maybe £300 to £400 each, they said. 'Anything of great personal importance?' I asked. 'No,' they said. 'Then leave it,' I said, 'it's not worth it.' But they wanted their stuff, and weren't as scared as I was. They decided to go back and get their packs and sleeping bags. In the event they were OK. I was wrong in my guess about where the police would strike.

Eventually everyone was in a group, and all the stragglers joined up with somebody. Chris Nineham, Bambery and I went back to Maria's, and then out to the only restaurant open.

I walked to the restaurant with a Catholic pacifist from Genoa. I was still feeling amazingly up because of the size of the demonstration. 'How do you feel?' I asked her.

'Terrible,' she said. 'The violence and the burning. The Black Block have spoiled everything. There are 300 people in the Black Block, and 20,000 police in Genoa. You know our police. You have seen what they do. They could stop the Black Block easily. But they have arrested no one. Why?'

Why indeed.

The Black Block have been on many demonstrations before,

in the United States, Germany and Spain. They are anarchists who demonstrate in black clothes, in a group, with black masks, either ski masks pulled over their heads or kerchiefs hiding their faces. Black has always been the anarchists' colour, just as red is for socialists and green for environmentalists.

In Genoa there were two main groups of anarchists. The larger, the Pink March, included people like Venus the Fairy. They were mostly pacifists, although some felt like the White Overalls that they should defend themselves if attacked. Their politics started from the idea that the mass of ordinary people were conservative. So they concentrated on building islands of opposition to the system. This meant peace camps, exciting and colourful contingents on marches, large squats as social centres, and networks of friends in the counter culture. The aim was to make these groups as large as possible, and gradually bring other people to them. The idea was to change by example, and to bring people over to a new way of living.

The Black Block were the smaller group of anarchists. They too felt that ordinary people were conservative. The important thing was to unsettle their fixed habits. On demonstrations, this meant going through and around other groups, challenging the police. Then the cops would attack everybody, and everyone would see the police for what they were. Some of the people, outraged, would then be attracted to the ideas of the Black Block.

Anarchists concentrate on changing individuals. They wanted to build islands of opposition outside the oppressions of normal life. Socialists like me concentrate on getting large groups of people to change their views, without changing their lives. We want to create opposition at the centre of the system, where people work for governments and corporations.

So that, roughly, is what the Black Block were about. But in Genoa things were more complicated. After the demonstrations many people were furious with the Black Block. Angriest of all were the Catholic pacifists and the White Overalls, who had been beaten, in part, because the Black Block were among them. People also said on Saturday, and again and again in the days that followed, that there were police among the Black Block.

News reports piled up. People reported seeing groups of men in black masks emerging from police buses. They had seen men in masks chatting with the police, and moving back and forth through their lines. There was film of the Black Block attacking the Marassi prison in the hills of Genoa, breaking prison windows and throwing Molotov cocktails, while the police stood around and did nothing.

Many people in the movement concluded that everyone in a black mask was a cop or a fascist. But I've talked to people who had friends among the Black Block in Genoa. Their friends were anarchists, not cops. They say there were two Black Blocks in Genoa, the real one and the cop-fascist one. Again, I don't think it's that simple. There must have been times when cops or fascists operated separately. Much of the time, though, the crowd in black must have been a mixture of infiltrators and genuine people. The real point is that what the Black Block wanted to do was the same as what the police wanted done. They provided an excuse for police attacks. They provided the trashed cars and burning buildings for the TV cameras. They were the pictures, a lone thug in disguise, that the police and the G8 wanted to go round the world. That's why the cops didn't arrest them, but left them the space to get on with it.

I had two beers in the restaurant and went back to Maria's. My friends from London stayed at the Convergence Centre, planning to catch their planes from Turin the next day. As dark fell the city was still smoking. Police helicopters circled above them, their floodlights playing on the protesters.

The people staying in the Centre were almost all foreigners. Most Italians had already got out of town. In the area around the Convergence Centre the Genoese were all indoors. In the suburbs they were watching television, or in the bars.

Rich Moth had been in Prague with me. The day after the big march there 800 people, mostly Czechs, had been arrested on the streets, and many badly beaten in prison. Now Rich thought the same thing might happen at the Convergence Centre.

So Rich Moth, Nicola, Richard Peacock and Ruard headed off up the hill towards the headquarters of the Genoa Social Forum, which had been turned into a dormitory for the night. Another friend from London, Richard Garrett, decided to stay behind. Earlier in the day, Richard Garrett had marched carrying a Greek socialist banner, laughing with the beautiful woman next to him. Now he stayed with his new friend and the other Greek socialists who had decided the Convergence Centre was as safe as anywhere.

The GSF's headquarters were in two schools across from each other on a small back road about 10 minutes walk from the Convergence Centre. The city of Genoa had given these schools to the Forum for the week of the demonstration, and the class-rooms had been turned into offices. To Rich, Nicola and the others, the Forum headquarters seemed a moderate, official place. They thought they would be safe there.

They all dumped their rucksacks in the school and went to a bar a couple of streets away. There they met a friend from Hackney, Laurence, and Kalpana, the geneticist from Globalise Resistance. They were staying in the school too.

They all had beer and chocolate cake, except Kalpana, who found the combination revolting. After one beer, Rich and Nicola went back to the school. She was tired. Richard Peacock, Ruard, Laurence and Kalpana decided to stay in the café for another beer. Suddenly 50 riot police in full gear ran by, going towards the school. Right behind them were several empty police vans. Ruard and the others knew people would be arrested. They went out into the street, to get back to the school and join their friends. The police met them with gas and batons, and they fell back. Many more police filled the street. They went back to the bar. The family that owned it pulled them in and closed the shutters. Peeking out, they could see the road outside was now blocked by a line of police vans, all the way to the school 150 metres away. That meant there were an awful lot of police converging on the school. The family told them there was no way they could go back out into that. Outside, wave after wave of police arrived.

Hundreds of them charged into the school, chanting: 'You're the Black Block, and we've come to kill you.'

11 | Globalisation

Until now we have been looking at the consequences of globalisation. This chapter tries to make sense of the process as a whole. First we look at the economics of the system, and then at the resistance globalisation is producing.

The word 'globalisation' is deceptive, because the world economy has been global for hundreds of years. A hundred years ago great colonial empires like Britain, France and Russia ruled most of the third world directly. International investment between countries is now much larger than it was in 1973, but it has not yet reached the level of 1914. Although people are moving all over the world, they also moved in the African slave trade and European migration that colonised the Americas. At least since 1950, almost every one in the world has been part of the global economy. There are no places left where people don't use money, buy things from shops, and produce for a national and world market. The power of the bank or the moneylender reaches into every village in the world.

What is happening is not that the world is becoming more global. Rather, the process called 'globalisation' is an attempt by the corporations, and particularly the US corporations, to do something about their declining profits. To understand why this is happening, we need to start with some basic Marxist economics.

Profits are the driving force of capitalism. A corporation spends money on three major things. First, they buy raw materials. Second, they buy machines, trucks, buildings and everything they need to work on the raw materials. Third, they pay wages to their workers. The workers use the machines, trucks, buildings and so on to make something new out of the raw materials. The corporation then, ideally, sells the new products for more than they spent on raw materials, machines and wages. That's their raw profit, what Marx called 'surplus value'.

At first sight, that raw profit seems to come from the skills of the people who manage the corporation. Marx's basic insight was that the raw profit comes because the corporations pay the workers less than the new value the workers are producing. If the workers all owned the corporation together, they could share out that raw profit in wages. Instead, the corporation then shares out that raw profit with other companies, rich owners and the government. They do this in several ways. They pay some of the raw profit out in rent. Some is paid in corporation taxes and taxes taken from the workers' pay cheques. Some is paid in interest to banks and bondholders who have loaned money to the corporations. In effect, the banks and bondholders are partner capitalists with the corporation. What's left after all those people and institutions are paid is 'net profit'.

Some of this net profit is paid to shareholders that own the corporation. The corporation invests the rest in new machinery, buildings and transport.

For the sake of the corporation, the more of this profit that is invested back into the company, the better. Every corporation competes with other corporations. In capitalist competition, generally either you expand or you die. Take the example of the grocery shops in my neighbourhood. Ten years ago we had two small grocery shops round the corner, and a Safeway supermarket just off the main road at the bottom of our street. The supermarket had invested far more than the little shops could. Safeway, a giant corporation, ran all their stores like one giant integrated production line in a factory. Cashiers checked out customers, trucks delivered from great warehouses in response to computerised tills monitored at headquarters, and the night shift stacked the shelves. That factory-like efficiency meant

Safeway was much cheaper than the small grocery shops, which began to go to the wall.

Then Sainsbury's built a bigger supermarket on the main road. We had more choice there than at the smaller Safeway, so we switched. Safeway responded by closing their old supermarket and opening a new one that surrounded the Sainsbury's on three sides. Sainsbury's had to close their store. But they opened a new one, even bigger, a mile down the road in Camden Road, with extensive parking. One of our two corner shops went broke. The other is struggling. On a national level, the big supermarket chains are starting to buy up each other.

The same process of competing investment and mergers is happening in many other industries. Some airlines go bust, and the rest join international alliances. Auto corporations in Korea go bust and are bought up by Ford and General Motors. And so on. The corporations have to keep competing, and to compete they have to invest.

Corporations are not only competing with other companies producing the same sort of goods. They are also borrowing money from the banks to invest. They have to pay this money back at a standard rate of interest that works across the economy. This means that a company making cars has to make the same rate of profit as a company making software or magazines. So every corporation is competing to make profits against every other corporation. Banks are lending and borrowing money all over the world. A corporation making glass in England is competing for loans with a company making cigarettes in Indonesia.

All this produces a world that seems to be dominated by greed. But this is not the greed of rich owners who want to consume. It's the greed of corporations that want to invest so they can compete harder. This greed, this need to invest driven by competition, drives the system.

That competitive drive for profit translates into constant pressure on the workers. Remember, the raw profit comes from the workers' work in the first place. To get more to invest, employers have to squeeze the workers harder. They can do this by holding down wages, making people work harder and longer hours, or cheating on the costs of safety.

The pressure is there in the public services too. The money that goes on taxes cuts into raw profits. The lower the taxes, the more the profits. So the corporations want public services delivered as cheaply as possible. That means both cutting the services and pushing public sector employees to work harder for less.

This increased pressure on workers and public services is not easy for the corporations, however. People resist. Every day, in every job, people try to slow down the pace of their exploitation. They take breaks, they cover for people who go off for a cigarette in the toilet, they tell new workers who are going too fast to slow down, they walk out on the job. More important, workers join together in unions to defend themselves. They campaign, demonstrate, strike and vote to protect public services. All these struggles keep the share going to workers up to at least the minimum people need to keep going.

The people who own and manage the corporations face another problem, however, that is built into their system. The more they invest, the harder they find it to make profits. Any one corporation that invests heavily usually makes better profits until the others catch up. But it's different if you look at the economy as a whole. At that level, all the corporations are spending a larger and larger proportion of their investment on machinery, buildings, tools, trucks and the like. They are therefore spending a smaller proportion on wages. They have more and bigger supermarkets in the grocery sector, for instance, but fewer workers. The trouble is that the raw profit of corporations as a whole comes from the labour of the workers they employ. If they employ fewer workers and spend more on fixed investment, the rate of raw profit they make goes down.

Marx called this the 'tendency of the rate of profit to fall'. It's only a tendency, a pressure built into the system. There are several ways the corporations can reduce the pressure on raw profits. As we have already suggested, they can pay lower wages and make people work harder. They can open new factories or stores in places where wages are low. So capitalism spreads to depressed regions of Britain, and to every corner of the third world.

The corporations can also make worse products more cheaply. They can speed up the process of production and distribution. For instance, they now use 'just in time' methods where the raw materials arrive at the factory gate hours or minutes before they are used, so there is no stockpiling. They can also speed up the efficiency of the trucks delivering supplies to stores.

The corporations can also look for areas of the economy where very little is spent on machinery, and most costs are wages. So capital moves out from industry to labour-intensive sectors like restaurants and stores. As they do so, of course, they turn McDonald's and Safeway into factories. At the level of the national economy, they can slow down the rate of investment by spending money on arms and soldiers (money that would otherwise go into productive investment). I will explain later how this works.

In some periods of the history of capitalism, these methods have kept the rate of profit up. From 1938 to about 1965, for instance, profits were healthy. The world economy grew as never before. In most of the industrialised world, there was nearly full employment except for a few regional black spots. Wages and benefits went up. The welfare state expanded.

There is dispute about why profits were healthy in these years, but the best explanation is a massive increase in arms spending. This began in the build up to World War Two. After 1945 spending on arms was far higher than ever before in peacetime. For most of the years from 1945 to 1970, the largest economy, that of the United States, put more money into military spending than on new capital investment. This was unprecedented. It had two effects. First, there was what is called the 'multiplier effect'. All the soldiers and sailors and workers in defence industries and their families spent more on food and cars and washing machines and the like. There were then more workers in grocery stores and car factories. They in turn spent more on toys, meals out, books, shoes, and so on. Toy sales staff, restaurant workers, writers, and so on, had more to spend. Military spending primed the pump of the whole economy.

Second, this new spending meant that much less went into capital investment. That slowed down the tendency of the rate of profit to fall. Between them, these two effects kept the world economy healthy.

But only for so long. In the long term, those countries that spent more on the military and less on investment found their industries had trouble competing. So the US, Britain and the USSR were in trouble. Those countries that spent less on arms, like Germany and Japan, started to do better. That meant the governments of the US, USSR and Britain wanted to cut back arms spending. And the reduction in the rate of investment had only slowed, not stopped, the tendency for the rate of profit to fall. After a certain point, the healthy profits produced by priming the pump gave way to the pressure from low invest-ment. Profits began to fall.

There are arguments even among Marxist economists about the exact year this fall in profits started, and about how severe the fall has been. It depends on which of many different accounting systems you use. But it is clear that profits held up pretty well from 1938 to 1960, and began falling seriously sometime between 1960 and 1968. This fall in the rate of profit has been documented for the United States, Canada, Western Europe, Eastern Europe, Japan and South Africa.

In 1973 this led to the first major recession since 1938. In good times and bad, the capitalist economy goes up and down in a cycle of boom and bust, with 5 to 10 years between each low point. In good times the bottom point of the cycle is not that bad. 1958 was a recession year, for instance. But nobody remembers it, because the system as a whole was doing well, so a recession was not that bad. 1929, on the other hand, happened in a bad period for profits and started the Great Depression. Once profits as a whole were in trouble after 1965, recessions led to mass unemployment in 1973, 1980, and 1989. Another recession is happening now. The high points of the booms between recessions, too, were nothing like as good as before 1973. Unemployment stayed higher in most countries than it had in the 1940s, 50s and 60s.

This long-term crisis created major problems for the corporations and the banks that lend them money. It has two effects we can see everywhere in the system: speculative bubbles and growing debt. Let's take bubbles first. It is important to understand here that the rate of profit is falling, but some profits are still coming in. There is still money in the system, and it is still expanding. But it is expanding more slowly. Those profits have to be invested somewhere. Because the rate of profit in industry is bad, the temptation is more and more to invest in speculation. So in Japan in the 1980s, for instance, investment poured into the property market, particularly in Tokyo. There was more money chasing land and houses, and prices rose. As this kept up, more and more investors were tempted to put their money into a rising market, and that drove the prices up further. The bubble spread to the Japanese stock market, where many companies were now valued in terms of how much real estate they held in Tokyo. Everyone was on to a good thing, and prices kept rising. The trouble with this kind of bubble, though, is that profits are rising without anything real or new being produced. So the bubble keeps growing as long as every one has faith in it. Then comes the moment when confidence falls, and every one in the know rushes to get out. The bubble bursts.

The same sort of thing happened in the American stock markets and the dot.com bubble in the 1990s, in the stock market booms of the last 20 years, in the world art market and in the property markets in Hong Kong (1990s), Bangkok (1997) and London (late 1970s).

The second effect of the crisis in profits is rising debt. Corporations now raise most of their money for investment by borrowing from banks or by selling bonds. As profits decline, they find it more difficult to pay back these debts. We see this increasing debt in many places. There are the debts of whole countries, like much of Africa, Turkey, Argentina, Indonesia and Russia. There is a continuing problem of massive bad debt in the Japanese banking system. Hanging over everything, there is the very large external debt of the US economy.

One solution to these debts would be to let companies and countries go bankrupt, and simply abolish their debts. But as the debt in the whole system grows, central banks, and particularly the US government, are increasingly worried by the possibility of a financial crash. This happened in the 1930s. If any major corporation or government was simply allowed to go bust, they fear that might mean major banks would follow, and a crash would radiate out through the system. To prevent this happening, governments usually help out corporations in trouble, and the banks endlessly reschedule government debts. These rescues, in turn, increase the amount of debt in the system as a whole. At the same time, central banks lower the rate of interest to encourage companies and individuals to borrow more. This is why banks keep sending letters offering new credit cards through my door. It's also why household debt in the US is now, for the first time ever, greater than household savings.

But bubbles are a short-term fix. They don't touch the underlying problem of profits. Nor does debt. The corporations need a long-term solution. Their answer has been 'globalisation'.

'Globalisation' is an attempt to restructure the whole global economy in the interests of corporations. There are several different parts to this strategy.

One is driving employees harder and paying them less. In Britain, for instance, most people's jobs have got more difficult in the last 20 years. Many have also got more dangerous; safety slows down work, and that costs money. But in most of the industrial world it has not been politically possible to drive down workers' pay.

The exception is the United States. Less than 12 per cent of American workers are in unions. Even these unions have accepted 'give-back' contracts, under which wages and conditions are cut. Many people who have lost jobs in productive industry have had to take much lower paying jobs in the service sector; steelworkers become waiters at Pizza Hut at a third of the pay. By the early 1990s 'real' hourly wages ('real' means wages measured in terms of what money can buy) were down to the levels of the 1950s. Wages have got slightly better since. But US working families have only been able to keep their standard of living up by working harder. Women have gone out to work in far larger numbers, and families now need two wages to cover what one did before. But men also work harder, an average of 200 hours a year more than they did 20 years ago. That's one month's extra work a year.

That squeeze on wages went some way to hauling profits back up in the United States. After about 1985 profits in the United States recovered about two-fifths of what they had lost in the 20 years before. That was enough to make the US economy stronger than those of Germany or Japan in the 1990s. But it was not enough to solve the problems of profit for American corporations. And in Japan and Germany it was politically impossible to make working people pay for the crisis in the same way. Even when Japan was stuck in recession in the 1990s, the government was careful to keep unemployment rates down to four per cent. This was high for Japan, but the same as the unemployment rate in the United States at the height of a boom.

In any case, attacking US workers' standard of living carried a cost for American capital. If US workers made less money, they could buy fewer goods. So any attack on them had to go hand in hand with an attempt to increase US exports and take over foreign markets.

Another part of the globalisation strategy is cutting taxes; both the taxes that come out of pay cheques and the taxes that corporations pay. If they can cut the amount going on government welfare state programmes as a whole, what they save can go to profit. This is what is driving the constant cuts in public expenditure: health, schools, public transport, and so on.

Corporations can also invest in places where the wages are low. This solves the problem for any one corporation for a short time. It does not solve the general problem of the falling rate of profit, for this new investment simply increases the proportion of capital tied up in long-term investment.

But corporations can move into new sectors of the economy where there is little capital investment in machinery, plant and trucks, and where the great majority of costs are wages. The part of the economy that looks like this is the welfare state: schools, colleges, hospitals, social work offices, support for the disabled, care homes, unemployment offices, and so on. So there is more and more pressure from the corporations to open these areas up to private management. This then lowers the average costs of fixed capital investment for the corporations as a whole. That is the driving force behind the privatisations seen all over the world.

Another important way any one corporation can keep up profits is monopoly. This does not solve the problem of falling rates of profit for the economy as a whole. But monopoly does help one company beat the others. Some corporations, like Microsoft, effectively do not face competition. More common is the situation where a few corporations control one national market and try not to compete with each other. The three big car companies in the United States (Ford, General Motors and Chrysler) are one example. They charge much the same prices, and try not to force each other out of business. Similar effective agreements cover many industrial sectors in most developed economies. The trend in any capitalist economy is for smaller companies to be bought and merge until a small number of players control the market. The problem then is international competition. The US car companies, for instance, had the American market wrapped up. Then Volkswagen, Nissan and Honda came along. The solution to this problem, from the corporations' point of view, is international monopoly. So car companies merge across borders, buying pieces of each other, until now Ford owns part of Honda and Daimler owns Chrysler. The same process is happening with airlines, software companies, media conglomerates, and across the board.

For US corporations as a whole, their solution to their crisis in profits is opening up the world economy and world trade. This is partly a matter of being allowed to sell their products anywhere. Then American car companies, for instance, can drive the local Malaysian car company out of business or take it over. The bigger company, with more and newer capital investment, will be able to take over the smaller. For this to work the American corporations need global free trade rules. In other words, they need an end to the Malaysian law that charges a high tax on imported cars. They also need changes to the Malaysian, Japanese and Chinese laws that used to forbid foreigners to buy a large proportion of the stock in national companies. And they need the national governments to sell off publicly owned industries like power utilities, telephone systems, post offices, railways and airlines. These sort of changes in the law is what the World Trade Organisation negotiations are about.

These changes are usually called 'free trade'. The term is inaccurate. What is happening is that weaker parts of the world economy are being opened up to the strong, while the strong protect themselves against the weak. The North American Free Trade Agreement, for instance, is over 300 pages long. A real free trade agreement would be one page long. In the NAFTA agreement all the other pages are devoted to exceptions, mostly so that parts of US capitalism don't have to compete. In the same way, the European Union insists that third world countries accept its industrial exports, even if these will destroy their industries. But the EU subsidises their own agri-business, and keeps tariff barriers high on third world agricultural produce.

The WTO and the IMF police this new system. It is increasingly weighted in favour of US corporations. The reaction of ruling classes and corporations in other countries is contradictory. On the one hand, they lose out to US capital. On the other hand, the IMF, the WTO and the ideas of 'neo-liberalism' strengthen capital in every country against their own workers. Indian capitalists may lose out by opening up their economy to US and Chinese products. But they gain from the privatisations in India, the cuts in public services there, and the assault on workers' wages and conditions. So local ruling classes are constantly torn between opposing US domination and accepting the fruits of that domination.

Nor do US or European workers gain from this process. They, like Indian or Nigerian workers, are getting it in the neck. The US union federation, the AFL-CIO, for instance, led a campaign against China joining the WTO. They said it would threaten US jobs. Many people said they were being greedy and protectionist. But the WTO hurts Chinese workers too. The Chinese government has joined the WTO because they think it will increase profits in China. The Chinese government also predicts that 20 million Chinese workers will lose their jobs as a result of joining the WTO. And as we have seen, globalisation and neo-liberalism have forced down US wages and working conditions.

This is important. Globalisation is in part an increasing competition between US capital and other corporations, as they try to solve their crisis at each other's expense. But it is also an attack by all capitalist owners and managers together on workers. Some parts of the anti-capitalist movement see globalisation as basically a conflict between the US and the rich countries, on the one hand, and the poor countries on the other. The difficulty with this analysis is that it cripples the anti-capitalist movement. In the US, if you think globalisation benefits American workers, then you cannot reach out to the unions, the main force that will fight on your side. In the third world, if you think the fight is between countries, then you cannot understand why your own ruling class backs the WTO. And you can all too easily end up supporting your local rulers.

The fall of the dictatorships in the Soviet Union and Eastern Europe has strengthened the whole globalisation project. The Soviet economy was already coming apart in 1989. The change to a 'market economy' only made things worse. Russia's much weakened economy means it is no longer an economic or military competitor on anything like the same scale as before. For the moment, the USA is the lone super power. That makes US corporate domination of the world far easier.

More important, many people, in many parts of the world, thought that Russian communism was the only alternative to western capitalism. In 1989 it became clear that system had not worked economically. Anyone could see how workers in Eastern Europe felt about 'communism'. Happy crowds of workers destroyed statues of Lenin. We watched on our TV screens as men and women tore down the Berlin Wall. They were not wearing suits. The men attacking the Wall with hammers and chisels clearly knew how to use the tools. These were workers, tearing down 'communism'. That same year, massive demonstrations in Tienanmen Square and right across China made it clear that Chinese workers hated their 'communist' government. And the 'communist' leaders of both Russia and China declared that socialism was dead.

I loved watching workers tear down the dictatorships. I was surprised how many people on the left were depressed. They had felt those systems were, in some partial or flawed sense, the alternative. It was not only communist party members, it turned out, who believed this. In Britain more or less the whole of the Labour left, and much of the centre, turned out to have had illusions about the Soviet Union. Now they said that communism had not worked, so there was no alternative to the market.

Across the world, the left, including most mass parliamentary parties, was similarly demoralised. For ten years after 1989, the ideas of the free market dominated the world. But at the same time, people were suffering more and more under that market. The politicians and the media told them they had to keep suffering, because the market left them no alternative. Whenever the government cut public services or a corporation closed a plant, they said the world market was forcing them to do so. People had felt there was no alternative to the market. Now they began to hate the market at the same time.

People learn from experience. The experiences that were creating the anti-capitalist movement are also creating widespread resistance by workers, particularly in the third world.

On 11 May 2000, I was in Darjeeling, India, doing research for a history of Sherpa climbers. The Indian trade unions united to call a general strike for that day. The strikers' demands were for controls on inflation, keeping the subsidies on fertiliser for farmers, against the introduction of tuition fees at public universities, against privatisation, against the increasing physical attacks on minorities, against the right-wing BJP government, against the IMF and against the WTO. These are the same demands that unions make in Italy or the United States.

The Indian unions expected 20 million people to follow their strike call. In the event it was closer to 30 million. This was still a minority of India's workers. But the strike was solid in several states, particularly in West Bengal, where Kolkota (Calcutta), one of the world's 20 largest cities, was shut tight for the day. Boys played cricket in the great avenues of the city. In Darjeeling every workplace and every shop was shut tight. You couldn't buy a pencil, a cigarette, a meal or a cup of tea in Darjeeling. 11 May 2000 in Indian saw the biggest one-day strike in the history of the world.

Six months later I was back in Darjeeling for three and a half weeks. It's a town of 60,000 people, traditionally conservative. During my 25 days there was a national strike for two weeks by India's 600,000 postal workers, trying to get equal rights and pension provisions for part-timers. There was an all-out local strike by truck drivers. The bank workers in Darjeeling all joined a national one-day strike in solidarity with the workers in the government bank, who were threatened with privatisation. There was a conflict between the majority on the local government council, and the minority who wanted a separate state for the Darjeeling region. Student supporters of the majority killed a supporter of the minority at the local college. He was the son of a worker on the tea plantations outside town, and the tea workers came into town the next morning and shut down everything in a one-day strike. The next week both majority and minority supported a three-day local general strike against the state government. The students occupied the small dental college in Darjeeling in protest at the lack of tools, facilities and the tendency of their teachers not to turn up. As I was leaving, the government had sacked all their teachers, but they had not yet won more dental chairs or tools.

This was in one small town, over 25 days. It is not that unusual for India now. There have also been many strikes and protests against globalisation in China. There workers in public sector jobs and state-owned industry have traditionally had 'the iron rice bowl': a guaranteed job with wages high enough to feed their children. But since 1980 there has been an explosion in industries owned by local governments and private companies who do not guarantee such benefits. Instead, they sweat people until they drop. As part of the preparation for China joining the WTO, the government has been closing down factories and public services all over the country. By 1998, 17 million workers had lost their jobs. In reaction, according to official figures, there were 8,247 strikes in 2000 alone, in a country where all strikes are illegal. As yet there is no national free trade union organisation. But the government is very worried there might be.

The last three years have also seen general strikes by workers in South Africa, Argentina, Greece, Ecuador, Peru and Nigeria. There are peasant rebellions in parts of Columbia, by the Zapatistas in Mexico, and one led by the Maoists in Nepal.

These are very large movements, particularly in China, India, Argentina and Nepal. In Europe and North America the last 10 years have seen large scale strike movements only in Finland, Canada, France, Greece and Turkey. In much of the rest of the industrial world the workers' movement is weaker. In some of the richer countries, like Britain, strike figures are at, or close to, historical lows. But in Britain, and in most of these countries, the trend is now towards rising numbers of strikes. Where the strikes have not yet come, you can feel the hope and anger boiling. And the ideas of the anti-capitalist movement are everywhere now. It is possible, again, to be against not just this or that injustice, but capitalism as such. The market may rule the world, but no longer rules our minds.

12 | **Sunday**

When Rich Moth and Nicola got back to the school to go to sleep on Saturday night, there were perhaps 100 people in the big hall on the ground floor. A few people were checking their e-mail on the computers in the far corner. There were a few whispers too, but most people were already in their sleeping bags, and everyone was trying to be quiet.

Every night so far on this trip Rich and Nicola had tried to zip their two sleeping bags together. Every night they had failed, probably due to drink. This time the zips worked. Rich took it as a good omen for their relationship. He went to brush his teeth.

As he came back from the toilet into the main hall there was a loud noise outside. Rich immediately thought someone must be trying to close the great iron gates of the school to stop the police coming in. Things had been tense enough all night that he knew it must be riot police. A few people moved to block the front door of the school. From what he had already seen that day, Rich knew eight people at the door weren't going to stop a force of riot cops.

Nicola thought there was some kind of rioting outside in the street. It didn't occur to her the police would come into the school. Some people were running out the back door of the hall. Nicola followed them, Rich right behind her.

When they got out of the hall, they saw the people weren't turning to go out the back door, but up the back steps instead. So Rich and Nicola followed them, up to the corridor at the back of the second floor, as high as they could go. People were climbing out an open window onto scaffolding (the school was being renovated). Rich said to himself 'No, not on the scaffolding. If I'm going to be beaten by riot police, don't let it be on scaffolding.' So he didn't go out. Nicola stayed with him. She thought they would stay here until the trouble outside blew over and then go back down. They waited in the corridor.

They could hear the sounds of people screaming as they were beaten on the ground floor. Rich took another look out the window. He saw the playground in the back was swarming with riot police. 'Oh, shit,' he said. In that moment Nicola knew what was happening. She closed her eyes and didn't look out the window.

The police came up the stairs, roaring. Rich and Nicola didn't understand the Italian, but did know, somehow, that they had to lie down on the floor. Nicola lay on her stomach. Rich crouched above her on his hands and knees, trying to shield her, his eyes closed. The police began beating them with clubs.

Rich crouched as low over Nicola as he could, but the police were aiming kicks and clubs underneath him on to her as well. He heard her screaming, 'No, no!' and 'Stop, stop!' But he didn't call out, just made a big grunt each time he was hit. They got his back, his legs and his head. Nicola found the way he grunted more frightening than if he had called out. Her wrist was broken as she held her hands in front of her face.

There seemed to be about eight cops in the group beating Rich and Nicola. After a few minutes they were done, and the group of cops moved down the corridor to the next person lying on the floor waiting. There were maybe eight other people in the corridor. Where they could, they were trying to get under tables or chairs to shelter themselves. Rich could hear people screaming as the police slowly and methodically worked their way down the line, and crying after the police moved on. He and Nicola said nothing to each other. A second group of cops came up the stairs and began beating them again. This time Rich felt less pain. Maybe it was shock, or maybe the fear was now so big it was blotting out the pain.

After the second group of cops worked their way down the corridor and left, everyone just lay there, not moving. Rich and Nicola were too shocked and frightened to whisper to each other. Then more police came up the stairs.

Nicola and Rich didn't know it, but 140 of the police were from the special national riot control unit used to put down prison rebellions. Their commander in the school that night was the head of the national riot police. The national commander of the anti-terrorist police from Rome was there too. Whatever this was, it was coming from the central government.

Nicola and Rich had got together six months before. They both worked for a housing association in East London that helped people with learning difficulties. Nicola's team worked with people whose main problem was not their learning difficulties but their poverty. A lot of her time was taken up in making sure people didn't fall too far behind in their rent. Mostly she sat in their houses and drank cups of tea and listened.

Rich's team provided close support to people who, in the jargon, had mental health problems as well as learning difficulties. Rich talked a lot about challenging behaviour and boundaries; he was tired of disturbed clients banging on the door of his hostel room at night and screaming 'Fuck you!' But he was good at what he did, because he was kind, and calm, and what people in the trade call 'centred'.

On Friday, the direct action day, Nicola and Rich had started out with one of the Globalise Resistance affinity groups that was not planning to confront the police. They had found themselves a few rows behind me as we marched up to the Red Zone. When the police charged in from the side street, Nicola decided it was time to leave. She and Rich went back to the Convergence Centre.

★

There were journalists and TV camera teams in the bar with Richard Peacock, Ruard and Kalpana. The journalists with press passes were able to go into the street outside the school during the beatings. They could hear the police chanting, and then the screaming, but were not allowed inside. The journalists came back to the bar and passed the news to Ruard and the others. At times the bar owners stood by the door, ready to intercede with their bodies and beg for the foreigners if the police came in. Richard Peacock and Ruard went on the street twice, but the force was too strong. They came back to the bar. Kalpana did what she could to calm Richard Peacock. The man had ants in his pants, she thought, wanting to go out there, desperate to help his friends.

At the Convergence Centre by the shore Richard G and the others had built a fire out of driftwood. They sat around, drinking wine, a couple of people playing musical instruments. They could see the police buses going up to the school. Gradually, word came down the hill. The protesters at the Convergence Centre held a quick meeting about what to do, and argued furiously among themselves. Some people said 'Those are our friends, our comrades. We have to go up and defend them.'

Richard Garrett made himself argue loudly, publicly, that nobody should go up there. They would only increase the number of victims. Richard Garrett knew, absolutely, that he was right. Yet it was the most difficult thing he had ever done in his life. He was a socialist back in Britain, but his friends were mostly Hackney anarchists, many of them artists, scoffers at authority. Richard Garrett had always scoffed at moderation and authority too. Now he was taking charge, because some-body had to, you couldn't just let people sacrifice themselves. There were a lot of people saying they ought to go up the hill, but there was nobody doing it. In a way, he was taking on the burden of guilt for the people who wanted to fight back but didn't dare.

Sunday

Richard Garrett's new girlfriend was furious with him, and he liked her very much. After the big meeting, they sat around the fire again, the waves breaking against the rocks behind them. 'How can we sit here?' she said. 'How can they play music, when that's happening to our comrades?' She was lashing out with words, and Richard kept trying to talk her down. The fire made them all feel safer, of course, and so did the music. And it made them seem less of a threat to the police outside the convergence Centre.

Back in the school, Rich and Nicola were lying wordless on the floor of the corridor on the second floor when the third wave of police came up the stairs.

These new police made them all stand up, their backs to the corridor wall, facing outwards. Of course they looked down, not such fools as to challenge the police by making eye contact. But Rich could see that many of the police were wearing civilian clothes under their riot gear and flak jackets. That made him think that these men were fascists. The police must have simply given them the gear and told them to go in and beat the people in that school. Much later he understood that these were plain clothes, or secret, police.

The police were yelling abuse. Rich understood 'Bastardi', but not most of the other words. The tone, though, he understood. One of the cops took out a knife. A young Spaniard with long hair past his shoulders was standing next to Nicola. A cop grabbed the Spaniard's hair in one hand and cut it off with the knife. Then he held the knife by Nicola's head. Rich didn't know what would happen next. Nor did Nicola. The cop took hold of her hair and cut it with the knife. Rich says now he remembers the sound of the hair being cut. 'It's strange, that,' he says, 'because it's such a quiet sound.'

Rich could feel the blood running down his head and around his ears as he stood there. He didn't reach up, but he knew it was blood. There wasn't a lot of pain at this point.

217

Then they were marched down the stairs one by one. The stairs were lined with police. As the prisoners went down, the police were hitting and kicking them, shouting abuse and 'Black Block.' Some people were thrown down the stairs, but not Rich and Nicola. Then they were led back into the main school hall on the ground floor they had fled from 30 minutes or an hour before.

There were suddenly much worse things to look at. There was a lot of blood everywhere. People were lying in pools of blood. There was blood on the sleeping bags. A hundred or so people were lying all over the hall, hurt. Some were crying, some groaning, some screaming and some were quiet. Rich and Nicola went over to the far wall and sat there. Upstairs they had said no words to each other. It seemed too dangerous. Here they spoke quietly. Rich now can't remember any of the words they used. The words didn't matter, the touching each other did. A young German man, maybe 18, was sitting against the wall to one side of them. He was freaked out, crying and making strange noises. Rich pulled him in and put his arms round the man. Rich sat against the wall, one arm around Nicola, her arm around him, and his other arm around the German.

At first Rich was trying to comfort Nicola. Later, he was sitting against the wall, falling asleep from the concussion and fear, and Nicola was slapping his hand to keep him awake, taking her turn to comfort him. Nicola hadn't told her family she was coming to Genoa, partly because she didn't want to worry them and partly because it would mean another political argument with her father. Rich had told his family in passing. It wasn't a problem; it was what they expected of Rich. The family had always held left-wing opinions. One uncle, 'Red George', had been a militant union man in Portsmouth dockyard. Now Rich felt responsible for Nicola being here, and full of guilt.

No one moved around the school hall. No one talked, but just whispered to the people near them. Police were all over the school, but they were not as bad as the police before. Every now and then one of the more brutal police would come back in, his club held high in the air, threatening, prancing, roaring, and the other police would talk to him and get him out of the hall. Then there would be a wait, and another one would come in. But they were less energetic now, the other cops would talk them down.

Paramedics went from one person to another. The medics seemed strange to Rich. They didn't seem to know what they were doing, and showed no concern for the people they were treating. Rich couldn't figure out if they were distant and fumbling because they were scared of the cops or whether the medics were just ordinary cops who had been told to do that job.

Rich tried to stand up and his leg buckled under. He couldn't walk. He thought maybe his leg was broken.

People were calling to the medics. Some were screaming, 'My friend is hurt! Come to my friend!' The medics were not really responding. But then they began to lay the badly injured, those who could not walk, in the middle of the floor. They didn't have enough stretchers, so they put the wounded on thin foam rubber carry mats, the ones you sleep on when you're camping. The medics put them in rows on the floor, row after row. Ambulance workers began coming in and picking people up in the carry mats, laying the mats on top of their stretchers, and carrying them out. Rich didn't know it, but the ambulances had been there a long time. The police had called them before they got to the school.

Nicola got busy finding Rich a place on the floor. The ambulance workers were taking people in order, working down one row and then the next. Nicola got Rich a place in the queue, on a carry mat. Then one of the ambulance people said there was just space for one of the walking people in an ambulance that was going.'

'Go!' Rich said to Nicola.

'No,' she said. She wanted to stay with him.

'Go!' he said. He thought she would be taken to hospital and then be out of this place. There she would be treated, and then released. He still didn't understand what was really happening. But he wanted her out of that place.

'Go,' he said again, and she went. He watched her leave. He felt good that she was out. But he also felt alone.

He was concussed. All he knew was he felt blurry and disconnected. He'd been dropping asleep and jerking himself awake. With Nicola gone, he didn't have to fight it any more. Rich went to sleep.

He woke up when they carried him out on a stretcher. Someone put a hand over his. There were bright lights shining everywhere and shouting. He felt too weak to take it in, couldn't turn his head to see. Then he was in the ambulance.

While Rich and Nicola were being beaten, other policemen were invading the part of the school across the road. The Independent Media (Indymedia) centre was based there. Indymedia broadcasts and runs a Web site for every big demonstration. The police smashed their computers and took their footage. People were made to stand against the wall here too, and hit a bit. But there were mainstream TV crews in the building watching, and a Green member of the European Parliament. The police were not ready to beat up an MEP in front of the cameras. Indymedia had already announced that the GSF legal team had film of the police disguising themselves as Black Block. Now the police went to the computers of the legal team and removed the disks and hard drives. No one who watched was in any doubt that the police knew what they were looking for.

As the injured were carried out of the first school, the people in the other school across the road hung out the windows, shouting 'Assassini, Assassini' at the cops.

All of the people in Rich's part of the school had been arrested: 93 people. The great majority had to be taken to hospital first.

Each ambulance took two people: one on a stretcher and one of the walking wounded. Enrico was in the ambulance with Rich. He was young, perhaps 18, Italian, and not so badly injured. Enrico spoke English, and through him the ambulance staff asked Rich if he was all right. That felt good. Their faces didn't look caring to Rich, but at least they had asked. And there was less fear in the ambulance, with no police there. Enrico talked to him kindly.

At the hospital there were police everywhere. The other prisoners from the school saw that the doctors and nurses were afraid. They would not look at the people they were treating, kept their faces impassive. If the police were out of the room, the nurses would soften, there would be concern on their faces. Rich was too groggy to grasp this fully.

They took Rich into a big room. He knew the police were there. He couldn't see the police, but he could feel their presence, black and circling round the edges. He was laid on a table, or something like it. The doctors and nurses were not caring, made no human contact, and tried to work quickly. Rich didn't know if they were afraid of the police, or just didn't like protesters. They began sewing his head up quickly, without local anaesthetic. Now, for the first time, it really hurt. Rich tossed his head from side to side as they tried to stitch. So they gave up on his head, and switched to sewing up his leg. People held his leg down. He could feel the pull of the needle as it sliced through, the long slow arc of the pull down through one side of the leg, and then back up through the other side. He screamed as they worked. They finished the leg and went back to his head. He threw his head from side to side again, screaming. Fed up, or frightened, they simply sewed the gauze and cotton bandages on his head to the scalp. It stopped the bleeding, but didn't close up the wound.

What the doctors and nurses could tell, and Rich could not, was that the police were some kind of elite unit from out of town. They were also very aware, as everybody in Genoa was by

Sunday morning, that nothing like this had happened in Italy for 50 years. The attack on the official headquarters, on sleeping people, was something new in Italy. The hospital staff knew the 'post-fascist' National Alliance was part of the government coalition. None of them was sure what would happen next.

(Later that morning, at 8.30, two lawyers from the GSF would go down to the relevant police station, following normal procedure after demonstrations, to ask who had been detained and where they were held. The police immediately arrested both lawyers, beat them up and then released them.)

After sewing the bandage to his head, they wheeled Rich on a trolley to a cubicle, where he waited. A Spanish woman came and comforted him. She was 65, and had been in the school too. She talked to him, lifted his head and gave him a bit of water, stroked the back of his hand and soothed him. She said she was worried that her daughter would find out what had happened to her. This struck Rich as funny. So many people worrying about what their parents would think, and she was worrying about what her child would think.

It was a long wait. Consciousness came and went. A nurse came to take him for an X-ray. Her face said sympathy. She was the first person outside the beaten who had looked at Rich like that. So he asked her to find out if Nicola had been in the hospital. She said she couldn't find that out. Rich asked her again, describing Nicola and giving her name. The nurse told him again that she couldn't get the information. Now Rich understood she was saying that it would not be safe for her to go up to the desk and ask that question.

But, she said, Rich could ask. When he went out into reception, there was a desk there. Rich could ask the person at the desk about Nicola and they would tell him. For her part, the nurse said, she had not treated anyone with that name.

After the X-ray, the nurse left him on a trolley in reception near the front door of the hospital. There were about eight or so other injured people sitting in plastic chairs. The police were sorting the injured as they came through reception. Those who could not walk were kept in hospital. The rest would be taken away. Rich did not understand this.

A policeman leaned over Rich's trolley and told him to get up. The cop used no words. He just beckoned Rich up with his hands. Rich indicated he could not stand. The man insisted, leaning over, beckoning harder. Rich was scared. He held out both hands, elbows bent, fingers grasping invisible handles, trying to tell the cop he needed a wheelchair. The cop went and got a wheelchair standing next to the wall. Rich got himself from the trolley to the chair. Then the cop had to push him over to where the others were sitting. Rich knew the cop was furious to be pushing the wheelchair, that he thought he was so tough and now here he was being the care worker. Rich didn't look back at the cop, but he knew.

Rich got Enrico to walk over to the reception desk and ask for Nicola. They said they had nobody by that name.

Once the police vans and buses had finally left the school, Richard Peacock, Ruard, Kalpana and the others left the bar and went to the school, looking for Rich and Nicola. Ruard went from room to room, looking at the pools of blood on the floors. A week later I sat on a bench in my local park in London, the one where I used to walk my dog Wesley, and listened while Ruard talked to a journalist from the *Observer* newspaper. The journalist asked Ruard what the pools of blood in the school looked like. 'Like human pools of blood,' Ruard said, as if we all knew what that looked like. 'It depended how they were lying when they were beaten,' he said. 'Some of them were really wide.' Ruard spread his arms wide, his hands held like a man measuring a fish. 'Some were narrower. And some were like splashes. There were marks where the police had tried to wash some of the blood away before they left. But they couldn't.'

They didn't find Rich and Nicola. The friends held a quick meeting and decided to split up. Ru would work the phones.

Kalpana, Laurence and Richard Peacock would check the hospitals. Suddenly the Spanish consul was there. Richard Peacock got in a taxi with him and went to search the hospitals. It was a brave and dangerous thing to do; he was likely to make one more victim.

Richard Peacock, Nicola and Rich Moth all knew a bit about violence. They had grown up working class, in tough towns and neighbourhoods. Richard Peacock was originally from Darlington, a northern town that was centred around the railway works before they closed down. Rich Moth was from Portsmouth, a naval base, working class, pretty right-wing, with a lot of fights in the pubs. Nicola's family was career military, in the ranks, so she'd moved around a lot, her childhood more respectable than the others, but with the background knowledge of violence that's always there in the services. All three of them had gone on to university, and their families were intensely proud of them.

Richard Peacock and the Spanish consul reached a hospital. Richard Peacock found Rich Moth sitting in reception.

Rich Moth was surprised to see him. It felt surreal. Peacock asked how he was. From the bandages sewn to his head and the wheelchair, Richard Peacock was worried Rich Moth had brain damage.

'Not so good,' Rich Moth said. 'Where's Nicola?'

'I don't know,' Richard Peacock said.

'Find Nicola,' Rich Moth said.

'I don't know where she is,' Richard Peacock said.

'Find Nicola,' Rich Moth kept saying. Richard Peacock was relieved. His friend could only say one thing, but his brain was working.

They had been talking two minutes. The police, standing against one wall of reception, were allowing this. Rich Moth didn't understand it, or where Richard Peacock had come from. Now Richard Peacock got behind the wheelchair and started to wheel Rich Moth right out of the hospital.

The cops were across the room fast. Rich Moth said to Richard Peacock 'Go now!', meaning 'or they'll take you too.' Richard Peacock got out the door.

A little while later the prisoners in reception were taken out front. Up to now Rich Moth had been thinking that maybe they were going to be released. He hadn't really allowed himself to think anything else. Now they were taken out to ordinary police cars, with those wire cages for people in the back. Two people went in the first car, and Rich and two German girls in the next one. The cops pushed Rich's wheelchair to the curb. He got himself out of the chair, carefully, bent over, and into the squad car.

They drove him to the special detention centre the riot police and the secret police had set up in Bolzaneto, 15 kilometres outside Genoa.

Those two beers Saturday night knocked me out. I collapsed onto an air mattress at Maria's. I left my new mobile plugged in to the wall across the room, recharging. Sometime after three it rang. I started out of sleep, groggy, confused by my first mobile phone. 'Somebody's trying to call you, Jonathan,' Bambery said from another bed, and went back to sleep. I couldn't get the message thing to work, but I took the phone into the sleeping bag with me. An hour or so later it rang again. It was Ruard.

He filled me in. I stood myself up, woke the others up and asked for advice. It was still dark. I rang up Marco, the Italian film producer. I needed someone who could speak Italian. I asked him to bring a cab. Someone had to go down and fetch our people. There was no question that it was me. Those were my friends down there, people I loved. Ru is a man, 27 years old. But I felt something of a parent's responsibility, the one that wrenches your gut.

Someone made me a coffee. I called Ru at the number he had given and said I was waiting for a taxi and would come as soon as I could. Marco came with the cab. It was half past five by the time we got to the school. There was a lovely early morning light. Ru and Richard Peacock were waiting for me, just inside the gates of the school where the GSF had held all its meetings.

Rich Moth and Nicola had been beaten in the part of the school across the road. Now perhaps 100 people were congregated in the forecourt of the main school. Richard Peacock and Ru said to wait for Laurence and Kalpana. They were still out looking for Rich and Nicola. I was tired and frightened. The only way I could deal with this was to imagine I was Chris Bambery, hard, strong, giving orders in a calm, authoritative voice, and burying my feelings six feet under.

My friend Uri, an Israeli anarchist, was in the forecourt of the school that morning. Days later he told me I had looked spaced out, and more afraid than I needed to be. 'I wasn't so worried,' Uri said. 'But then I was in the Israeli army. That was worse. And I was one of the cops in Israel. It's better to be one of the protesters.'

We held our taxi, and got the driver to call another one. We waited on the pavement, just outside the school. There were a lot of people there, including an obvious undercover cop. He was standing in the middle of the road, loud, boisterous, clowning around. No one who was not a policeman would have had the courage for that. I remembered what Nancy said about living in Syria. They leave one undercover cop standing in public for you to see, to scare you. They have another you can't see to deal with you.

Laurence and Kalpana arrived as the second taxi did. I told them to get their things and get in the cab. They had been to every hospital in Genoa, with the family from the bar. Kalpana hadn't found Nicola, and thought Richard Peacock had been looking in the wrong hospital for Rich Moth. She was trying to tell us this. I couldn't listen, frantic to get out of there. She and Laurence went back into the school to get their bags. We bundled into the taxi and back to Marco's flat.

Marco was staying a block from the Red Zone. As we got

near the flat Marco said the area was crawling with undercover cops. We should get out of the car, get into the house, not talk, nobody speak in English, just do it. Marco had forgotten his keys in the rush. He hoped someone would answer the bell quickly. They did. We were in.

It was another old, lovely flat, cool with high narrow windows. Marco drew the curtains so nobody could see us from the street. Ru turned on the TV. Over and over it showed the killing of Carlo and pictures of people being taken out of the school. There was a clip of a man on a stretcher, bloody. It looked something like Rich Moth, but I told myself the man in the picture was bigger than Rich. (It was him.) There was another of a woman, from the back, walking funny, who looked a bit like Nicola. (It was.) The same pictures, over and over. I wanted that TV off, so I could forget my fear and think.

We had a little meeting. Fiona was there, making us all tea, being calm. I told everybody they would wait here. I would go back to the school and see what I could do with the GSF. When things looked quieter, we would get everybody out of Genoa. That might be in a few hours, or it might be tomorrow.

I got Ru to call his mother. We needed her help. But first and foremost, I needed to let Nancy know Ru was safe. I don't know why: she didn't know what danger he'd been in.

Ru called Nancy and filled her in. Then I got on and asked for help. I gave her a couple of key phone numbers of people in England who might be able to help exert pressure to get Rich Moth and Nicola out of jail. Nancy got busy.

I called Chris Nineham and Martin, told them I was going back to the school. They agreed to meet me there. I then tried to ring some of the GSF. Marco asked me to use only the mobile, not the landline. He explained that I was one of the leaders of the protests. He and Fiona thought the undercover cops in the street outside were monitoring calls. If they knew I was calling from here, they would be round within minutes. He explained that if the police came, they might do things to me, but they would certainly hurt the other people in the house. 'Please do not put us in danger,' he said. I stuck to the mobile.

I was talking on the phone all the time, to people back in London, to Nancy, to people in Genoa, to the press. It was time to go back to the school. I dumped my old small backpack. It was torn, and looked scruffy. I wanted to be respectable. One of the women on the film team gave me a bag of hers to carry. I left behind every socialist newspaper, and the red bandanna I had worn on all the marches.

First Marco had arranged an interview with a TV team for me. We would meet in public, on a scenic lookout point above central Genoa. Marco said 'We will walk fast, along the street. Follow me, don't say anything, don't talk English.' We got a few blocks away from the Red Zone and relaxed. There was nobody at the lookout point. Marco was suddenly very worried. It felt just like a movie about the resistance in World War Two. I looked out over Genoa like a tourist, pretending to be calm. Marco was on the mobile, unable to raise the TV team.

There is something quite odd about being with someone who is very afraid because he is standing next to you.

Pause a moment here, to look at this fear, his and mine. It was not just ours. The Italians Marco was asking advice from, his friends and co-workers, were telling him to be afraid. He had worked as a stockbroker for several years in Rome and London, before going back to graduate school. He was not helpless, and knew the ways of the powerful.

The attack on the school had been designed to produce this fear. The headline in the first Italian paper I saw said 'Genoa Social Forum Attacked'. That summed it up. The police had gone for the moderate headquarters of the movement. There they had woken sleeping people who thought they were safe because the school was moderate and official. The police had beaten people in there in ways that allowed the media outside in the street to understand, report and film what was happening.

The message was: no one is safe.

The fear we were feeling all around us was what they wanted ordinary Italians to feel. What magnified it was that nothing like this had happened in Italy since the time of Mussolini. The rules had been well and truly broken now. No one knew what would happen next. Anything could, people felt.

The TV team finally arrived. We were relieved. The reporter was blonde, trim, dressed in a blue power suit. Before we started filming I asked her if I had food on my face. 'No,' she said, 'do I have food on mine?' 'No,' I said.

From that morning on, the journalists who had been in Genoa were on our side. It didn't necessarily show up in their published and broadcast reports. Those get edited. But they were all trying as hard as they could to get the truth out. Whatever we asked for as we tried to get Rich and Nicola out of jail safe and alive, they did for us.

Marco went back to the flat. I got a ride to the school, and went inside. The leaders of the GSF were meeting at the school. I said goodbye to Chris Nineham, who was due to leave Genoa that morning. Martin stayed as backup, working the phones back at a hotel, out of the way.

I gave an interview to American TV and then went out into the school forecourt. Richard Garrett was there. He had come up from the Convergence Centre, hoping I'd be there and know what to do. Richard Garrett was clearly done in. I told him what I knew about Rich and Nicola, but that our other close friends were all right. The BBC wanted an interview. I looked at Richard Garrett's face. I said 'I know you have terrible feelings right now. I can't deal with them and keep coping. Please just stand over there and I'll get you out of here as soon as I can.' I answered questions into the BBC mike. Richard Garrett stood upright in the sunlight, a muscular young man in a T-shirt, his face beautiful, his shoulders shaking gently, crying to himself in a disciplined way.

The leaders of the GSF were meeting upstairs. I figured the meeting would be in Italian, and I had to get Richard Garrett to safety before I did anything else. And I was scared. The interview finished, I called Marco and Fiona. They had decided to get everyone out of the flat. Marco suggested we meet them at Bolzaneto, the nearest railway station still open. We didn't know it, but that's where Rich and Nicola were being held. I called a taxi. We waited by the gate of the school, the obvious plain-clothes cop clowning two or three paces away. The taxi came through the crowd in the street. I breathed as we left Genoa and got onto the motorway, in a valley between the mountains. Finally, safe.

In Bolzaneto, a small suburban town, there seemed to be a lot of police on the streets. We found Marco, Fiona, Ru and the others at the train station, standing outside waiting for us. They took a swift look at Richard Garrett, and arms went round him and held Richard as he cried. A friend from London walked up from the other side and said 'Hullo, Jonathan.' Three people hissed at him 'Your T-shirt!'. He was wearing a 'Save Mumia' T-shirt.

'Turn it inside out!' they hissed. He didn't understand. Two women pulled it off him, turned it inside out, put it back on him and then explained that a political T-shirt might provoke the police.

Marco, Fiona, Richard Garrett, Richard Peacock, Kalpana, Ru and Laurence got on the first train out of town. Then they changed again for Turin, found a hotel and started getting flights home.

Martin had told me to go to the Genoa youth hostel, high in the hills above the city. It was an oasis. I sat on the patio, looking out over the city and the water, blue far below. The hostel was closed until three, and there was hardly anybody there. I watched the distant water, took solace, and smoked.

While I was hiding out up at the youth hostel, the Italian leaders of the GSF were being braver. They met for three hours at the school. Then they held an international press conference down by the shore, on the Piazza Martin Luther King. More than 1,000 journalists and camera crew stood for over three hours asking questions. The media workers knew that every hour they stood there normalised things, and made the leaders of the GSF safer.

Everyone in the GSF understood what had happened. Vittorio Agnoletto, the main spokesperson of the GSF, speaking firmly, called for the resignations of Berlusconi and the minister of the interior, laying the blame for the attack on the school defiantly at their door. It helped, probably, that he had been a doctor treating patients with HIV for years. He knew there are worse miseries and fears. He kept saying to the press, nothing like this has happened in my lifetime. Agnoletto is 43. He meant nothing like this had happened since fascism.

In Genoa, all over Italy, many people feared the return of that power. Over and over in the next few days, people said there is nothing Italian about this. This is new, and very frightening. And, they said, it should be stopped.

From Saturday night people put up home-made banners, bigger than sheets, all over Genoa. They hung them in the parks, over the street markets, from lampposts across the streets. On them was one word: 'Assassini'. Now, on Sunday, they hung one of those banners in front of a local police station in the centre of Genoa.

The police did not dare to take these banners down. They went in and out of the police station, under the banner. They stood on the street in groups, a banner flying above them. The police knew what the people of Genoa felt.

The banners had not gone up after Carlo died on the Friday. They began on the Saturday, after the march of 300,000. That was what gave people the confidence. When there is a march of 30,000, most people in the country learn what happened from the media. When there is a march of 300,000, almost everyone in the country knows someone who was there: a woman they work with, a neighbour, a friend down the café, a nephew. They know what to believe. The word gets out.

Those 300,000 had the confidence that came from the numbers on that glorious day. The leaders of the GSF were able to meet down by the sea, and the journalists to stand with them, because they had felt that strength. That's also what got Richard Peacock into the hospital looking for Rich Moth.

It could have gone either way. But all over Italy people said to each other: 'If this stands, we live in Pincochet's Chile'. They did not say, directly, 'in Mussolini's Italy'. It was too scary to say that. But in every indirect way they could, they told each other stories about the prisoners forced to sing old fascist anthems.

The banners made the difference. Sunday evening they began to go up all over Rome. No police force, and no government, can stand firm against that, unless they are prepared to kill very large numbers of people and pretty sure they can get away with it.

The force began to flow our way. But Rich and Nicola were still in jail. We were increasingly worried about what the police were doing to them.

The police car drove Rich into a compound in Bolzaneto Sunday morning. There were long barracks in a compound, and he could tell it was not a normal police station.

Rich got out and was made to stand there. He saw Nicola in a police van. Rich told himself she had just been processed here, and was now being released. The van was going to drive her out of the compound and release her. Then they took him to the holding cell.

There were 30 men and women in the cell, but no Nicola. The front of the cell had open bars, and there were always several policemen watching. During the hours that followed Rich felt fear, all the time. Not anxiety, not worry, but real stomach-clenching fear. The fear drove out anger, or sadness, or concern. The police would come and bang on the bars. They came into the cage, many times, forcing people to lean up against the wall, their arms spread above their heads, and say things over and over. After a few minutes the pain in the arms and shoulders was excruciating.

Mostly the police were asking details of who they were, but trying to make them say things differently, trip them up. The police yelled at them a lot. They were not beaten that morning, but they were waiting for it, all the time.

Rich wanted to move around and talk to people. You could move a little, talk a little, when the police were paying less attention. There seemed to be every nationality in Europe in the cell, more Germans than anything else. Rich tried talking to two Spaniards. They had been arrested in Prague, and they were the people in the cell most fearful about what was likely to happen next. Listening to them wound Rich up.

The police would come in and tell them they would be released, and then come back and say no, they had been in the school and they were all going to prison for a long time. Some of the younger Germans, who had allowed themselves to hope, were crying and screaming. Rich wanted to tell them the police were playing mind games with them, but he couldn't while the police were there. He was angry with the screamers because he wanted to scream too, and might. So he talked to some German students, who had it together, sort of.

Enrico, the Italian prisoner who had been in the ambulance, was moving around every group, slowly, as best he could. He was bringing comfort, and translating what he was hearing from the Italian police. Rich started to move around too, in part to bring comfort, and in part to find it, since he was on his own, not part of any group.

Rich saw the police take Nicola down the corridor to the toilet. He did not call out. They made no eye contact; it wasn't safe. He didn't know if she had seen him. Again, it was a strange double feeling knowing she was there. He felt good for himself, and bad for her. But not that bad. He had told himself she had been let loose, but he really knew that she hadn't.

After about 10 hours the guards began to let up. Maybe it was because they were coming to their end of their shift, bored and tired and looking forward to going home. Maybe it was something else. The prisoners began to hope.

The guards brought food for the first time. Only bread rolls and water, but it was something. It showed things were getting better.

Enrico told Rich 'Now I can see your face. Before there was only fear on your face; I could not see who you were. Now your face moves, I can see you,' Enrico said. 'I know you.'

Enrico already knew that his girlfriend was in the next big holding cell along the corridor. Now that the police were easing up, Enrico asked for permission to be with her. The police put her in Enrico and Rich's cell. She told Rich that Nicola was in the next cell. Rich immediately asked, through Enrico, for permission to join Nicola.

'No,' the police said.

The police finally agreed to let him stand outside Nicola's cell and talk to her for about 30 seconds. As soon as she spoke, he could feel she was strong. She would be all right.

Then the shift changed, and the new police were fresh and eager. The banging on the bars, the standing against the wall, increased. The fear grew. Rich did not say to himself that the police might take them away and use pain until they got a confession. When they whispered to each other about what might happen, no one said it to him. But it was in his head, and theirs, unspoken, unformed in words.

At about two in the morning, the guards began taking them away one by one. The prisoners immediately started memorising each other's names, repeating to each other the names of the people who had been taken away, so they would all carry a record in their heads. In case someone didn't come back, and was lost. They did not say, but it was in their minds, that someone might be permanently lost.

★

In London that night, Nancy, Silva and Pim were working the phones in our flat. Pim was making lot of tea, too. He is a gentle Dutchman and a student of graphic design. Silva has worked for NGOs in wars and crises for years. She's also Italian. She was ashamed of, and furious about, what had been done in her country.

Nancy got the number of the British consul in Turin, who had been sent down to Genoa. He told us the Italian authorities were refusing to say where Rich and Nicola were held, or if they were held at all.

Jim Nichol, a human rights lawyer in London, called and told me to call the Press Association. Give them a story they could use. That meant Rich and Nicola's full names and ages, Jim said. Put in their jobs. I said they were support workers for people with learning disabilities, and this was Nicola's first demonstration. 'Put that in,' Jim said. 'It's a story. The PA will send it out over the wire. Then all the media will get someone to call the Foreign Office, and they'll have to respond.'

We sat on that idea. I was worried about Nicola and Rich losing their jobs. We got hold of Rich's parents in Portsmouth by afternoon, but no one could find an address or phone number for Nicola's family. Her flatmate went through her room, drawer by drawer and envelope by envelope, and found nothing. My memory was they lived somewhere in Kent. I didn't want to tell the papers without telling them first.

This was stupid. I wouldn't do that again. Next time I would know the only thing that really mattered was getting them out as fast as possible. That's how I would feel if it were my child.

That night I went down and stayed in a hotel room near the Red Zone, with Martin and his partner Sue. It seemed safe. Things were getting quiet. At nine that evening I phoned the Press Association with the story. I told them the Foreign Office was being no help, and we were worried. Within 15 minutes the media were calling us and the Foreign Office. Martin, Sue and I tried to eat out. We had to leave the restaurant in the middle of the meal, because our mobile phones never stopped ringing.

Sue was resentful of Martin paying no attention to her. They'd been apart all week. This was their day to be together in Italy. He told her this was his job. It didn't occur to Martin, or me, to hand Sue the phone and say 'This is important, help us.'

The next morning a radio station in London woke me at five to seven in my hotel room, in Genoa, for an interview. I was groggy, not thinking straight. During the interviews the night before the journalists were all sympathetic. I wasn't ready when the interviewer tore into me, saying wasn't it true Carlo Giuliani had been attacking the police, and how could I justify the violence. I botched the interview, sounding surly and defensive.

Half an hour later Nancy called. She said maybe I needed to get out of Italy now. She'd been glued to the media: TV, radio, papers. Nancy wasn't watching for the news, but for slant. The night before, she said, it was OK, and Channel 4 was sympathetic. That morning the spin had changed completely. The papers were hard against us, so were the TV and the radio. Blair, like Bush and Berlusconi, was backing the police. Nancy said the word must have gone out from Downing Street and down through the media corporations last night, must have, for the slant to change so abruptly. 'That means you're in danger,' she said.

All the way through Nancy was utterly reliable, and very useful, because she understands power. She's an anthropologist, and has lived in the USA, Britain, Turkey, Syria and Afghanistan. Her family back home in Missouri are working-class people, carpenters and schoolteachers, union members. But she also spent 25 years married to a man who went to Eton. Nancy knows what the ruling class can do to ordinary people, and how they think. She knows they can turn on a dime, move from democracy to repression. Her experience in Turkey is especially important in looking for the subtle signs of instant repression. She lived through a coup there, and much uneasy and partial democracy.

At the same time, Nancy knows repression is not automatic. We can move the powers that be too, if we build enough pressure. In the days that follow it will be very important that she knows both these things as she works the phones. Someone who believed or trusted the Foreign Office would be useless. A person who didn't understand they could be pressured from below would be no use too.

I tell Nancy I want to stay, but I'll ask Martin's advice. Only a fool makes these decisions on his own, and I trust Martin's judgment. Martin says he can't be sure what will happen to me. But the police have not arrested any of the leaders of the GSF. 'Or any old people,' he says gently.

Oh. I'd forgotten I was old.

'They want everybody to think their enemies are young people,' Martin says. 'You should be fine.'

So I stay.

The only GR person arrested on Friday was Margaret from Glasgow. She lost hold of the arms of the people next to her, and went down under the police. They beat her and took her away. She's in hospital in Genoa, and will have reconstructive surgery on her nose. But the police have not charged her, because she's 48 and a woman.

Martin flies out; the airport is open today. Sue takes over the phone from him. She's happy now, useful and steady. We can't afford another night in the hotel, so we move up the hill to the youth hostel where I found peace two days ago.

Back in London a lot of people are busy on the phone. Silva is doing an extraordinary job of keeping us linked to Italian organisations. Richard Peacock and Ruard are back in their shared flat, working two mobiles and a landline. Guy and Despina stagger off the train from Genoa, physically done in, and on to the phones at the GR office. Nicola's flatmate Jonny is stuck by his phone. Rich's family get mobilised in Portsmouth, harrying the Foreign Office. Doing something helps them get through the anxious waiting. Jonny calls Nicola's work, and her union steward and her boss both get going. Rich and Nicola are both in Unison, the public sector union, with 1.3 million members. Unison supported the Genoa protests. Now the GR office encourages Unison members all over the country to press the union leadership to act.

It's a strange campaign, because there's no coordination, no orders. We all just do it, taking decisions on the hoof, calling each other for advice if we're not sure. The urgency means there are no meetings. We don't even ring round and ask people to throw themselves into our phone campaign. We just enlist whoever calls up and get them moving. At the heart of any good defence campaign are those who love the people in trouble.

Italian law says the police have to lay charges within 48 hours. Monday night the police charged all of the 93 people arrested at the school on the same four counts: resisting a public official, criminal association, possession of offensive weapons and possession of arms. These are all collective charges. They are not charged with doing these things themselves, but with being in the presence of unspecified people who were.

The cops show the press and TV the weapons they found in the school. There are several Swiss army knives, ordinary knives for buttering bread, and two empty wine bottles the police say are Molotov cocktails. They also produce a sledgehammer and a pickaxe. The school, as anybody would know who's been inside it, is currently being repaired. These are building workers' tools.

The collective charges relieve one worry in my mind. They're not doing Rich separately for assault. I still don't understand that everybody was much too afraid to resist in any way. The thing that surprises me most is the Italian police didn't bother to plant any real weapons on the people they arrested. I assume the British or US police would have manufactured evidence. What can be wrong with the Italians?

I don't think the charges will stand. These people were settling down or asleep when they were arrested. What worries me is the police have no evidence, so they may well be beating people for confessions.

I emphasise to all the journalists I speak to that Nicola is innocent, on the first demonstration of her life. She would never hurt anybody, I say. The *Mirror*'s man in Genoa calls us. He knows they're a couple, and wants to get a big spread in the paper about innocent young British love in a foreign prison. For that he needs a picture of the two of them together. Nicola's flatmate tears her room apart again. No picture of them together. Pim ransacks Rich's room. Nancy finally finds a photo she took of Rich and Nicola together. The next morning Nicola's parents open the paper and learn where their daughter is.

As Monday goes into Tuesday we get more worried. Five of the detainees are British. One, Sky, is under arrest in hospital with 10 broken teeth, eight broken ribs and a punctured lung. The rest (Rich, Nicola, Dan and Norman) are being held somewhere else. The consul tells us he can't find out where.

By this time we know that the Spanish consul, the German consul and the US consul have all seen at least some of their detainees. The Foreign Office in London won't tell us, or Rich's family, anything. The British consul in Genoa keeps telling us that the Italian police won't tell him where Rich and Nicola are held, so he can't speak to them. Late Tuesday afternoon two senior journalists on two different British national newspapers ring Nancy from Genoa. They have it on good authority, they say, that the consul and the Foreign Office are lying to us. The consul knows where Rich and Nicola are being held and is refusing to visit them. The journalists think we should know this. So, by implication, does the person in the Foreign Office who leaked this information to them.

Silva calls the GSF lawyers in Genoa. Their guess is that the reason the British detainees have not been produced is that one or more of them have been badly beaten in custody, and are in a military hospital. Maybe they can't be seen because of what they would look like. Maybe the British authorities know this, and are covering it up, the GSF people say.

In Genoa, I get a call from Nicola's dad in England. He's very angry. But he's trying to hold on to himself so he doesn't piss me off, because I might be able to help his daughter. He asks who I am, what my part is in this. I tell him. He says he can't help blaming Rich. I say I think Rich is probably blaming himself, but Nicola's a grown woman, and a strong one. She made her own decision. Of course I feel guilty, I tell him.

'I don't know you,' he says. 'But I know my daughter. She wouldn't hurt a fly.'

Back in London we now have a leading human rights lawyer, Louise Christian, working for free. The consul is lying to her too. The Foreign Office isn't answering calls from the families. They tell Louise there is no point in getting a lawyer in Italy, as Italian law says a lawyer can't visit a foreigner in custody for the first four days. She believes them.

One of the British detainees, Dan, has held on to his mobile phone in the chaos. In an act of foolhardy bravery, he secretly calls his father from jail. His father Bill is a former physician to the Queen. Bill gets his boy one of Italy's leading human rights lawyers, fast, and the man gets in to see Dan on Tuesday. Dan asks him to represent all 92 other detainees too. He says he will, but doesn't get to see them.

By this time Rich's parents and sister, Nicola's father, mother and brother, Nancy, Dan's parents and Norman's girlfriend are all calling each other back and forth, calling their MPs, anyone else who might help. Rich's parents tell me it's been good to talk to Nicola's mother. At least there's someone who's coping worse than they are, and so they can be of use to someone. Nicola's mother tells me exactly the opposite. Rich's mother seems unable to cope, she says, so she was glad to be of some use. These are decent people who have never met each other, doing everything they can.

Dan's dad Bill has all the class confidence and nose for the ways of the powerful a man can have. He really gets to the media and says, in a voice of solid authority, that we have direct evidence the Foreign Office are lying to us.

In Germany, Spain, the United States, Norway and I don't where else, families, friends and comrades are mounting similar campaigns.

Tuesday night I flew home from Genoa. All I could do in Italy was man the phones in the youth hostel.

Monday night, with no official protest called, 30,000 people turned up in the centre of Milan anyway. Monday morning Berlusconi had been right behind his police force. Tuesday he said in Parliament that he knew nothing of the attack on the school before it happened. Scajola, the interior minister, said the same thing. The banners were doing their work. The governments of France, Germany and Russia were now making critical noises. Only Blair and Bush were holding firm.

The GSF called for demonstrations all over Italy on Tuesday night. The GSF estimated 500,000 people in all came out on the streets. In Rome there were 40,000, in Milan 100,000. Richard Peacock and Ruard had written a joint witness statement of what they had seen. On Wednesday a Green MP read a translation of their statement out in the Italian Parliament, to Berlusconi's face.

The British press had turned against the government and the Italian police. The general line, though, was 'What could you expect from Italy? They have different customs.' Only some reports made it clear that the British government still had not criticised the police.

On Wednesday morning I called Rich and Nicola's union headquarters. At three I was in the office of the Unison deputy general secretary. I said 'Do you want to know who I am?' 'I know who you are,' he said. 'You're the Genoa Social Forum.'

He asked me what was happening. I told him. I said I didn't want Unison to endorse anti-capitalism. I just wanted to make

sure Nicola and Rich weren't lying somewhere, badly beaten
and without medical care. One phone call from Jack Straw, the
Foreign Secretary, to the Italian government would get them
out. I wanted him to ask Straw to make that phone call. He said
he had a taxi waiting outside to go to Whitehall. Forty-five
minutes later someone in his office released the text of a stinging
letter from him to Jack Straw. Everything I'd said was in that
letter, but the deputy general secretary had added angry words
about police brutality.

Still Straw didn't make that phone call. But the pressure was
mounting in Italy. And there were demonstrations outside Italian
embassies and consulates in dozens of countries, from Germany
to Los Angeles.

Wednesday afternoon, though, I was getting frantic. The
consul and the Foreign Office were telling us they now knew
where Rich was, but couldn't get in to see him. They said they
didn't know where Nicola was. Nancy and I sat across the
kitchen table in London, me on the mobile, her on the landline.
She kept telling me to write a summary of every call I made. I
kept not doing it. She got angrier and angrier. I didn't understand why. I said 'Lay off! This is going too fast to take notes.'
Nancy said 'We have to make a record.' Then I understood.

'Oh!' I said. We looked at each other.

'Silva's been talking to Italy,' Nancy said. 'I think we should
make a record of every call. Let's be very careful to do this. Ask
everybody who they have talked to at the Foreign Office, and
when. Write down the names and the times.'

'We don't know where Nicola is,' I said.

'No, we don't.'

'Do we have any evidence at all that she's alive?' I said.

'No,' Nancy said.

I called Richard Peacock and said that to him. There was a
silence, and then he said 'That fits.'

I called Liz, a socialist lawyer, for advice. Liz said 'Call everybody in the press or with influence you can. Don't tell them you

think there is a conspiracy and a cover-up. They already think left-wingers are paranoid. Just tell them you're worried. Say all the other consuls have visited their people and the British have not. You are worried something may have happened to one of the British detainees. They may be in some sort of trouble. The Foreign Office doesn't seem to be helpful.'

I tried that. I called one of the two senior journalists who had leaked to Nancy the day before. I said what Liz told me to say, and ended: 'Do you think I'm being unnecessarily alarmist?'

'Who do you want me to call?' he said.

I called the other senior journalist and said the same thing. 'How can I help?' he said.

I called a Labour MP, not a left-winger, who was helping one of the families. I got his assistant. 'Am I being unduly alarmist?' I asked. She said the MP had told her to wait for our call. He was in a meeting with a minister, desperately trying to get to Jack Straw.

Now I was really worried.

Louise Christian, the lawyer, called the consul in Genoa. Aware that she had been systematically lied to, and furious, she gave him a piece of her mind and said he had to see Nicola immediately. He turned his mobile off as she was talking.

The consul immediately rang Nicola's father. He told Nicola's dad that he was going, right now, to the prison where Nicola was held. He would stand outside the prison, for however long it took, until Nicola was released into his custody. He promised Nicola's dad that.

Nicola's dad immediately called her flatmate with the information to pass on to us.

Now we knew that the consul had cracked. He was clearly feeling guilty, and very worried. He did know where Nicola was. For some reason he was still not going to ask to see her.

On Sunday at Bolzaneto the police had taken Nicola, Rich and the other detainees off one by one. They had fingerprinted them, filled out forms, and taken them back to other cells. That night Nicola and the other women in her cell lay on the cold marble floor, covered by a few blankets, holding each other for warmth. Because so many of them were injured, they found it painful to lie on one side for any length of time. So every so often they would all wake up together and roll over to lie on the other side, and then hug each other again.

Nicola didn't get a lot of sleep that night. She kept having thoughts about what might happen: torture, for instance. But she tried not to say anything. Some of the other women in the cell with her did talk about their fears. Nicola didn't want to hear. Talking could only make it worse. When her fears, or other people's, began to overwhelm her, she lay on the ground and shut her eyes and pretended to sleep.

Later on Monday the police took Nicola and the other women off in mini-buses. They drove a long way, and came to a prison. They were taken to a room one by one. There were three women warders in the room. They filled out a form on Nicola, and gave her a cup, a bowl, a plate and a spoon, all plastic. And a towel. She could tell by looking at the prison officers that they weren't going to be like the police. She was still worried about going to jail for years. But she wasn't afraid of being beaten any longer.

She had a shower. The women were allowed to choose their cellmates, and Nicola ended up in a room with three other calm people. They sat on their beds, wrapped in towels, putting off the moment when they put their clothes back on. The clothes stank. Nicola hadn't smelled old blood before, and it repelled her.

They spent the next 48 hours wondering if they would be released or go down for years. When the going got rough, they told jokes. When that didn't work, all four of them lay on their beds and closed their eyes and let sleep come.

There was a TV in the cell, and Nicola's cellmates watched the news. They saw the raid on the school on the TV, and pictures of all the weapons they were supposed to have had. There was footage of the demonstration in Milan demanding their release. Nicola couldn't bear the television, but the other women wanted it.

For part of the day, all the women detainees from the school were allowed out in the exercise yard together. They had meetings out there, trying to decide how to deal with questions from the magistrates, trying to guess what would happen to them.

The men were held in another prison, two to a cell, in a special corridor with no contact with the ordinary prisoners. Except for Rich, who was in a cell by himself. He didn't like that, and wondered why. The next day they were all moved around, and again Rich found himself the only with no one in the other bunk. Now he was pretty sure he was being somehow singled out. The prisoners could shout to each other down the corridor. All Rich had to do was kneel by the heavy solid metal door, push up the flap the guard passed his plate of food through, and shout down the hall. He found out that many of the other detainees had been visited by their consuls. Rich decided that he had not seen a consul for the same reason he was in solitary. The British and Italian governments had agreed to make an example of him. He decided, in his mind, that it would be five years.

All this time it had never crossed his mind that this ordeal would hurt his relationship with Nicola. Now he thought that five years inside might split them. He worried about how his family would react. And Nicola's family. He'd never met them.

In the second cell there were pornographic pictures on the wall. Rich took them all down. It wasn't political correctness, or anything like that. He just couldn't stand them being there. They looked so alienated, so made into objects. Like him. He was very careful and gentle in taking them down. It seemed important not to tear the pictures, and he didn't want to make a noise. He was worried it would bring the guards.

★

Over at the women's prison, one of the detainees was very withdrawn. She sat, clutching her knees, not speaking. A Kurd, she had been tortured in a Turkish prison. Now she thought the same thing would happen to her again. She had a rare disease, and if she didn't take her medicine she would go blind. Her medicine had been left behind in the school. The guards would not get her more. The other women decided they would go on hunger strike to get her the medicine.

And then the magistrates came. The women were taken down one by one. The magistrate Nicola saw was a woman. She told Nicola she was being released with all charges dropped. Just before Nicola left the room, the magistrate said to her, 'The people who did this will pay.'

They took Nicola to a holding cell, and there was an agonising wait to find out if the other women were being released too. They were. The Bristish consul was allowed into the prison, and Nicola was very pleased to see him. Then they were taken to another police station, there were some more forms, and then Rich was there too.

At nine Wednesday night we got the news in London. They were all out. Rich and Nicola were alive, and walking.

Then we understood. Our paranoia had been misplaced. All that had happened was the British government had been determined to do as little as possible for their nationals. The American, German and Spanish consuls had seen their people. The British had not, and the consul and the Foreign Office had lied to us about it. We had not been able to make the jump to understand that this was because New Labour was more hostile to the demonstrators than Bush's State Department.

Everyone I have talked to who dealt with the British consul in Genoa felt, as I did, that he was a decent man doing the best job he could. In any case, it is not possible that in a situation of this political delicacy he would have made the decision, on his own, not to see the detainees and to lie to the families, saying he didn't know where they were. That decision must have been taken at a much more senior level. I personally think it was made by Jack Straw, the Foreign Secretary, but I have no evidence for this whatsoever. It is possible that the decision was taken by a senior diplomat in the Foreign Office, though we should not forget that another senior diplomat leaked the information to the journalists. Jack Straw was, however, the man in charge, the minister responsible.

The families, Nancy, Silva and I met all five British detainees at Heathrow airport the next morning. Dan's father, Bill, brought the press. Bill wanted to nail Jack Straw any way he could for what had been done to his boy. Rich and Nicola came out, looking tired, bewildered and alive. Rich still had his bandages sewn to his head. He handed me a statement the five British detainees had written for the press. 'We're too far gone to read it out,' he said. 'You do it.' They disappeared round the corner, and I read their statement to the cameras. Then I cried, finally. Nancy held me.

We had a little party with Rich and Nicola and their families back at her place. Ruard and Richard Peacock came over too. It was a bit like a wedding, with everybody celebrating and trying to be nice to people they had never met but would have to live with for a long time.

Since their return home to Britain, none of the detainees, their families, friends or lawyers, have received a phone call or a letter from the Foreign Office asking how they can help.

After every major protest, on almost every issue, the police arrest and charge some people. A few of those always end up in prison. But none of the people arrested in the school was going to jail after Genoa. And no one was charged with anything. This side of a revolution, there had never been such a spectacular collapse of a political case.

When everyone else was released, an Austrian street theatre

group with them in prison were kept in. They had been arrested on Sunday with a van full of props the police said were weapons. An American Quaker was arrested with them. She was writing a thesis on street theatre. In Portland, Oregon, the Quaker's home town, an Italian ship sailed into the docks. The local movement threw a picket line across the docks to stop the ship being unloaded. The longshoremen (dockers) refused to cross that picket line. When their national union officials found out, they insisted the longshoremen go into work. But the point had been made. The American and the Austrians were released.

In the Italian parliament the opposition did a deal. They withdrew their demand for the resignation of the interior minister. In return the government agreed to an official parliamentary inquiry. The investigating magistrates, the rough equivalent of a British or US prosecutor, launched eight separate investigations into police brutality. All the senior policemen involved said they had not been in charge of anything. The head of the anti-terrorist squad and the national head of the riot police said that yes, they had been at the school, but just hanging out, observers really. Both men were transferred out of their jobs. So was the policeman who had been in charge at Genoa. Six months later all three policemen had new jobs as senior figures in the intelligence services.

In cities all over Italy people set up their own Social Forums, modelled on Genoa's. Two thousand came to the first meeting in Rome, too many for the hall they had booked. They moved out into the piazza and had the meeting there.

We had won. The authorities, spurred on by and using the fascists, had tried to break the anti-capitalist movement. They had failed, spectacularly. What made the difference was not the direct action on Friday. It was 300,000 people, and the courage that gave many more to protest about what happened in the school.

It all comes down to who you think can change the world. In Italy, after it was over, the people in the movement who were most disoriented were those who had thought they could defend themselves on the streets. Many felt defeated or confused. Those who look to the majority of Italians, and understood that Saturday mattered more than Friday, knew we had won a major victory over Berlusconi and the G8.

The G8 had tried to stop the anti-capitalist movement with fear. We had been afraid. But that very fear had convinced hundreds of thousands of people in Italy that they had stop what was happening to their country before it was too late.

That reaction by the Italian working class, white collar and blue collar, answered every argument about tactics in Genoa. In the end, what must determine our tactics on the street is the fact that we need public support. Not that we need media support. We usually can't get that. But what made the difference in Genoa was that 300,000 people went home, and they knew 10 million. No, the 300,000 said to the 10 million, we weren't violent, the police were. We have to stop this.

13 | **Another world**

This last chapter will try to answer three linked questions. What would another world look like? What went wrong in the Soviet Union and China? What do we do now?

We'll take the USSR and China first. In communist Russia and China political opponents were shot, tortured and sent to prison camps. In Cuba homosexuals were sent to prison. Fear and corruption pervaded the state machine. People were not allowed to say what they thought or worship as they chose. Women were forced into abortions in some communist countries, and denied abortions in others. All of these are critical matters. No regime behaving in these ways could call honestly call itself socialist.

But what was wrong, at root, with the 'communist' countries was not this or that defect, but the central lack of democracy. For Marx the defining fact of socialism would be that the working class, the large majority of ordinary people, had taken power. Marx believed in elections. He always argued that the 'emancipation of the working class is the task of the working class itself'.

In the midst of the Russian revolution of 1917, Lenin wrote a book, *State and Revolution*, while he was in hiding in a worker's house outside Petersburg. The book is well worth reading, to see that then Lenin was no dictator. In it Lenin was wrestling with the question of what society would look like after a revolution. He took democracy for granted. He came to the conclusion that workers would have to do away with the all the old government, army and police. In its place there would be direct democracy. In his formula, we would build a society that any cook could understand and any cook could administer.

Two months later the Russian communists were elected to power by a national meeting of elected representatives from local councils of workers and soldiers. It was not a coup. The Russian communists were still followers of the ideas of Karl Marx. As part of that, they believed they could not build socialism in one country. Either there would be a revolution across the developed world, they said, or their isolated experiment would go under. That world revolution did not happen. The landlords, generals and businessmen launched a civil war. Fourteen foreign countries, including all the powers of Europe, invaded to support the right-wing 'White Army'. But the Russian peasants had already shared out the land. The communists, and the Russian workers, won the civil war because the majority of peasants sided with the Red Army in order to keep their land.

At the end of the civil war and the invasions, though, the Russian urban economy had been destroyed. The majority of workers had lost their jobs and returned to the countryside. Most people were now peasants. In the cities there were now more government bureaucrats than factory workers. The leaders of the working class on the shop floor, the shop stewards and the communists, had either died in the civil war of become bureaucrats themselves.

Lenin was incapacitated by a stroke six years after the revolution, and died in 1924. His last writings complain furiously about the bureaucracy and lack of democracy in Russia. Revolutionary movements failed to take power in Germany, Italy and Hungary. By 1924 it was clear there was going to be no successful workers' revolution outside Russia for many years to come. The old communists left in the government knew that they had to compete with the Western capitalist powers, and that sooner or later the Western powers would invade again. Stalin, the leader who replaced Lenin, argued that Russia had to have modern arms, and therefore a modern industrial economy. The only way to build that in a poor country was to sweat the workers and peasants. And the only way to force them to work so hard for so little was brutal dictatorship.

Most of the old communists could not stomach that. In the absence of a world revolution, they could not see what else to do. But they hated what they were doing. A few of them changed, under the pressure of what they were doing, into men and women fit to run a new dictatorship. But Stalin had to kill all but two of the surviving members of the communist central committee, and the overwhelming majority of the hundreds of local activists who had attended party conferences in the revolutionary years.

Stalin's dictatorship built a new society that worked like the old capitalism. In a Soviet car factory, the foreman spoke Russian, but he issued the same orders as a foreman in Detroit, in the same tone of voice. Stalin's government was driven to make the economy grow by military and economic competition with the West. So they, in turn, drove the workers to produce more and consume less, so the profits could be invested and the economy grow. Working in a Soviet factory was like working for a giant General Motors, one more mega-corporation. This is why the transition from 'state capitalism' to 'market capitalism' after 1989 in Russia was not that great an upheaval. The system was already driven by profit, just the profit of the state, and not an individual company.

Once this Stalinist system was in place, all the communist parties in the world changed to resemble it. This was not a simple process. But all over the world the prestige of the Russian revolution was enormous. The great majority of people who really wanted to change the world joined communist parties and looked to Russia for a lead. Stalin's dictatorship purged all those parties, installing new leaders. Most of the activists in the parties went along with this; they could not bear to face what had happened to the Russian revolution.

Moreover, in much of the third world the example of the

Stalinist state had an appeal to middle-class nationalists like Mao Zedong who wanted to build a strong modern developed industrial state. They were not interested in democracy, but in development. What appealed to them were the very things that were wrong with state capitalism: the dictatorship, the exploitation of the workers and peasants, the subordination of every human value to profit and investment.

So once the Stalinist system was in place, the new communist states that took power later followed the model of dictatorship and state capitalism. Some, like China and Cambodia, were monstrous states. Mao, for instance, allowed 20 to 30 million peasants to die of famine between 1958 and 1960 because he was trying to develop the country at breakneck speed. Others were gentler and more ordinary dictatorships, like Vietnam, Cuba, the states of Eastern Europe, and the Soviet Union after the death of Stalin in 1953. But all were places where strikes were banned, peasants were taxed heavily and workers were exploited as in private capitalism. Marx and Lenin would have recognised none of them as socialist.

So what would a genuinely socialist world look like?

A socialist world would be one where the rule of profit was replaced by the rule of votes at work. Of course, we already have democracy and parliaments in many countries. People in Britain or India still feel they have little control of their lives. Of course, even those limited choices are better than living in a dictatorship, as anyone who has ever lived under one knows. The real problem is that you are allowed a limited choice every few years over the political rulers of society, but no choice over the economic rulers. In our day-to-day working lives, there is no democracy. We spend more than half our lives getting ready for work, going to work, working and coming back from work. If the relationships between human beings at work are undemocratic, boss rule and authoritarianism infects the whole of society.

Socialist democracy would be based on democracy at work. The workers in each company would elect the company bosses. They would elect their foremen and senior managers. This would happen in the public sector too: nursing managers would be elected by nurses, head teachers by teachers and school cleaners, and so on.

The workers in each workplace would also elect representatives to larger parliaments, or councils. In a large city these representatives would all meet in one big building, probably the football stadium. From there they would elect representatives to national meetings. And those would be the power in the land.

These elections would be regular. People would meet at each workplace each week to consider the national issues, and re-elect or replace their representatives. The football stadium meetings would hold new elections each week too. People would elect people they knew and worked alongside: cleaners, plumbers, and data clerks, not lawyers.

Of course students and retired people won't have jobs. Some farmers, and some other people, work for themselves. But it wouldn't be hard for groups of all these people to meet and elect their own representatives.

Democracy on its own would not be enough, though. The other crucial thing necessary would be a world economy no longer driven by profit and competition. Then the elected representatives of working people could meet and decide what to do with the economy so that it met people's needs.

We can't tell now what decisions people would make in that situation. It would be a different world. Quite new things would be thinkable and possible. But we can have some idea of the sort of choices people would make.

First, if the system is not driven by profit, it does not have to grow. So the new democracy would debate whether to increase the wealth of the world, or to hold it steady in the interests of the environment. I take it for granted that everyone would have to work or study, and that everyone would be paid the same. But we wouldn't have to work as hard. There would be enormous savings of human labour from eliminating unnecessary jobs. Advertising is a good example. It's a large industry, full of talented artists perverting their creativity. We could eliminate ads and let all those people make the art they want to. The financial services industry, and all those highly intelligent brokers playing the margins, could devote the same skills to the worlds of pure maths or astronomy. Public transport would be free, and that would save millions of jobs selling tickets, checking tickets, and building cars that fall apart. Those people could get jobs driving more buses, smaller buses, more regular buses. Or they could get jobs making live music on the platforms.

Or perhaps the savings of labour could be spread across the society, so everybody works less hard. We could eliminate Monday. With technological progress, maybe we could even eliminate Tuesday working. That would mean more time for sports, or worship. Perhaps we would worship different things and other powers: perhaps each other or the land.

But some people would argue then that instead of working less hard we could work at different things, meeting human needs. Maybe we would put far more of our work into care for the elderly that would enable them to live proud lives at home. Or there would be an explosion of counselling, and people who had previously been policemen or managers could listen carefully to the damaged and the desperate.

Maybe cooking would become more important. Maybe people would get fed up with competitive sports and spend their time dancing instead. Maybe the world would go football mad.

There could be a great increase in free childcare. The people who work in the nurseries could have fewer children to look after, time to read books to individual children, time to sit and crayon quietly and hold a lonely child. Maybe, instead, parents could have far more time off work to look after their own children. But if we close city streets, and people take more responsibility for others' children, it could be like country areas where children spend their time playing with each other and parents don't feel trapped. Who knows? All we know is the debates would be spirited.

Certainly, it would be a world where people were secure. The fears of being without work, without medical care, lonely and helpless in old age, without money to buy your child a nice doll at Christmas, without money, without value in the world: these would go. And with security, people would change. Many of these changes we cannot now imagine. But some we can guess at. Nowadays people at the sharp end of the economy are more likely to get the diseases of stress, to smoke, to drink too much, to go mad, to stay insane, to beat up their children, to beat up their wives, to kill themselves.

There's an American proverb: when poverty walks in the door, love flies out the window. In every country I have lived in, the strongest force breaking marriages is poverty. It isn't just those tight anxious fights about money. When people worry all day about the future, it is far harder to stop escalating fights over other things, and those terrible fights over nothing.

It's not that people don't have demons in their past and their heads that drive them to smoking or to madness. But those demons (sexual abuse, fearful and lonely childhoods, drunken parents, the memory of the bombers overhead, a father's fear of his father's madness) are all easier to deal with if you can take time off work when the voices start to scream in your head. If there is someone with all the time in the world to listen. If you don't have to hear your children crying for things you cannot give them. If you don't feel anxious all day about losing a job you hate.

None of this means we, or the world, would be perfect. But life would be easier.

Then our democracy could argue about the problem created because there were some jobs people really wanted, and some they didn't. These wouldn't necessarily be the same jobs as now. Our world is now dominated by people who do mental labour, so mental work is valued over physical. In a world where manual workers had won dignity, the human body would be honoured. Suddenly an eye surgeon who did the same squint operation over and over again, day after day, might allow himself to become bored. A master carpenter might take pleasure in his work. In a world where dirt and bodies no longer stood for the oppressed, emptying the rubbish bins along the streets in the dawn light might turn into a job many people enjoyed. In a world where people said thank you to plumbers in the same way they do to doctors, we might have enough plumbers.

With democracy at work, with the election of supervisors, foremen and managers, the whole world of work would be restructured. In every job I've ever done, the people I worked with had detailed ideas about how to do this. The only chance they ever had to express these ideas was after work in the pub with a few drinks inside them.

Even then, even when waitresses were not insulted and humiliated, even when there were no waitresses, some jobs would be better than others. Maybe we could share out the stuff we don't like, with everyone doing one or two days a week of a hard job, or four months a year. Maybe people in difficult jobs could work fewer hours, or fewer weeks, and have six months holiday a year. (Maybe all the rest of us could gang up and force young people to do them!) Maybe we could focus all of human scientific endeavour on how to get rid of those jobs.

The hardest debate would probably be over the inequalities between countries. Getting the kind of alternative world we're talking about here would need a revolution. That revolution would have to start somewhere. But we live in a world economy, and a world system of power. Any revolution that was limited to Britain, or Nigeria, or even the United States would be strangled. However, in a newly democratic world workers in some places would be a lot richer than workers in others. How would we deal with that? Would we level down to begin with, sharing out the world's income? Or would we hold the standard of living steady in the rich countries, and raise it in the poorer ones? That could be done. Look at how fast Japan, for instance, moved from being a poor country to the world's richest. But would it be fair?

And I think we would vote for freedom of movement around the world.

The disputes in our democracy would be endless. Hundreds of millions of people worldwide, maybe billions, would be changing their jobs. Some people would want one thing, some another. They would have different interests, and individuals are also different. The point, though, is that the decisions would be made by discussing and voting together, not by a few men obeying the laws of profit.

In Genoa, for the first time, I felt that world is possible in my lifetime.

Two months after Genoa came September 11. The papers and the TV said that wrecked the anti-capitalist movement. What happened in Britain was that most people in Globalise Resistance threw themselves into the anti-war movement. This was bigger than the anti-capitalist movement had been in Britain. On Mayday 10,000 had demonstrated in London. Now 50,000 marched against the war in London in October, and 100,000 in early December. The crowds were young, mixed, and full of workers.

On the first march, I was with 400 students and staff from the School of Oriental and African studies. The staff brought their union banners. Next to us were 200 Bangladeshi Muslims from East London, chanting '*Allah Akbar*' (God is Great) and carrying Stop the War and Socialist Worker placards. We all shouted all the way. The loudest roar was anger as we passed the Ritz. You could feel that powering this march was not just a longing for peace, but class anger.

In many parts of the world, the activists were looking in their address books and computer memories for the people they already knew, trying to build a peace movement. That move-ment was strongest where the anti-capitalists had been strongest. In Berlin 50,000 marched. In South Asia the largest demonstra-tion overwhelmingly was in Hindu Kolkota (Calcutta), where 80,000 marched. In Italy there was a ritual peace march every year to Assisi, because the peaceful St Francis came from there. In October 2001, after Genoa, and after September 11, 200,000 people joined that march.

The anti-war movement was weaker in two places. In France ATTAC's public position was that Islamic fundamentalism and George Bush were equally bad. They organised nothing against the war, and there were almost no protests. And it was harder in the US, for obvious reasons. But the anti-capitalists in New York met right after September 11 to decide what to do. That weekend 1,000 of them held a peace vigil as close to Ground Zero as they could get. It was small. But no one in New York tried to prevent them. There were then peace demonstrations on over US 160 campuses and in over 200 cities and towns. These too were small, and after the bombing of Afghanistan started things got harder.

Then, in January 2002 the Davos Forum met. This is an inter-national club of leading bankers, politicians and corporate executives. Usually they meet every year in Davos, Switzerland. This year they met in southern Manhattan, at the Waldorf, in sol-idarity with the dead of New York, and perhaps also to escape the demonstrators in Switzerland the year before. Now the anti-capitalists marched as close to the Waldorf as they could get. The symbolism was lost on no one. The marchers were close to Ground Zero. The TV and the *New York Times* had told them it would be utter disrespect to demonstrate. Twenty thousand came. The anti-capitalist movement was back in the US. In April an anti-IMF protest in Washington joined with a march against Israeli attacks on the Palestinians, and together they were 100,000 strong.

In Europe December saw the regular summit of EU leaders,

like the one in Gothenburg six months before. This time it was in Brussels. One hundred and thirty thousand Belgian and French trade unionists marched outside. Their slogan was 'For a Social Europe', and from the platform the trade union leaders said it was one struggle for the working class, North and South, rich countries and poor. The next day 20,000 marched against war and capitalism.

In December Argentina rose against IMF restructuring. All over the city of Buenos Aires over 2 million people demonstrated. The police fired, killing many, and the demonstrators did not retreat. The government fell. A new government tried to continue the IMF policies. The people demonstrated again, and that government fell within the week. There have been three more governments since then. Each one tries to do the bidding of the IMF. The politicians put off an election for as long as possible. The revolt goes on, with hundreds of local neighbourhood committees meeting. The weakness is that the union leaders still support the politicians.

In January 80,000 people went to the World Social Forum meeting, the counter-conference to Davos for our side, in Porto Alegre, Brazil. In March the EU leaders held a quick summit in Barcelona, Spain. Again there was an official trade union march, and then an anti-capitalist one two days later. This time there were 140,000 on the union march. On the anti-capitalist one there were 500,000, including 30,000 from the unions. Two hundred and twenty chartered buses had been stopped at the borders, and few people came from outside the region of Catalonia. Most of the crowd were from Barcelona itself, a city of three million people. This was a whole city joining the movement. The official slogan was 'Against Capital and War'.

In Italy 300,000 had marched in Genoa, and 200,000 against war in October. Then the school students went on strike across the country. The pupils occupied the school where Rich and Nicola had been beaten. One of their demands was that the school clean up the blood in their classrooms, which still smelled. When the school would not do it, the kids did it themselves.

Then Berlusconi tried to change the law that protected workers against unfair dismissal. The unions called a demonstration in Rome, and 3 million people came. It was a sea of red flags, and everywhere there were Palestinian scarves. The unions called a general strike, and 12 million people came out. The local branches of the Italian Social Forum that had grown out of the GSF surrounded non-union workplaces so the workers there had an excuse for joining the strike. In Britain 100,000 marched in London for Palestine.

I write this in early May. All things seem possible now, from another world fit for human beings, to a hell run by the likes of George W. Bush. Genoa seems long ago, and small. But it was a turning point. We stopped them. Because we did, we now have a chance to change the world.

When we marched in Genoa, even in our fear we chanted:

'We Are Winning, Don't Forget.'

And we chanted another idea:

'They Make Misery, We Make History.'

Further reading

The books and articles that follow are not a comprehensive bibliography. Instead, the intention is to tell you where you can find the ideas set out in this book at more length, and some of the evidence to back up the arguments. Place of publication is London, unless otherwise specified. If you have trouble finding any of these books or journals, ask for help at the Bookmarks bookshop Web site, www.bookmarks.uk.com.

IMF and World Bank

The best starting place is a study of one country, Patrick Bond (2000) *Against Global Apartheid: South Africa Meets the World Bank, IMF and International Finance*, University of Cape Town Press, Lansdowne, South Africa. Walden Bello (1994) *Dark Victory: the United States and Global Poverty*, Pluto, gives an overview of US policy. Catherine Caulfield (1997) *Masters of Illusion: the World Bank and the Poverty of Nations*, Macmillan, and Susan George (1986) *How the Other Half Dies: the Real Reasons for World Hunger*, Penguin, are both very useful.

Foreign aid and NGOs

Three stunning books with long angry titles: Graham Hancock (1989) *Lords of Poverty: the Freewheeling Lifestyles, Power, Prestige and Corruption of the Multi-billion Dollar Aid Business*, Atlantic Monthly Press, New York, is about the government aid agencies.

Michael Maren (1997) *The Road to Hell: the Ravaging Effects of Foreign Aid and International Charity*, Free Press, New York, is mainly about the collusion between NGOs and the US invasion forces in Somalia, by a former aid worker there. Alex de Waal (1997) *Famine Crimes: Politics and the Disaster Relief Industry in Africa*, James Curey, Oxford, is mainly a careful anthropological study of one famine in the Sudan.

James Ferguson (1994) *The Anti-Politics Machine: 'Development', Depoliticization, and Bureaucratic Power in Lesotho*, University of Minnesota Press, Minneapolis, is a thoughtful analysis of why aid projects consistently fail, and how development theorists write about the subject.

AIDS

The best place to start on the generic drugs issue is the Web site of the Treatment Action Campaign in South Africa, www.tac.org.za, and the Oxfam pamphlet by Kevin Watkins (2001) 'Patent Injustice: How World Trade Rules Threaten the Health of Poor People'.

On the politics in the early years of the epidemic see Jonathan Neale (1991) 'The Politics of AIDS', *International Socialism*, and the magnificent book by Randy Shilts (1988) *And the Band Played On: Politics, People and the AIDS Epidemic*, Penguin, New York. For recent years Chris Beyrer (1998) *War in the Blood: Sex, Politics and AIDS in Southeast Asia*, Zed, London, and Sidarth Dube (2000) *Sex, Lies and AIDS*, Harper Collins, on India.

Edward Hooper (1999) *The River: a Journey back to the Source of HIV*, Penguin, argues convincingly that HIV got into people as a result of American field tests of polio vaccines in New Jersey and central Africa. Everyone interested in AIDS should read the book, and then make up their own minds. If Hooper is right, the US government is legally liable, in American courts, for the costs of all treatment for all people with HIV in the world.

Star Wars and global warming

On Star Wars there is a magnificent pamphlet, Karl Grossman (2001) 'Weapons in Space', Open Media Pamphlets, Seven Stories Press. Follow the references. Dinyar Godrej (2001) *The No-Nonsense Guide to Climate Change*, Verso, is an excellent introduction. Jeremy Leggett (1999) *The Carbon War: Global Warming and the End of the Oil Era*, Penguin, is about how the oil, coal and auto companies organised to stop controls on global warming, written by the Greenpeace scientist who confronted them.

Middle Eastern politics

Start with Said Aburish (1996) *The Rise, Corruption and Coming Fall of the House of Saud*, St Martins, New York. Also useful, by the same author, are (1997) *A Brutal Friendship: the West and the Arab Elite*, Orion, and (1999) *Arafat: from Defender to Dictator*, Bloomsbury.

On Iran, Assaf Bayat (1987) *Workers and Revolution in Iran: a Third World Experience of Workers' Control*, Zed, and Phil Marshall (1988) *Revolution and Counter-Revolution in Iran*, Bookmarks. On Israel, John Rose (1986) *Israel: the Hijack State: America's Watchdog in the Middle East*, Bookmarks. For daily life for workers in an oil state now, Joma Nazpary (2002) *Post-Soviet Chaos: Violence and Dispossession in Kazakhstan*, Pluto. On sanctions and Iraq, Antony Arnove, editor (2000) *Iraq Under Siege: the Deadly Impact of Sanctions and War*, Pluto.

Afghanistan and September 11

Three articles in the special issue of *International Socialism* for December 2001: John Rees, 'Imperialism, globalisation, the state and war', Jonathan Neale, 'The Long Torment of Afghanistan', and Anne Alexander, 'The Crisis in the Middle East'.

The best book on Afghanistan is Ahmed Rashid (2000)

Taliban: Militant Islam, Oil and Fundamentalism in Central Asia, Yale University Press, New Haven. See also Jonathan Neale (1981) 'The Afghan Tragedy', *International Socialism* (this article is available online at www.marxists.de) and Jonathan Neale (1988) 'Afghanistan: the Horse Changes Riders', *Capital and Class*.

Marxist economics

Karl Marx, *Capital*, Volume 1, is much easier to read than you might think. If you find philosophy difficult, start at chapter 4, and from there the book gets steadily easier and more concrete as you go along. Then read the first three chapters once you finish. I find the Penguin edition easiest. If you have trouble, Paul Baran (1973, first published 1957) *The Political Economy of Growth*, Monthly Review Press, New York, is a simplified guide to Marx's *Capital*.

For Marx's ideas on the falling rate of profit you need to read *Capital*, Volume 3, chapters 1–15. Or you can start with Chris Harman (1999) *Explaining the Crisis: a Marxist Reappraisal*, Bookmarks. Harman's book requires work, but it does make sense of everything. For a simpler, and more readable, version of the same ideas, see Chris Harman (1995) *Economics of the Madhouse: Capitalism and the Market Today*, Bookmarks.

For recent data on falling profits see first Robert Brenner (2002) *Turbulence in the World Economy*, Verso, a newer version of a book-length article in *New Left Review* in 1999. Readable and interesting, though I disagree on the causes of falling profits. See also the special number (2001) of *Historical Materialism* on Brenner's book, especially the articles by Anwar Shaikh, Chris Harman, Fred Mosely, and Ben Fine et al. Then try a more technical book, Anwar Shaikh and E. Ahmet Tonak (1994) *Measuring the Wealth of Nations: the Political Economy of National Accounts*, Columbia University Press, New York.

For the assault on wages and conditions for US workers, see Laurence Mishel, Jared Bernstein and John Schmitt (1999) *The*

State of Working America 1998–99, Cornell University Press, Ithaca. A new edition of this useful book is published each year.

What happened to 'communism'

Start with Mike Haynes (2002) *Russia: Class and Power 1917–2000*, Bookmarks. On Russia also try Tony Cliff (1987) *Revolution Besieged, Lenin, 1917–1923*, Bookmarks, and Ante Ciliga (1979) *The Russian Enigma*, Ink Links, by a former communist prisoner in Stalin's gulag.

There is no one good book on Mao's China. But see Harold Isaacs (1961, first published 1938) *The Tragedy of the Chinese Revolution*, Stanford University Press, Stanford, for the 1920s; Nigel Harris (1978) *The Mandate of Heaven: Marx and Mao in Modern China*, Quartet, for the 60s and 70s; and Charlie Hore (1991) *The Road to Tienanmen Square*, Bookmarks, for the 1980s. Zhisui Li (1994) *The Private Life of Chairman Mao*, Arrow, by Mao's personal physician, is about far more than the title indicates.

For Vietnam see Jonathan Neale (2201) *The American War: Vietnam 1960–1975*, Bookmarks.

Links

Globalise Resistance: www.resist.org.uk
Socialist Workers Party: www.swp.org.uk
International Socialists: www.internationalsocialists.org, or go to
    www.swp.org.uk and click on International
Treatment Action Campaign in South Africa: www.tac.org.za
World Development Movement: www.wdm.org.uk
Stop the War campaign: www.StopWar.org.uk
Campaign for Nuclear Disarmament: www.cnduk.org
Left Turn (US anti-capitalist group): www.left-turn.org
Bookmarks bookshop: www.bookmarks.uk.com

Index

Index

Non-Governmental Organisations
(NGOs) 40–43, 177, 263
non-violence as tactic 24–25, 141
training in 92
North American Free Trade
Agreement (NAFTA)
207–08
North Korea 76, 106
Northern League (Italy) 19, 70
nuclear energy 108

Obasanjo, Olusegun 29
Observer 223
oil 117, 153–58
US power over, restored after
Gulf War 166
Oxfam 40, 42

Pakistan 106, 118
Pakistan, health, education and debt
spending in 39
Palestine 156–57, 163, 166–70, 171
Palestine Liberation Organisation
(PLO) 157–58, 161, 167, 170
Patna railway station 1–3
Peach, Blair 125
Peacock, Richard 99, 101, 102, 216,
223–24
People and Planet 42
Peru 212
Pfizer 79
pharmaceutical industry ('Big
Pharma') 74–75, 77, 79–82
Pink March 141, 192
police violence 125, 126, 182–86
on central government orders
215
and inquiry called by govern-
ment 248
in school HQ 194–95, 213–22
passim, 228
poll tax 184
Powell, Colin 165
Prague 10, 12–13
public services, cuts in 44–45
Putin, Vladimir 175

Qatar 10

Ribicoff, Senator Abraham 59
Rossi, Bruno 17
Ross, Jimmy 126
Ruard (author's stepson) 57,
99–101, 123, 134, 181, 216,
223, 225–26
Russia 9, 108, 109, 117, 209
see also Soviet Union

Sadat, Anwar al- 158
Saddam Hussein 162–65
and Israel, bombing of 166
see also Iraq; Kuwait
Sam (protester) 91, 92
Saudi Arabia 117, 153–55, 156, 162,
163, 170–71
US troops in 166
and princes' hypocrisy 154–5
Save the Children 41
Seattle 9, 42, 76, 83, 179
Sen, Amartya 29
September 11 attack 172–74, 259–60,
266
see also Bin Laden, Osama;
United States of America
Socialist Party of Italy 18
Socialist Workers Party 11, 14–15,
59–60
Solu Khumbu aid project 36
South Africa 76–79, 84, 85–86, 212
and the African National
Congress (ANC) 76, 78
see also AIDS and HIV
Soviet Union 9, 105–06, 108,
251–54
and Afghanistan, invasion of
170–71
see also Russia
Spain 261
Sri Lanka 108
and AIDS and HIV 88
Stalin, Joseph 252–54
'Star Wars' *See* Strategic Defense
Initiative
State and Revolution (Lenin) 251–52
Strategic Defense Initiative ('Star
Wars') 105–12, 265
Straw, Jack 242, 247

273

About the author

Jonathan Neale was one of the organisers of the July 2001 protests in Genoa against the G8. He was born in New York, and grew up in Connecticut, Texas and India. He has written 11 plays, mostly for young people, and eight books. His most recent books are *The American War*, about Vietnam, *Tigers of the Snow*, about Sherpa climbers, and *Lost at Sea*, a novel for children.

Jonathan studied anthropology at the London School of Economics, doing fieldwork in Afghanistan, and social history at the University of Warwick, writing a thesis on mutinies in the 18th century navy. He worked in clinics and hospitals in London as a porter, occupational therapy technician, abortion counsellor and HIV counsellor.

Jonathan has been an active socialist for many years, mainly as a shop steward in various unions, but also in student occupations, squatter politics, the Anti-Nazi League, the campaign against the poll tax, the peace movement and now anti-capitalism.